CONTENTS

Complicating Categories:
Gender, Class, Race and Ethnicity

Edited by
Eileen Boris and
Angélique Janssens

Complicating Categories: An Introduction
Eileen Boris and Angélique Janssens
                                                                    I

Family Concerns: Gender and Ethnicity in Pre-Colonial
West Africa
Sandra E. Greene
                                                                    15

Narratives Serially Constructed and Lived: Ethnicity
in Cross-Gender Strikes 1887–1903
Ileen A. DeVault
                                                                    33

Competing Inequalities: The Struggle Over Reserved
Legislative Seats for Women in India
Laura Dudley Jenkins
                                                                    53

"The Black Man's Burden": African Americans, Imperialism,
and Notions of Racial Manhood 1890–1910
Michele Mitchell
                                                                    77

Sex Workers or Citizens? Prostitution and the Shaping of "Settler"
Society in Australia
Raelene Frances
                                                                    101

From Muscles to Nerves: Gender, "Race" and the Body at Work
in France 1919–1939
Laura Levine Frader
                                                                    123

"Blood Is a Very Special Juice": Racialized Bodies and Citizenship in
Twentieth-Century Germany
Fatima El-Tayeb
                                                                    149

NOTES ON CONTRIBUTORS

Eileen Boris, Studies in Women and Gender, University of Virginia, 227 Minor Hall, Charlottesville, VA 22903, USA; e-mail: eboris@virginia.edu

Ileen A. DeVault, School of Industrial and Labor Relations, Cornell University, Ithaca, NY 14853-3901, USA; e-mail: iadl@cornell.edu

Fatima El-Tayeb, Djambistraat 5 hs, 1094 AW Amsterdam, The Netherlands; e-mail: sfruit@xs4all.nl

Laura Levine Frader, Department of History, College of Arts and Sciences, Northeastern University, 249 Meserve Hall, Boston, MA 02115, USA; e-mail: lfrader@lynx.dac.neu.edu

Raelene Frances, School of History, University of New South Wales, Sydney, NSW 2052, Australia; e-mail: R.Frances@unsw.edu.au

Sandra E. Greene, Department of History, Cornell University, Ithaca, NY 14853-3901, USA; e-mail: seg6@cornell.edu

Angélique Janssens, Vakgroep Geschiedenis, Katholieke Universiteit Nijmegen, Postbus 9103, 6500 HD Nijmegen, The Netherlands; e-mail: A.Janssens@let.kun.nl

Laura Dudley Jenkins, Department of Political Science, University of Cincinnati, PO Box 210375, Cincinnati, OH 45221-0375, USA; e-mail: jenkinla@email.uc.edu

Michele Mitchell, Department of History, University of Michigan, 1029 Tisch Hall, Ann Arbor, MI 48109, and/or Center for Afroamerican & African Studies, University of Michigan, 200 West Engineering Hall, Ann Arbor, MI 48109, USA; e-mail: mmitch@umich.edu

international review of social history

Supplement 7

Complicating Categories: Gender, Class, Race and Ethnicity

Edited by Eileen Boris and Angélique Janssens

Published by the Press Syndicate of the University of Cambridge
The Pitt Building, Trumpington Street, Cambridge, CB2 1RP
40 West 20th Street, New York, NY 10011–4211, USA
10 Stamford Road, Oakleigh, Melbourne 3166, Australia

*A catalogue record for this book is available
from the British Library*

Library of Congress Cataloguing-in-Publication Data

Complicating categories: gender, class, race and ethnicity / edited by Eileen Boris
and Angélique Janssens.
    p. cm.—(International review of social history. Supplement; 7)
Includes bibliographical references.
ISBN 0–521–78641–X (pb.)
    1. Working class—History. 2. Women—Employment—History.
3. Minorities—Employment—History. 4. Social classes—History.
I. Boris, Eileen, 1948– . II. Janssens, Angélique. III. Series.
HD4851.C625 1999
331.11′43—dc21   99–055823 CIP

ISBN 0 521 78641X (paperback)

Printed in Great Britain by the University Press, Cambridge

International Review of Social History 44 (1999), Supplement, pp. 1–13
© 1999 Internationaal Instituut voor Sociale Geschiedenis

Complicating Categories: An Introduction

EILEEN BORIS AND ANGÉLIQUE JANSSENS

This 1999 *Supplement* of the *International Review of Social History* focuses on complicating central concepts in the understanding of economic and social history: class, gender, race and ethnicity. In concentrating on industrial workers, their politics, and institutions, labor and working-class history had tended to ignore gender, race, and ethnicity as discursive and material forces. It discussed the woman or black or immigrant worker as a subset of worker, assumed to be male, white, and of the dominant national or ethnic group. Only during recent years have historians began to ask how gender, race, and ethnicity as categories of analysis change narratives of class formation and working-class experience. This question has become particularly salient as the European Union and the United States seek to grapple with the human consequences of colonial and imperialist legacies both within and beyond national boundaries in an increasingly global economy.

Over the last few decades, feminist scholarship has demonstrated most powerfully the analytical power of gender to disrupt conventional understandings of worker identity, class formation, proletarianization, and a host of other prominent issues. Simultaneously, it has shifted the terms of discussion from the workplace to the home and family and back to other locations of labor. Its findings have seriously undermined the class paradigm in the study of labor and working-class history. We have moved beyond debating the explanatory primacy between class and gender to consider their mutual constitution. Still the field has more often studied gender apart from race and ethnicity, marking woman as belonging to the dominant racial or ethnic group as surely as labor history had treated the worker as male, and ignoring the ways that racial and ethnic differences turned class or gender divisions into solidarities.

More recently, scholarship on "race" and ethnicity as sometimes related and sometimes distinct categories of analysis (depending on time and place) has expanded knowledge of class formation and gender construction. These developments have led scholars and activists to question the precise relationship between all of these concepts and the possibilities or impossibilities to unite and/or integrate them. What would this process of integration look like? What kinds of historical insights and histories would emerge from such a process of integration? Or is integration even the appropriate metaphor for interrogating the meaning of each of these categories in itself and in relation to the others? This *Supplement* highlights attempts to write a richer history that complicates categories, suggesting how class, gender, race and/or ethnicity combine across a wide range of economic and social landscapes.

GENDER, RACE AND THE NEW LABOR HISTORY

The now old new labor history came of age with a silence at its core. In the excitement of recovering the culture and agency of laboring people, it failed to recognize the actual subject of working-class history. In their survey of labor history before gender analysis, Laura L. Frader and Sonya O. Rose have found "a story of exclusions" – of women and non-whites, whether native-born, colonial, or immigrant. Working-class women were marginal, for example, to E.P. Thompson's magisterial *Making of the British Working Class*. As Joan Wallach Scott argued, Thompson constructed class "as a masculine identity, even when not all the actors were male". Indeed, Scott exposed the gendered dynamic at the heart of Thompson's story: the coding of work, production, and "rationalist" politics as male and the locating of domesticity, coded as female, as "outside production" and connected to expressive religious movements that undermined "true" class consciousness.[1]

In parallel fashion, David Roediger returned to the pioneering insights of W.E.B. Dubois to chart "the wages of whiteness" that were all but ignored by Thompson's American followers who focused on artisanal labor. But Roediger did not merely point out racial silences in texts or the ways that some workers constructed themselves as white against the black slave. His critique of the new labor history condemned its "overemphasis" on class over race. Its main narrative had black as well as white workers acting on the basis of class interests over cultural or racial ones, as if the former was not framed by the later – and both by gender, as we argue throughout this volume.[2]

By the time Scott's critique appeared, a growing band of women historians were already casting women into the story of working class formation as active agents on their own terms. While most contextualized their studies in light of worksite, ethnicity, and other sociodemographic factors, whiteness lurked as a subtext with the black or racial ethnic worker a special case of the woman worker.[3] By focusing on the dyad male and

1. Laura L. Frader and Sonya O. Rose, "Introduction: Gender and the Reconstruction of European Working-Class History", in Laura L. Frader and Sonya O. Rose (eds), *Gender and Class in Modern Europe* (Ithaca, NY, 1996), p. 10; Joan Wallach Scott, *Gender and The Politics of History* (New York, 1988), pp. 72, 79. See also Sally Alexander, "Women, Class, and Sexual Difference", *History Workshop*, 17 (1984), p. 131.
2. David R. Roediger, *The Wages of Whiteness: Race and the Making of the American Working Class* (New York, 1991); *idem*, "'Labor in White Skin': Race and Working Class History", in David Roediger, *Towards the Abolition of Whiteness* (London, 1994), p. 25; *idem*, "The Crisis in Labor History: Race, Gender and the Replotting of the Working Class Past in the United States", in *Towards the Abolition of Whiteness*, pp. 69–81. Similarly, see Herbert Hill, "The Problem of Race in American Labor History", *Reviews in American History*, 24 (1996), pp. 189–208; Nell Irvin Painter, "The New Labor History and the Historical Moment", *International Journal of Politics, Culture, and Society*, 2 (1989), pp. 369–370.
3. Evelyn Brooks Higginbotham, "African-American Women's History and the Metalanguage of Race", *Signs: A Journal of Women in Culture and Society*, 17 (1992), pp. 251–274; Dana Frank, "White Working-Class Women and the Race Question", *International Labor and Working-Class History*, 54 (1998), pp. 80–102.

female, feminist thought during the 1970s and 1980s replicated exclusions of race, ethnicity, and nation that distorted working-class history as a whole. For many sought to supplement class analysis by turning to the concept of patriarchy as a system in which men as a sex group controlled the productive and reproductive labor power of women. And patriarchy was a concept blind to race and ethnicity. These writers concluded that women's oppression emanated not from industrial capitalism but predated it and indeed its locus lay elsewhere. Patriarchy, more than capitalism, had kept women subordinated. By the early eighties, however, attempts to integrate a feminist analysis of patriarchy with the Marxist analysis of class had produced an unhappy marriage on the verge of divorce. Some questioned the interpolation of the term patriarchy to class society in the first place; others rejected dual systems theory as replicating Victorian notions of separate spheres and saw gender "imbricated" in economic and social systems as a whole.[4] While theorists moved in separate directions, with class analysis suffering a crisis from the collapse of the eastern-European communist regimes and the weakening of traditional labor movements, gender emerged into the analytical limelight by the early 1990s.

Initially women's labor history, focused on the last two centuries, had charted occupational segregation by sex, trade union exclusions, and employer exploitation. It further recovered the history of women as wage earners and their roles in productive as well as reproductive or family labor. It highlighted the relationship between female wage earning and capitalist development, the family wage and trade unionism.[5] These were materialist histories, sure that they had captured women's experiences and voices even as they questioned the terms of labor and working-class history. What did deskilling mean for women, defined as unskilled in the first place? Perhaps women's skill just was unrecognized because others determined the boundaries of "skill". The public/private dichotomy broke down, or at least became more complex. The home stood as a workplace not only for the family but also for the market. It became a space not only for the fashioning of goods but also for the making of people, a socialization process as significant to class formation and resistance as the housewife's indirect work for the employer. Resistance no longer belonged only to unions and parties but occurred in the family. Consumption became a site of struggle.[6]

4. For history, Alice Kessler-Harris, *Out to Work: A History of Wage-Earning Women in the United States* (New York, 1982); Joan Wallach Scott and Louise Tilly, *Women, Work, and Family* (New York, 1978); for theory, Michele Barrett, *Women's Oppression Today* (London, 1980); Lydia Sargent (ed.), *Women and Revolution: A Discussion of the Unhappy Marriage of Marxism and Feminism* (Boston, MA, 1981); Sylvia Walby, *Theorizing Patriarchy* (Oxford, 1990). For the dual systems critique, Frader and Rose, "Introduction", p. 19.
5. For one summary of old and new directions, Pamela Sharpe and Harriet Bradley (eds), *Labour History Review*, 63 (1998), special issue on "Gendering Work: Historical Approaches".
6. Excellent summaries of the literature are found in Frader and Rose, "Introduction", and the remaining essays in *Gender and Class in Modern Europe*; see also Ava Baron, *Work Engendered: Toward a New History of American Labor* (Ithaca, NY, 1991). For the home, Eileen Boris, "The

This gender turn came in tandem with the linguistic turn. To the dismay of some, gender exists even without women. Attention to manhood and masculinity as well as a concern with gender as a marker of difference and signifier of power has distinguished literature that relies on gender as a category of analysis. So has a shift to the cultural, an emphasis on meaning derived from understandings of gender as a process or relation, one that shapes institutions no less than characterizes representations. Certainty as to voices and experiences disintegrated, as identity became more negotiated and less fixed. These developments also tended to disrupt certainty as to the meaning of class, race and ethnicity.[7]

Gender itself stands in conjuncture with other social signs – class, race, ethnicity, and sexuality – in ways that are still being problematized. In part, this trajectory – from description to theorization – follows a necessary course. Empirical research deepens analysis. But this trajectory also reflects the history of feminist scholarship itself. Having cast aside Marxist accusations of neglecting class differences between women, feminists increasingly found themselves under attack for ignoring differences of race and ethnicity. The universalizing rhetoric of gender claimed to embrace all women when in fact it derived from the standpoint of usually middle-class white women in North America or northern Europe. These claims had no reality for women of color faced with a set of problems resulting from their gendered positions within specific ethnic or racial communities as well as their racial position within the larger society.[8] White women in the metropoles partook of white privilege based on the exploitation and oppression of women of color at home and abroad. During the last century and a half, the labor of women of color in domestic, service, and other low-waged work has enabled white women to gain leisure or enter the workplace, usually on better terms than those available to racial "others".[9]

Despite a rich historical literature on women of color in the United

---

Home as a Workplace: Deconstructing Dichotomy", *International Review of Social History*, 39 (1994), pp. 415–428.

7. Scott, "Gender: A Useful Category of Historical Analysis", in *Gender and the Politics of History*, pp. 28–52; Ava Baron, "On Looking at Men: Masculinity and the Making of a Gendered Working-Class History", in Ann-Louise Shapiro (ed.), *Feminists Revision History* (New Brunswick, NJ, 1994), pp. 146–171.

8. Some recent critiques include Ann duCille, "The Occult of True Black Womanhood: Critical Demeanor and Black Feminist Studies", *Signs: A Journal of Women in Culture and Society*, 19 (1994), pp. 591–629; Susan Stanford Friedman, "Beyond White and Other: Relationality and Narratives of Race in Feminist Discourse", *Signs: A Journal of Women in Culture and Society*, 21 (1995), pp. 1–49; see also Chandra Talpade Mohanty, "Under Western Eyes: Feminist Scholarship and Colonial Discourses", in Chandra Talpade Mohanty, Ann Russo, and Lourdes Torres (eds), *Third World Feminisms and the Politics of Feminism* (Bloomington, IN, 1991), pp. 51–80.

9. For example, Phyllis Palmer, *Domesticity and Dirt: Housewives and Domestic Servants in the United States, 1920-1945* (Philadelphia, PA, 1989).

States, much of it focused on work, family, and politics,[10] the historiography of class and race often considers gender as an afterthought.[11] Eric Arnesen noted in 1998 that race and class represents "an academic growth industry".[12] US labor historians have addressed "the intersections of race and class, racial segmentation of the labor market, and the impact of race on culture and community", Alan Dawley and Joe William Trotter, Jr previously explained.[13] With theories of social constructionism discrediting biological explanations for racial difference, the historicizing of race in a period of multiculturalism has framed this burgeoning literature. "White" not only developed in relationship to the category "black", but definitions of "white" have changed over time and place. In some cases, class advancement whitens individuals. And the binary of white/black embraces only some racial hierarchies. The construction of race has differed among Anglo-American societies as compared to Iberian ones, for example. The burgeoning whiteness literature has explored European ethnic groups in the United States as "inbetween people", explaining the development of "whiteness of another color" and "how Jews became white folks".[14]

To their credit, Dawley and Trotter recognize that race "is about kinship, courtship, recreation, education, and who marries whom – in short, social reproduction".[15] Martha Hodes more recently has asserted: "the history of

10. Notable examples include Jacqueline Jones, *Labor of Love, Labor of Sorrow: Black Women, Work, and the Family* (New York, 1985); Tera W. Hunter, *To Joy My Freedom: Southern Black Women's Lives After the Civil War* (Cambridge, MA, 1997); Evelyn Nakano Glenn, *Issei, Nisei, War Bride: Three Generations of Japanese American Women in Domestic Service* (Philadelphia, PA, 1986); Vicki L. Ruiz, *Cannery Women, Cannery Lives: Mexican Women, Unionization, and the California Food Processing Industry, 1930–1950* (Albuquerque, NM, 1987); Laura Tabili, *"We Ask for British Justice": Workers and Racial Difference in Late Imperial Britain* (Ithaca, NY, 1994) genders black working-class men. Recent work in Australia also has reclaimed the history of Aboriginals. See Ann McGrath and Kay Saunders, with Jackie Huggins, "Aboriginal Workers", special issue of *Labour History*, 69 (1995).
11. For example, the forum on Bruce Nelson, "Class, Race, and Democracy in the CIO: The 'New' Labor History Meets the 'Wages of Whiteness'", *International Review of Social History*, 41 (1996), pp. 351–374, which dismisses the comments of Elizabeth Faue.
12. Eric Arnesen, "Up from Exclusion: Black and White Workers, Race, and the State of Labor History", *Reviews in American History*, 26 (1998), pp. 146–147.
13. Alan Dawley and Joe William Trotter, Jr, "Race and Class", *Labor History*, 35 (1994), p. 486.
14. James R. Barrett and David Roediger, "Inbetween Peoples: Race, Nationality and the 'New Immigrant' Working Class", *Journal of American Ethnic History*, 16 (1997), pp. 3–44; Mathew Frye Jacobson, *Whiteness of a Different Color* (Cambridge, MA, 1998); Karen Brodkin, *How Jews Became White Folks and What That Says About Race in America* (New Brunswick, NJ, 1998); Raymond Gutierrez, *When Jesus Came, the Corn Mothers Went Away: Marriage, Sexuality and Power in New Mexico, 1500–1846* (Stanford, CA, 1991).
15. Dawley and Trotter, Jr, "Race and Class", p. 492. For examples, Kevin Boyle, "The Kiss: Racial and Gender Conflict in a 1950s Automobile Factory", *Journal of American History*, 84 (1997), pp. 496–523; Eileen Boris, "'You Wouldn't Want One of 'Em Dancing With Your Wife': Racialized Bodies on the Job in WWII", *American Quarterly*, 50 (1998), pp. 77–108.

racial categories is often a history of sexuality as well".[16] Indeed, race itself is gendered. As Tessie Liu also contends, it "functions through controlling sexuality and sexual behavior".[17] Race and gender share much as categories of analysis – both are socially constructed through the assignment of meaning to bodies and thus take material forms in their terms as well as their consequences. But their functioning within social formations varies, as does their relationship to and reformulation of class.

COMPLICATING CATEGORIES

Race, gender, and class may be conceptualized as systems of domination or systems of inequality. But they may also be cultural identities. How do these systems of difference relate to each other? Despite a growing empirical literature, authors more often connect dyads rather than consider historical phenomenon from the tryad of class, race, and gender.[18] The category of race has served to divide white women from women of color, while the category of gender has separated non-whites into males and females. Differences in class distinguish both racial and gender groups. Meanwhile, definitions of deviant gender relations and behaviors have shaped racial relations and racial systems of domination. These are contingent, provisional categories and identities. Their form and content differ according to time, place and historical circumstances, but also depend on the dimensions of experience and identity that the historian wishes to illuminate.

However, bringing all three factors into the analysis is extremely difficult. Feminist theory, as Ann Curthoys has argued, inclines to focus on gender as the primary concept, viewing class or race/ethnicity as secondary distinctions. If treating gender together with either race or class is not already difficult, trying to bring into play a third factor makes the analysis too complex to handle. To circumvent what Curthoys calls "the three body problem", we need to reject conceptions of race, class and gender as three separate structures of domination, which can just be "added on" so that black working-class women are constructed as threefold oppressed, as women, as blacks and as working-class. Rather each of these experiences and relationships influences the others, transforming the meaning of what it means to be black, to be a woman or to be working-class. So if we start

16. Martha Hodes, "Introduction: Interconnecting and Diverging Narratives", in Martha Hodes (ed.), *Sex, Love, Race: Crossing Boundaries in North American History* (New York, 1999), p. 1; see also Peggy Pascoe, "Miscegenation Law, Court Cases, and Ideologies of 'Race' in Twentieth-Century America", *The Journal of American History*, 81 (1996), pp. 44–69.
17. Tessie Liu, "Teaching the Differences Among Women from a Historical Perspective: Rethinking Race and Gender as Social Categories", *Women's Studies International Forum*, 14 (1991), p. 271.
18. For one attempt that privileges race, Floya Anthias and Nira Yuvaly-Davis with Harriet Cain, *Racialized Boundaries: Race, Nation, Gender, Colour and Class and the Anti-Racist Struggle* (London, 1992).

by considering race and class in a dyadic approach, each of these influences the other. However, if we bring a third factor seriously into play, such as gender, the third term will influence the second and therefore the first in such a way that the original basis for the analysis changes and one has to start all over again.[19]

Ethnicity sometimes designates the other instead of race, especially other-ness associated with nation, citizenship, religion, or culture. Sandra E. Greene notes in her contribution that definitions of the "ethnic other" change under the influence of political and demographic developments that relate to social hierarchies and family formation. Essays by Michele Mitchell, Raelene Frances, and Fatima El-Tayeb particularly highlight the conjunct-ure of race and citizenship in colonial or imperial settings. United States historiography especially distinguishes race from ethnicity. Ethnic conflict occurs between European immigrants, seen in Ileen A. DeVault's study of cross-gender strikes. Some Europeans were not always judged to be white, as Frances shows for Australian immigration policy.[20]

History reveals the instability of these categories, warning against any reification of them. Within one and the same boundaries of time and space, gender or race may don many meanings. Race, class, and gender do not conform to categories that exist in and by themselves. However, the inherent instability of categories should not automatically lead us to the postmodern-ist assumption that these categories do not exist outside of the historian's texts. Race, class and gender do structure people's lives, their relationships with other individuals and/or groups and the objects surrounding them. Moreover, since these categories structure domination and inequality, this automatically implies that social, economic and political resources are div-ided unequally between the groups distinguished by such categories, as is demonstrated by Laura Dudley Jenkins in her paper on Indian women.

The instability of categories such as race, class and gender becomes appar-ent when one category becomes inflected by another. Laura L. Frader, for example, demonstrates what happens when race mediates gender. In early twentieth-century France, the gender of Asian male workers became "femin-ized" through an association with softness and submissiveness. Class, race and gender intertwined to the extent that Asian workers could never qualify as "real men". Often loss of masculinity denotes race and class oppression. Fighting for group liberation becomes a way to express real manhood, but just plain fighting will do, as Mitchell uncovers among elite and aspiring class African-American men a century ago.

What about women? Men have taken the category ethnicity/race away

19. Ann Curthoys, "The Three Body Problem: Feminism and Chaos Theory", *Hecate*, 17 (1991), pp. 14–21.
20. See also Ruth A. Frager, "Labour History and the Interlocking Hierarchies of Class, Ethnicity, and Gender", *International Review of Social History*, 44 (1999), pp. 217–247.

from women, who at the same time are responsible for maintaining ethnic/ racial identity. Does this work of race serve to maintain gender systems? Certainly white men used racial difference to discipline women of their own race and class by constructing racialized sexual identities in which white women represent chastity and women of color, promiscuity. These representations operate to ensure the sexual control of white women while justifying the sexual exploitation of women of color by white men. Whiteness, as well as blackness, is profoundly gendered. Still whiteness functions in relation to class, with behavior and character traits parceled out on the basis of social position as well.[21]

The privileges of whiteness have differed by gender and class. In demanding equal rights, white women threaten white men's control of racialized definitions of gender. White men may then stress normative gender systems which demand greater effort by whites. Working-class men, El-Tayeb suggests, benefit from their maleness in the process. This German example nicely demonstrates the "intersectionality" of gender and race. For women of color, however, positioning themselves in one system of struggle/ inequality also situates them in another system of inequality. They have to become engaged in a complex constellation of different interrelated struggles for power. Women of color therefore are caught between competing and unstable systems of male domination. White men try to regulate systems of race, gender and class to ensure their position within a classified, racialized, and gendered system of privileges. In response, men of color may try to regulate their own system of inequality based on gender divisions to ensure the continuation of family and community lives and to construct a politics of resistance in their struggle within the racialized system of inequality. Women of color identify more with men of their group than with white women. These processes exist for other ethnic, religious, and group divisions, as Jenkins's discussion of India reveals.

These divisions among women, and within ethnic or racial groups, derive from the relationships of these groups to the white men who hold much of the power in Western societies. The idea that these divisions come solely from the relationships between or within these social groups only operates to sustain the legitimacy of white men's power, can ignore the privileged status of white women, and precludes an analysis that takes into account the complex interrelationships between all three systems of inequality. It tends to hide the workings of class in the conflation of class with gender and race.

21. Julia Clancy-Smith and Frances Gouda (eds), *Domesticating the Empire: Race, Gender, and Family Life in French and Dutch Colonialism* (Charlottesville, VA, 1998); Earl Lewis and Heidi Ardizzone, "A Modern Cinderella: Race, Sexuality, and Social Class in the Rhinelander Case", *International Labor and Working-Class History*, 51 (1997), pp. 129–147.

INTERSECTIONALITY, SERIALITY, MATERIAL IDENTITIES

The collected essays divide into two loose groupings. The first – Greene, DeVault, and Jenkins – offers three approaches to complicating categories. The next four – Mitchell, Frances, Frader, and El-Tayeb – address the conjuncture of racialized gender and sexuality in relation to colonialization and nation-building. Class is present but undertheorized as these scholars highlight the ways that race and gender define citizenship within diverse class societies – post-emancipation United States on the verge of imperial prominence and in the consolidation of legalized segregation, settler-state Australia, World War I and 1920s France, and Germany in three periods.

Pre-colonial Africa constructed hierarchy in ways distinguished from modern capitalist society. It measured social stratification through lineage, age, ethnicity, and religion, all of which shaped the meaning of gender. Elder women in the lineage could hold power over younger men, sisters over wives. The means and mode of production, and indicators of wealth, also differed. Religious authority, for one, functioned as an important source of power and prestige. Through analysis of eighteenth- and nineteenth-century Anlo society (in what is now Ghana), Sandra E. Greene advances the approach of intersectionality, most associated in the United States with the legal studies movement of critical-race feminism. Arguing against an additive model of race, gender, and class, such scholars consider all of these components together as part of a single identity.[22] Greene explores the intersections between gender and ethnicity, moving African women into the middle of the concept of ethnicity. She counters the construction of ethnicity as something belonging to men and the political bodies that they regulated, a bias in African history analogous to conceptions of class and class formation within histories of capitalist societies.

In this account, gender and ethnicity operate as systems of identification invoked to confront social transformations generated by warfare, the slave trade, political instability, and the resulting influx of large numbers of immigrants. Greene demonstrates the important ways in which gender and ethnicity intersected and the ways in which gender, through marriage choice and household relations, contributed to the process of defining and redefining the "ethnic other". Both men and women were active agents that helped support or undermine boundaries distinguishing "us" and "them", including young women who joined religious groups to regain control over their lives. This account clearly reveals how ethnicity is a labile category, constructed and reconstructed according to the exigencies of external circumstances and reinforced or redirected according to family and group interests.

22. For a sample, see Adrien Katherine Wing, *Critical Race Feminism* (New York, 1997).

Drawing upon the work of feminist philosopher Iris Marion Young and historian Sonya O. Rose, Ileen A. DeVault fruitfully deploys John Paul Sartre's concept of *seriality* to analyze the significance of ethnicity in cross-gender strikes in late nineteenth-century United States.[23] She asks how and why historical actors decide to act upon one identity, for instance class, at one stage in a specific process, only to cast it aside for another identity, for instance ethnicity, at a later stage in the same process, or in circumstances that appear only slightly different. *Seriality* suggests that all individuals are members of various categories of identification conceptualized as "series", which lie waiting to be "ignited" by external events. Members of the working class or employees in a given workplace are also members of other series, such as gender or ethnicity or community/family. Individuals may act out of each of these series, varying in their response between events, during the unfolding of events, or even over the course of their lives. Identities form out of specific material circumstances, specific events, and by way of the historical narrative, itself a manifestation of seriality. Every individual at any one time has an array of choices of identity and can be an active agent in their construction.

Gender and ethnicity may at times reinforce each other; at other times gender divisions compliment ethnic ones, both of which are intensified by divisions of labor. Still other combinations are possible, as when family and community positions "mute" gender and ethnic divisions. DeVault's cases reveal how workers constantly use notions of ethnicity, class and gender, not only to rally support, but also to identify the enemy, to persuade co-workers to strike or to justify their own cause. The concept of seriality fruitfully directs us away from discussions over which category is the dominant one. Moreover, it accounts for contingency, for "the course of living, that is, of creating historical narrative", as DeVault so elegantly explains.

Laura Dudley Jenkins further highlights the materiality of identity. Rejecting the classification of class as a materially-based category and gender and ethnicity as "identity" categories with no such dimension, she calls for synthesizing economic and cultural analysis. New social movements based on collective identities such as gender, religion, or race, she contends, are material. By moving from Europe or North America to "the developing world" and focusing on women's struggles amid intense cultural diversity and material disparities, Jenkins disrupts current theorizing about identity movements. Identity politics has material consequences, especially when some groups argue for rights on the basis of being "more *un*equal" than others.

---

23. Iris Marion Young, "Gender as Seriality: Thinking about Women as a Social Collective", *Signs: A Journal of Women in Culture and Society*, 19 (1994), pp. 713–738; Sonya O. Rose, "Class Formation and the Quintessential Worker", in John R. Hall (ed.), *Reworking Class* (Ithaca, NY, 1997), pp. 133–166.

In India after Independence, no less than during British rule, the category "woman" fractured along religious and caste lines. Asserting rights equal to men's, some Indian women joined to gain "reservations", or parliamentary seats allocated according to group identity. Their demand, initially fostered by the British to counter more divisive religious and nationalist identities, has pitted women against "other backward classes" and Muslims in the politics of nation building. The Indian experience suggests how groups based on gender, ethnicity, caste, or religion may rally around shared interests. However, as identities overlap, material interests may become as unstable as identity is usually thought to be. Though the construction of women's interests and identities changed over time, the importance of keeping the nation intact triumphed over women's rights. "Competing inequalities" then stymied the development of coalitions to fight structural inequalities.

GENDER, RACE, AND NATION

Post-colonial studies and policy history offer new directions for historians of class formation and working-class lives.[24] They have revealed the intricate ways in which race, gender and sexuality connect to citizenship and nation building. The final four articles present intriguing variations on this theme. For Michele Mitchell, racialized discourses of manhood informed the African-American quest for citizenship in the era of imperialism. Indeed gendered notions of respectability for women and manliness for men – as well as education and morality for all – were central to the African-American construction of class, here the silent term behind racialized gendered articulations. Denied the political, civic and economic rights of "real men" at home, elite and aspiring class African-American men advocated their running of empires in Africa and the Philippines. As Mitchell explains, no contradiction necessarily grew from condemning subjugation at home while embracing imperialism as a providential opportunity for uplift of the race. By uncovering the conversation among black elites, she reminds us that men have gender and elites have class but race and nation complicate their meanings. That this story of masculinity and race takes place simultaneously with DeVault's strike narratives highlights the multiple dimensions that exist in one nation at any given time.

Investigation of prostitution, a form of sex work, allows Raelene Frances to chart changing state constructions of class, race, and gender and their

24. For example, Ann Laura Stoler, "Carnal Knowledge and Imperial Power: Gender, Race, and Morality in Colonial Asia", in Micaela di Leonardo (ed.), *Gender At the Crossroads of Knowledge: Feminist Anthropology in the Postmodern Era* (Berkeley, CA, 1991), pp. 51–101; Anne McClintock, *Imperial Leather: Race, Gender and Sexuality in the Colonial Conquest* (New York, 1995); Eileen Boris, "The Racialized Gendered State: Conceptions of Citizenship in the United States", *Social Politics: International Studies in Gender, State and Society*, 2 (1995), pp. 160–180.

shifting intersections. A settler society, Australia suffered from a gender imbalance as well as a dearth of workers. Establishing class hierarchy and maintaining heterosexuality initially dominated the nation-building project. But popular racism, as well as actual circumstances, turned racial hierarchy into a major issue after settler triumph over indigenous people and importation of non-white laborers. Inequalities in access to women, with the availability of Aboriginal women for white men but management of the sex industry to remove white women from non-white men, expressed social hierarchy in racialized gendered terms. In the early twentieth century, "white Australia" immigration policy became a vehicle for racial and sexual purity as officials deployed it against the entrance of white women reputed to be prostitutes. With the deportation of immigrant colored laborers, labor demands encouraged new attitudes toward the Aboriginals. This change meshed with white middle-class women's fight against the traffic in women, which by the late 1930s sought to end sexual exploitation of non-white women as well. Control of its sex industry allowed white Australia to cast itself as a "civilized" nation without disrupting racialized and gendered hierarchies of class power. Sex workers would not be citizens.

In early twentieth-century France gendered and racialized bodies became sites of modernization, which reconstructed class relations in the process. Laura L. Frader demonstrates that the new "science of work" was hardly gender or race neutral. In fact, it involved clearly gendered and racialized bodies in interaction with equally gendered and racialized notions about laboring capacity, muscular power, skill and technology. Frader considers gender, race, and class to be mutually constitutive categories of difference. Through the examples of the feminization of racialized colonial male labor during World War I and the deployment of French female labor in the telephone services during the 1920s, she exposes the silence of gender in the first case and race in the second. Asian workers lost their masculinity, as they became associated with softness and submissiveness, which made them suitable for unskilled labor in light industries and agriculture. Women's distinct physical and "natural" qualities made them good telephone operators, but as representatives of the French state they could also not be anything else but French and therefore white, and more often from middle-class backgrounds. The Asian worker was inferior not on the basis of race but for not being French. The abstract universalism of the Revolution obscured recognition of the racialized gendered basis of French citizenship.[25]

While adoption of French culture can confer a French identity, Germany still defines citizenship not on the basis of birthplace or culture but in terms of blood. Like pre-World-War-II Australia, Germany connected civilization, racial purity, and national identity. Fatima El-Tayeb joins Frader in

25. Joan Wallach Scott, *Only Paradoxes To Offer: French Feminists and the Rights of Man* (Cambridge, MA, 1996), p. 6.

exposing the racialized gendered assumptions behind science. Such attitudes shape state action, here seen through a sweeping history of Germany's response to interracial relations in three periods: the colonial experience in Africa of the imperial state before World War I, the French occupation of the Rhineland at the time of the Weimar regime, and discussions about *Besatzungskinder* ("occupation children") of German women and black American soldiers during the Federal Republic. Attitudes toward interracial mixing were surprisingly consistent from the closing decades of the nineteenth century, when German society almost exclusively perceived Africans in terms of their alleged sexuality. El-Tayeb concludes that the definition of Western identity is still very much dependent upon a binary model of "race". Gender and class antagonisms, she argues, are secondary to the West's conception of itself and the way the West perceives its past, present and future. Black people would always be the "other", whatever their gender, class or religion. Race supersedes divisions of gender or class, even when constructed through concepts of gender and sexuality. The only real male was a white male; both the association with non-white sexuality and female sexuality posed a serious threat to manliness. Sexuality here emerges as a socially-constructed category distinctly interrelated with race, class, and gender. From such strands is nationhood and citizenship built.

What happens to class when historians focus on race and gender? It sometimes fades into the background, assumed rather than actively present. This represents a shift from only a decade or so ago when Karen Brodkin Sacks could reasonably claim that "feminist theories and case studies [...] can be read as sustaining the centrality of class and class struggle as key forces for social transformation".[26] While such scholarship expanded the locations of class, and studies of race and ethnicity have transformed knowledge of social reproduction, class formation, employer strategies, and working-class resistance,[27] a thoroughgoing rethinking of class is still on the agenda.[28] We offer these essays as provocations rather than answers.

26. Karen Brodkin Sacks, "Toward a Unified Theory of Class, Race, and Gender", *American Ethnologist*, 16 (1989), p. 534.
27. See, for example, "Workers in Racially Stratified Societies", thematic issue of *International Labor and Working-Class History*, 51 (1997).
28. See essays in Hall, *Reworking Class*.

International Review of Social History 44 (1999), Supplement, pp. 15-31
© 1999 Internationaal Instituut voor Sociale Geschiedenis

Family Concerns: Gender and Ethnicity in Pre-Colonial West Africa

SANDRA E. GREENE

For at least the past twenty years, historians of pre-colonial Africa have studied gender and ethnic relations, but have focused on either gender or ethnicity without making reference to the other. This essay redresses this neglect by demonstrating that changes in gender and ethnic relations within pre-colonial Africa so profoundly influenced each other that it is impossible to understand one without also taking into consideration the other. Documenting this intersection requires more than simply reconstructing how ethnic groups (in their efforts to compete with others for social and political status) altered gender relations within their societies by handling differentially the affairs of their female and male members. It involves more than analyzing how those disadvantaged because of their gender used the prevailing ethnic relations to ameliorate their own situations, and how these actions in turn altered ethnic relations in the societies in which they lived. It requires as well that we reconceptualize the very definition of ethnicity.

All too often, terms that define particular social categories provide an exclusive racial, ethnic, class or gendered definition. We ignore intersections among these categories. In far too many African historical studies, for example, African men have been defined as representatives of their ethnic groups and as such are described according to their ethnicity. Women are simply women, an undifferentiated and marginalized mass that by implication played no role at all in shaping the content of their own identities or that of others.[1] By analyzing as intimately connected the changes that were occurring in both gender and ethnic relations among the pre-colonial Anlo-Ewe (in what is now south-eastern Ghana), I explode this notion and prove instead that among the Anlo, both men and women were viewed and viewed themselves as integral members of their clan, a social unit that also provided them with their ethnic identity and social standing within Anlo society; and it was because of this degree of identification that males and females alike throughout the history of the Anlo were deeply involved in both supporting and undermining the boundaries that defined "we" and "they" in pre-colonial Anlo. One cannot speak of ethnic men and non-ethnic women. Gender and ethnicity overlapped in ways that determined

---

1. John Lonsdale, "When Did the Gusii (or Any Other Group) Become a Tribe?", *Kenya Historical Review*, 5 (1997), pp. 123-133, and "African Pasts in Africa's Future", *Canadian Journal of African Studies*, 23 (1989), pp. 126-146; Leroy Vail, "Introduction: Ethnicity in Southern African History", in Leroy Vail (ed.), *The Creation of Tribalism in Southern Africa* (London, 1989), p. 15.

the course of social change among the Anlo during the pre-colonial period. One cannot as well speak of men and women as if these categories were defined simultaneously by both gender and ethnicity alone. In pre-colonial Anlo, age differentiated younger women from older women, younger men from older men. Age gave individuals authority over the young, especially in their own families. Similarly personality differences played a role in how individuals chose to respond to specific situations. All these factors (gender, ethnicity, age, and personality) operated in ways that defined a society that was stratified less by economic differences and more by social standing within the community. Some (those who were elderly, respected, and of a particular ethnicity) found their voices much more influential than others because of the combination of social and individual characteristics that came together in their persons. Others found themselves disadvantaged because of their gender, ethnicity, age, and/or personality. Still others fought against their disadvantaged position by challenging the norms that governed social hierarchical relations in Anlo society.

Documenting these events as they unfolded in late seventeenth-, eighteenth- and nineteenth-century Anlo involves a creative use of sources that rarely speak directly to the issues of gender, ethnicity and social stratification. As an oral society, the Anlo have maintained extensive traditions about the history of various clans and how these clans were defined ethnically, but rarely do these traditions speak of the changes that were occurring in the ways the Anlo ethnically defined "we" and "they". Similarly, the oral traditions say virtually nothing about the role women played in defining ethnic categories or changing the number and content of those categories. What we do know, from more recent missionary and ethnographic accounts, however, is that marital arrangements were key to maintaining and challenging ethnic boundaries and that young women were central to these challenges since it was their bodies over which so many sought control. By combining these bits and pieces of information – oral accounts about "we" and "they", written accounts about the role of marriage in structuring and destroying social boundaries, the predominant emphasis on female recruitment to religious orders developed and maintained by ethnic outsiders, and the incredible competition that developed during the era of the slave trade for control over women – it is possible to reconstruct through both circumstantial and direct evidence how gender and ethnicity (along with age) were profoundly and intimately connected in pre-colonial Anlo.

To consider gender and ethnicity as historically inseparable where both men and women, young and old, were primary actors in generating change allows us to avoid the all too frequent tendency to martyr the disadvantaged as they resist their marginalization and to demonize those in power. This tendency exists in a number of studies in pre-colonial African women's history.[2] In my own work, I document, as do so many other scholars, how male-dominated patrilineages and clans exercised far more control over the productive and reproductive capacities of the young women than the young men in eighteenth- and nineteenth-century Anlo. But I avoid demonizing African men or those African elders (older men and older women) who controlled the fate of the young women under their authority. I do so by discussing the increasing pressures felt by family elders as a result of demographic changes and the competition for prestige that arose because of the expanding influence of the Atlantic slave trade. Rather than excuse or deny the negative impact that decisions made by largely male elders (but also by female elders) had on young women, I emphasize the particular historical context in which these elders acted in order to meet specific challenges, not simply to make the lives of the young women in their families miserable. Social history thus becomes a field that examines the relationship between the powerful and the average, where both are given a voice, where the role of the historian is to unravel the complex reasons why individuals and groups acted as they did. This definition avoids creating stark oppositions between good and bad individuals, oppressor and oppressed that is largely incongruent with the complex realities of human relations.

By focusing on both gender and ethnic relations as intimately connected phenomena (where age and personality also played a role), I also bypass the failure of some women's studies scholars to acknowledge the fact that gender relations in Africa historically have been deeply and intimately affected by such issues as race even when race as a category meant little in the social hierarchies of the pre-colonial societies studied. As a field, African history – including African gender and women's history – has laboured under the racial stigmas that have been imposed on Africa and Africans since at least the eighteenth century. These stigmas vilify both African women and African men, associating them with some of the most venal stereotypes reserved for those defined as the ultimate "other" of Western culture and civilization. In the last twenty-five years, however, the growth in women's studies as a field has generated a massive body of scholarship that counters these myths especially as they pertain to African women. This literature documents the extent to which African women often held powerful economic, religious and political positions within their societies, how they resisted exploitation by both African and European men, how they organized their own institutions to reinforce existing social hierarchies or to develop more egalitarian self-help institutions, how class, age and racial

2. I. Wilks, *Wa and the Wala* (Cambridge, 1989); Robert Launay, *Traders without Trade* (Cambridge, 1982); Kwame Arhin, "Strangers and Hosts: A Study in the Political Organization and History of the Atebubu Town", *Transactions of the Historical Society of Ghana*, 12 (1971), pp. 63–81; Toyin Falola, "From Hospitality to Hostility: Ibadan and Strangers, 1830–1904", *Journal of African History*, 26 (1985), pp. 51–68.

differences among women have been used by some women to enhance their own positions and/or disadvantage others.[3] In contrast, the literature on African men as gendered individuals is quite limited[4] – an imbalance that bolsters a particularly negative image of African men since there is little to counter the stereotypes that have been generated for centuries. More significantly, much of the literature on African women reinforces this negative imagery by highlighting the disadvantaged situation of African women vis-à-vis men by vilifying the latter. By considering gender and ethnic relations as historically inseparable phenomena, I can better challenge both explicitly and implicitly racist formulations that describe African men as demons devoted to the subordination of African women for no apparent reason.

To illustrate the significance of the intersections of gender and ethnicity and their importance for understanding the history of pre-colonial African social stratification, I begin by documenting political changes in the late seventeenth century in what was then known as the lower Gold Coast. These changes sparked demographic shifts, a reconfiguration in ethnic boundaries and transformed the way Anlo families managed the affairs of the young men and women under their authority. Anlo youth were increasingly encouraged to marry individuals chosen by their male and female family elders, whether they agreed with the choice of their marital partner or not. However, young women bore the brunt of this system. Additional disadvantages accrued during the late eighteenth and nineteenth century as families came under increasing pressure to restrict even further the marital options for their young. Reactions of some young men and many young women to these familial actions generated major changes in Anlo society that not only altered their own lives as gendered individuals, but also profoundly changed the nature of both gender and ethnic relations in Anlo society during the pre-colonial

3. For a brief discussion of the history of African women's history in relation to other area histories within women's studies, see Sandra E. Greene, "A Perspective from African Women's History: Comment on 'Confronting Continuity'", *Journal of Women's History*, 9 (1997), pp. 95–104.
4. This, of course, has much to do with the fact that scholarly interest in masculinity is relatively recent in comparison with the more developed field of women's studies. Some recent studies on African masculinity include Janet Bujra, "Men at Work in the Tanzanian Home: How Did They Ever Learn?", in Karen Tranberg Hansen (ed.), *African Encounters with Domesticity* (New Brunswick, NJ, 1992), pp. 242–265; Gerald Keis and Salisu A. Abdullahi, "Masculine Power and Gender Ambiguity in Urban Hausa Society", *African Urban Studies*, 16 (1983), pp. 39–53; Shire Chinjerai, "Men Don't Go to the Moon: Language, Space and Masculinity in Zimbabwe", in Andrea Cornwall and Nancy Lindisfarne (eds), *Dislocating Masculinity* (New York, 1994), pp. 147–158; Lisa Lindsey, "'No Need [...] To Think of Home?': Masculinity and Domestic Life on the Nigerian Railway c.1940–61", *Journal of African History*, 39 (1998), pp. 439–466; and the special issue on masculinities in Southern Africa in the *Journal of Southern African Studies*, 24 (1998). There is, in addition, a growing literature on homosexuality among African men, a topic that at times also touches on issues of masculinity.

period. We see this in the late eighteenth century when young Anlo women – either on their own or with encouragement from their mothers – joined the Dzevi's Nyigbla religious order. Many did so to gain more leverage as wives in their marital households, but the results of their actions also successfully challenged the social boundaries that had stigmatized the Dzevi as outsiders. We see it again in the mid-nineteenth century when young women flocked to ethnic outsider Elias Quist's Yewe religious order in defiance of their parents' wishes. Again many of these young women joined this order to marry whom they wished, but in being so successful in recruiting and retaining so many young women, Quist successful entered the social elite of Anlo society and altered the boundaries that defined "we" and "they". Both examples illustrate the extent to which gender and ethnic relations, and changes therein, were intimately and profoundly connected with one another.

GENDERED RESPONSES TO ETHNIC CHALLENGES: ANLO IN THE LATE SEVENTEENTH AND EIGHTEENTH CENTURIES

In 1679, an undetermined number of refugees flooded eastward out of the lower Gold Coast in an effort to escape the advancing armies of the Akwamu state to dominate the trade in slaves, gold and European commodities at Accra. Many sought and received permission to settle in Anlo, an area situated like their own former homelands, on the Atlantic littoral but located just east of the Volta River. In 1702, however, Akwamu conquered Anlo as well. Akwamu citizens entered the area as administrators; they forcefully established themselves in the Anlo capital, Anloga, and then assumed the right to maintain order and to muster troops for additional military campaigns.

For those who had been resident in Anlo well before any of these developments, the presence of large numbers of refugees, and new residents who exercised considerable political power over the area, required a response. Earlier resident families grouped themselves together into new social units known as *hlowo* (clans) as a means of socially distinguishing themselves from others. They acted to protect their rights to the limited arable resources in the area, a course taken because of the geographical characteristics of the Anlo area. The total land area of Anlo in the late seventeenth century was approximately ninety-four square miles. Three-quarters of this consisted of swamps, creeks and low-lying salt-laden, clayey soils that could support little cultivation. The areas suitable for farming, less than twenty square miles, were placed under a system of shifting cultivation that yielded one crop per year. This method necessitated that each household have land in sufficient quantity to allow portions to be fallow, while the remainder provided the food requirements of the household.[5] Even these lands were subject to periodic flooding – a situation that often forced the Anlo to obtain food from the northern side of the lagoon. One such flood occurred in 1683, four years after the first wave of refugees moved into the area from the Ga and Adangbe districts of Accra and Ladoku.[6] Because of the scarcity of arable land resources, the increase in population resulting from the three or four successive waves of refugees between 1679 and 1702 and the floods in 1683, the earlier residents of Anlo organized themselves into clans in order to guarantee for themselves and their future generations access to the land needed for their subsistence. Control and distribution of clan land for the benefit of clan members was at the heart of the development of the clan system.

In creating the clan system, the earlier residents of Anlo not only developed a new social unit within their society, they also altered the way in which the community defined we/they relations. Anlo oral traditions indicate that when the first Ewe-speaking immigrants entered Anlo from the town of Notsie (presently located in south-central Togo), they encountered others already occupying the area. Numbering seven in all, this autochthonous population is said to have lived alongside the Ewe immigrants for some time. Later, however, they disappeared. In recognition of the notion that the autochthons as the first inhabitants of the area had spiritual authority over the land on which the immigrants were now resident, several of the Ewe lineages deified the autochthons and took responsibility for their worship.[7] These accounts – as is often true with other oral traditions – may or may not depict in precise historical detail the events described therein. They are important, however, because they do indicate that the Anlo population at one time, identified itself as a community composed of two groups: one associated with a set of gods that had power over the land, and another set that had custody of those gods brought to Anlo by immigrants from the town of Notsie. The entrance after 1679 of additional immigrants challenged the prevailing conception of we/they relations. Faced with the threat of having to compete for the limited arable land resources in an area that they had occupied for some time, the earlier resident groups retained their identities as lineages affiliated with either autochthonous or immigrant gods, but they elevated to much greater importance invented traditions that they were nevertheless all descendants of the same set of related ancestors and shared

5. For a more detailed discussion of this see, Sandra E. Greene, "Land, Lineage and Clan in Early Anlo", *Africa: The Journal of the International African Institute*, 5 (1981).
6. See Sharon Elaine Nicholson, "A Climatic Chronology for Africa: Synthesis of Geological, Historical and Meteorological Information and Data", (Ph.D. dissertation, University of Wisconsin, Madison, WI, 1976), p. 125.
7. See Sandra E. Greene, *Gender, Ethnicity and Social Change: A History of the Anlo-Ewe* (Portsmouth, NH, 1996), introduction and ch. 2.

an association with Notsie, their common ancestral home.[8] As a group, they stood as one, ethnically distinct from all others. Those who entered the area after 1679 were denied access to land and socially stigmatized as "other". They came late; they had different geographical and genealogical origins; they were ethnic outsiders.

Clan formation also generated changes in the way in which earlier resident Anlo families managed the lives of their young. Studies of the lineage inheritance system that obtained among the Anlo and other Ewe-speaking peoples in the area indicate that at one time all practiced patrilineal inheritance, where daughters as well as sons received from their mothers and fathers land which they could pass to their own children even if the latter, by descent, were members of a different patrilineage. This is said to have been the case in the 1860s and 1870s; it was also true in the early 1900s. Land could be inherited from both father and mother.[9] In most cases, the brothers of a woman who received land from her patrilineage would attempt to retrieve the land after her death or after the death of her children so that the property was not lost to their patrilineage. Among the Anlo, however, the land given to a daughter would be left with her and her children to be absorbed into the latter's patrilineage. No mechanism existed within the Anlo lineage system of inheritance to limit the transfer of property to a different patrilineage, save through the diminution in the amount of land allocated to the daughter.[10]

If this same system existed in the seventeenth century, the influx of refugees that entered and remained in Anlo after 1679 would have severely tested the provision that allowed land to pass out of the control of a particular lineage. Arable land was limited and it is almost certain that marriages occurred between local women and some of the immigrants. Traditions that discuss the particularly close relations that existed between specific stranger groups and earlier residents indicate that it was not uncommon for relations between these two to be reinforced through marriage.[11]

---

8. *Ibid.*, introduction.

9. Cited in J. Dickson, "Marital Selection Among the Anlo Ewe of Ghana: From Parental to Individual Choice", (Ph.D. dissertation, Duke University, Durham, NC, 1982), pp. 79–80.

10. A.K.P. Kludze, "Family Property and Inheritance Among the Northern Ewe", p. 208; D.K. Fiawoo, "Ewe Lineage and Kinship: Sub-Ethnic Group Variation", p. 165; T. Kumekpor, "The Position of Maternal Relatives in the Kinship System of the Ewe", p. 213; all in Christine Oppong (ed.), *Legon Family Research Papers: Domestic Rights and Duties in Southern Ghana*, (Legon, 1974); G.K. Nukunya, "Land Tenure, Inheritance and Social Structure Among the Anlo", *Universitas*, 3 (1973), p. 72, and *Kinship and Marriage Among the Anlo-Ewe* (London, 1969), pp. 43–44, 46. Michel Verdon, *The Abutia Ewe of West Africa: A Chiefdom that Never Was* (Berlin, 1983), p. 125, and Dickson, "Marital Selection", pp. 81–82; note the existence of the separate system of homogeneous transmission as applied to personally acquired, less valuable property.

11. Sandra E. Greene, Field Note 16: Interview with Togbui Le II, 16 August 1978, Anloga, (on deposit with the author), Special Collection (SC) 14/2, pp. 125–127, 187; SC 14/3, p. 272, (Ghana National Archives, Accra, Ghana).

Residential proximity to one another within the wards, and a preference for in-ward marriages that seems to have existed among all Ewe groups, facilitated such a development. The generation produced by these marriages (a generation that the Anlo defined technically as strangers) would have been in a position to compete quite effectively for the limited resources in the area. The descendants of an immigrant male and a local woman would have had three avenues of access to land. They could inherit property from their fathers, who in turn might have gained access to the same because it was unclaimed land or because it had been given to them as a gift. They could inherit from their mothers. Like their fathers, they could claim land that had not been possessed by others. These were the same avenues open to the children born of two local parents.

Given the competitive pressures probably created by geographical constraints and an inheritance system not structured to maintain access to land within a particular patrilineage, the Anlo developed not only a clan system to protect their interests. They also created a preference for clan endogamy to deal with the competition over limited resources and the inadequacy of the lineage system in coping with the problem.[12]

Unfortunately for the young women in these earlier resident lineages, the development of the clan system and the preference for clan endogamy came at their expense. For while both young males and females were increasingly forced to marry members of their clan whatever their wishes, the polygynous character of Anlo society allowed males, no matter their actual financial means, to at least aspire to contracting additional marriages with women of their own choosing. Women had no such options. This preference for marriage within the clan joined the already pre-existing preference for marriages between families that lived in the same residential areas. Thus with the development of the clan system and the preference for clan endogamy, ethnic insider women found their ability to influence their own marriages increasingly restricted. The development of the clan system rendered a woman's clan affiliation irrelevant for her children (since – unlike the lineage system – the children took their affiliation only from their father) yet in the context of marriage, her clan affiliation became more important than that of her brothers. If a woman's brother was betrothed to a woman of a different clan, the land he inherited from his father would remain in the clan because those who could inherit from him included his own children and the children of his sisters. If, however, a woman married a man of a different clan, her land would be lost to her clan because her children belonged irrevocably to the clan of their father. Thus, the earlier resident families in Anlo chose to defend their rights to the arable resources in the area by strongly encouraging – and in some instances forcing – the women

12. D. Westermann, "Die Glidyi-Ewe", *Mitteilungen des Seminars für Orientalische Sprachen*, 38 (1935), p. 144; Nukunya, *Kinship and Marriage*, p. 74.

in their families to marry someone who both lived in the same ward as the woman's family and was also a fellow clan member.

During the eighteenth and into the nineteenth century ethnic outsiders, for very different reasons, also increased control over the women in their families. This is most evident with the Amlade, a group that entered the Anlo area from Anexo as part of this state's invasion and conquest of the Anlo in 1742. In 1750 Anlo managed to free itself, but many from Anexo who stayed coalesced into their own clan known as the Amlade and established a reputation for themselves in Anlo as a group associated with particularly powerful gods. They installed in their new homeland their god, Togbui Egbe, which had the ability to incapacitate seriously those with whom the Amlade argued. Another god, Sui, proved powerful enough to demand payment for its services in the form of a *fiasidi*, a young woman who remained as a servant associated with the Sui shrine for the rest of her life and who on her death had to be replaced by her family with another female family member. Of greater importance here is that the Amlade – despite their ethnic outsider origins – were able to obtain membership in the highest political and religious circles in Anlo by reinventing the traditions that recounted their origins. They did so with the help of a number of allies within the Anlo political elite, but also by exercising much greater control over the women in their families.[13] Nineteenth-century descriptions by German missionaries noted that the Anlo expected a wife to know a great deal about her husband's clan. It was her responsibility to introduce their children into the culture of the father's clan.[14] Failure to do so could lead to potentially harmful consequences for those children. This education imperative appears to have affected how the Amlade families managed the marital affairs of their daughters.

Strongly urging daughters to marry within the clan in order to retain land holdings could not have been the factor that motivated the Amlade to adopt this practice, however. They did not possess any land as a corporate unit, even though they did indeed favor marriages within the clan as did other ethnic outsider clans in Anlo.[15] Several possibilities exist to account for this preference. Perhaps the various patrilineages that together formed the Amlade clan were few in number and therefore to strengthen their numerical position within Anlo they chose to betroth their daughters to men within the clan. A second possibility may have involved the imperative the Amlade must have felt to maintain control over the socialization of their children because of the change in identity they were attempting to affect

13. For a more complete discussion of Amlade origins and their history in Anlo, see Greene, *Gender, Ethnicity and Social Change*, pp. 61–67.

14. Westermann, "Die Glidyi-Ewe", p. 143; J. Spieth, "Von Den Evhefrauen", *Quartalblatt der Norddeutschen Missionsgesellschaft*, 6 (1889), p. 6.

15. Westermann, "Die Glidyi-Ewe", pp. 142–145; Greene, Field Note 16: Interview with Togbui Le II, 16 August 1978, Anloga; Nukunya, *Kinship and Marriage*, p. 23.

during the late eighteenth century. As ethnic outsiders, they were technically barred from holding any high position within the Anlo polity. Yet by the early nineteenth century, they had the right to enstool the paramount chief, the *awoamefia*, and to pray on behalf of the entire polity. They accomplished this by working with political allies to alter their history to emphasize a connection by descent to the original homeland of those who traditionally held authority in Anlo. They also used their connections with powerful gods to threaten those who offended them. They then supplemented these efforts by giving their daughters in marriage to men within their own clan. By doing so, Amlade parents could more safely assure that their own daughters would teach their children to view themselves as members of a clan that was indeed genealogically and spatially connected to the earliest Anlo families in the original homeland, Notsie. This latter effort required that Amlade young women sacrifice their own marriage plans for the sake of the clan. That many Amlade women willingly and/or unwillingly married fellow clan members is supported by the fact that they practiced clan endogamy at the same rate as others in Anlo. Thus, when the Amlade redefined themselves as ethnic insiders, they also reordered gender relations within the clan in order to reinforce their new ethnic identity. This reordering, however, had the same impact on gender relations as the reordering that occurred among the earlier immigrants to Anlo: families opted to alter the ways in which they handled the affairs of the young men and women over whom they had authority by placing far more restrictions on their young women than their young men. Thus, by the end of the nineteenth century, young women of Anlo – whether members of ethnic insider or ethnic outsider families – found their voices increasingly silenced in comparison with their brothers when it came to decisions that affected their own bodies. This situation developed in large part from the changing character of ethnic relations with Anlo society.

The construction and reproduction of these new ethnic and gender relations was not solely the concern of male household heads. Older women actively participated in the decision-making bodies of their clans and lineages and participated actively in both designing and implementing the way in which gender relations would be altered to support the ethnic interests of the family. Many mothers, for example, supported the decisions made by male and even older female family elders by encouraging their children, especially daughters, to acquiesce in the limitations imposed on them by the various preferences that came to govern Anlo marital relations. Included as part of this education was an emphasis on the desirability of marrying someone within one's own clan. Children whose mothers and fathers belonged to the same clan expressed great pride in that fact.[16]

16. Gottlob Binetsch, "Beantwortung mehrerer Fragen über unser Ewe-volk und seine Anschauungen", *Zeitschrift für Ethnologie*, 38 (1906), p. 13; Spieth, "Von der Evhefrauen", p. 6; Westermann, "Die Glidyi-Ewe", p. 143.

Older women's interests in supporting the Anlo preferences for clan endogamy and even young women's willingness to go along with this socialization suggests that most women took seriously the ideology that family members, male and female, should support their kin-group over their individual interests when family interests were threatened and when the family had the opportunity to benefit from particular conditions or changes. This ideology is evident in the strong prescriptions that outlined the responsibilities each clan member had to support and defend the *hlo*.[17] So many families were successful in encouraging their daughters to accept many restrictions on the powers they had over their own bodies. Thus, older women and younger ones protected the interests of their kin- and ethnic group, even if this meant sacrificing their own interests or the interests of their daughters.

ETHNIC AND GENDERED RESPONSES TO THE CHALLENGE OF MARGINALIZATION: ANLO IN THE LATE EIGHTEENTH CENTURY

By the end of the eighteenth century, Anlo women – whether members of ethnic insider or ethnic outsider families – found their voices increasingly silenced by the elders within their lineages and clans. Rivalry during the eighteenth century between earlier residents and those who entered Anlo after 1679 had prompted both to form themselves into separate sets of clans and to urge their young women strongly to marry fellow clan members. Late eighteenth- and nineteenth-century European accounts have indicated that by this period some young women had begun to challenge successfully certain aspects of this system. The history of the Dzevi clan and the Quist family, both defined by the Anlo as ethnic outsiders, best reveal these challenges. The Dzevi entered Anlo as Ga- and Adangbe-speaking refugees after 1679. The Quist family defined themselves and were defined as ethnic outsiders because they were the patrilineal descendants of a Danish officer who had been stationed on the west African coast during the late eighteenth century. Both significantly were also associated with influential religious orders during a pre-colonial period when political influence was inextricably linked with religious authority in Anlo. The more powerful one's reputation for exerting spiritual influence over worldly events, the more influential one became.

In 1769 an unprecedented event occurred in Anlo when an ethnic outsider clan, the Dzevi, rose to power. This clan demanded with the support of the Anlo population that the *awoamefia* – the most powerful leader in Anlo – share authority with them. The Dzevi could make such demands because their god, Togbui Nyigbla, had brought them victory in battle at a

---

17. For a more detailed discussion of these prescriptions, see Greene, *Gender, Ethnicity and Social Change*, p. 31.

particularly critical time for the political and economic welfare of the entire Anlo polity.[18] Significantly, the Dzevi priest of the god Nyigbla, and his supporters, were able to maintain his position within the most powerful political and religious circles in Anlo throughout the remainder of the eighteenth and into the nineteenth century by successfully claiming that their god was responsible for additional military victories. Of greater importance here is the fact that the Dzevi obtained massive support from the women of Anlo for reasons that had little to do with its spiritual role on the battlefield.

Family pressure on women over marriage choice had increased throughout the eighteenth century, particularly after 1750 when the Anlo became more involved in the Atlantic slave trade. In order to compete better for prestige gained from conducting successful trade relations with Europeans, many Anlo families began to encourage their daughters not only to marry men from the same residential ward and fellow clan members, but also the sons of their mother's brothers. Such marriages would ensure that the labour of the children born to such marriages stayed within the family and such labour could generate the commodities that would facilitate more extensive involvement in the Atlantic slave trade. Thus, by the end of the eighteenth century, young women in Anlo were also encouraged – and at times, forced – to marry maternal cousins. Under such conditions, divorce also became more problematic, since these marriages brought families the potential to enhance their social and economic standing within the community. Divorce would undermine such efforts and thus became more difficult as the social stakes associated with maintaining marriage were raised.

This situation changed for many women when the Nyigbla order began to gain prestige within the Anlo polity. As part of the efforts to institutionalize its position among the political and religious elite, the Nyigbla order of the Dzevi clan began to recruit (with the support of most Anlo families) at least two women from every Anlo clan every year. According to nineteenth-century accounts, the Nyigbla order attempted to maintain the impression that the god itself called the recruited women. However, members of the order would encourage others to join and then the priest would instruct the recruits how to behave. This involved the young woman learning to behave as if she were slightly off-balance mentally. As one elder noted, "they were not normal any more, but not so abnormal that people thought they were totally crazy [...]. They would roam about [...] so parents were not totally surprised by the possibility [that they had been caught by the god]."[19] Every year women responded to this recruitment effort and every year these new members, known as *zizidzelawo*, recruited others. Young

18. *Ibid.*, pp. 82–86.
19. See H. Seidel, "Der Yewe Dienst in Togolande", *Zeitschrift für Afrikanische und Oceanische Sprachen*, 3 (1897), pp. 166–167, and Greene, Field Note 65: Interview with Togbui Dzobi Adzinku, 6 January 1988, Anloga.

women undoubtedly had many reasons for joining this order. They gained prestige from affiliation with one of the most powerful gods in Anlo; membership may have provided an expanded set of contacts with potential social and economic benefits; others may have joined simply at the urging of their mothers. Of particular significance for our discussion here are the benefits that came to wives. Married women affiliated with this order gained considerable freedom of action within their husband's households. Accounts about such religious orders among the Ewe explain that:

> [...] the *kosio* (the prepubescent initiates) and the *vodu-viwo* (the children who had been dedicated to the god) either did not marry or their marriages contained the potential for great instability because, as European traveler A. B. Ellis noted, "[...] the husband [...] [could] not punish her or reprove her for any excesses, sexual or other[wise] [...]".[20]

Similarly, studies on Akan priestesses in the Fanti area indicate that "the husband of a priestess [had] to be extremely cautious not to 'abuse' her, lest he offend her deity and then have to appease it be a series of costly gifts".[21]

Women closely associated with gods, including the Nyigbla deity, thus gained considerable leverage within their marriages. By joining Nyigbla or encouraging their daughters to do so, many Anlo women took advantage of the opportunity to better protect their own interests in a climate where their natal and marital families were less prepared to do so. In pursuing this course, then, some young Anlo women, with the support of their mothers, not only took advantage of Nyigbla's popularity by consciously joining an order to gain greater freedom within their marital households. They also – wittingly or unwittingly – began to challenge those changes in gender relations that had begun to deny them the ability to participate in discussions about the fate of their own bodies. The support these women give to Nyigbla also challenged the prevailing character of ethnic relations in Anlo because this support helped institutionalize the Nyigbla priest's position within the Anlo political and religious hierarchy. With the inclusion of the Dzevi as ethnic outsiders in the ranks of the most influential political and religious groups came the first expansion in the definition of people deemed eligible to hold high political and religious office within the Anlo polity. The Dzevi's elevation to the position of sharing power with the Anlo *awoamefia* redefined the boundaries that separated ethnic insider from outsiders and which limited the latter's ability to wield influence within Anlo. Ethnic origins were still important, but service to the Anlo polity became an equally important marker of status. This change, in turn, opened

20. A.B. Ellis, *The Ewe-Speaking Peoples of the Slave Coast of West Africa* (Chicago, IL, 1890), pp. 141, 142; see also Greene, Field Note 33: Interview with Boko Seke Axovi, 3 October 1978, Anloga.
21. Robin Law, *The Slave Coast of West Africa, 1550–1750* (New York, 1991) p. 114; and James Boyd Christensen, "The Adaptive Function of Fanti Priesthood", in W.R. Bascom and M.J. Herskovits (eds), *Continuity and Change in African Cultures* (Chicago, IL, 1959), p. 268.

the door during the nineteenth century for other ethnic outsiders, like the
Quist family, to become centrally positioned within the Anlo social hierarchy.

GENDERED AND ETHNIC RESPONSES TO THE
CHALLENGE OF MARGINALIZATION: ANLO IN THE
NINETEENTH CENTURY

Nyigbla's stature in Anlo declined precipitously in the early 1800s. But it
still played a prominent role within the political and religious cultures of
Anlo between the early 1840s, when it again led the Anlo in battle, and
1874, when Anlo's defeat by the Europeans marked the beginning of its
final decline as a war god. During this period, the Yewe religious order
actively competed with Nyigbla by offering wives as well as young unmarried girls better support than available in the Nyigbla order. Affiliation with
the Yewe religious order also proved central to the social elevation of the
Quist family.

Because Nyigbla provided no recourse for young women who would have
liked to refuse their elders' choice of a husband, the Yewe order took advantage of this and offered women the opportunity to select their own spouse
and the time when they would marry.[22] Yewe also offered married women
a means to check the behaviour of abusive husbands when their own families
were unwilling or unable to assist them. In both situations, advantages
stemmed from the belief that an offence given to a Yewe member was an
offence to her god. Evidence that the god had indeed been offended took
the form of the Yewe woman behaving in an obviously possessed state.
Thus, if a husband quarreled with his Yewe wife, beat her or insulted her,
she could declare herself *alaga*, that is, someone who has gone wild, a right
of all members of this religious order. Young unmarried female members
also had this option. Former Yewe member, Stefano Kwadzo Afelevo, later
explained that they were instructed to "go wild if [their] mother or father
said something offensive to [them]".[23] Only by paying a fine to the Yewe
priest or *hubono* could parents or the husband of a female *alaga* rectify the
offence. According to a number of accounts from the late nineteenth century, these fines were often so large that the offender was forced to borrow
the sum or place a relative in pawn.[24] No doubt this action did much to

22. Stephen H. Kwadzo Afelevo, "Ein Bericht über den Yehwekultus der Ewe. Herausgegeben
mit deutscher Übersetzung und Anmerkungen von D. Westermann", *Mitteilungen des Seminars
für Orientalische Sprachen*, 33 (1930), p. 27.
23. Cited in Seidel, "Der Yewe Dienst", p. 170.
24. To pawn an individual means that a person hand a relative, usually a child, to another in
exchange for a loan. The child would live with the lender, working for him or her. The work the
child performed for the lender would serve as interest on the loan. The child could not return to
his or her family until the loan principle was repaid. For a more extensive discussion of pawning,

strengthen a woman's voice in her natal and her husband's household, but it had other consequences as well. By the end of the nineteenth century, the ethnic outsider Elias Quist had become a major economic power and respected figure in Anlo in large part because of his association with Yewe and because of the support his Yewe order received from women who sought to challenge the way in which their families handled their marital affairs.

The history of Quist's association with Yewe began shortly after 1847 when he was traveling westward from the coastal town of Anexo to Accra by boat. The vessel on which he was a passenger sank. A diviner attributed his near drowning to one of the Yewe gods, who was calling him to its service. Oral traditions indicate that these events set the stage for his involvement with the Yewe order. Heeding this call, he established a Yewe shrine and became its *hubono*, owner.[25] Such a position required him to support financially the activities of the members of the order, to adjudicate disputes between members and non-members, and to manage many of the ritual affairs of its members.[26] He undoubtedly also – as required of *hubonowo* – continued to provide assistance to and gain adherents from others the god had helped, but Quist did more than simply assume the expected role of a Yewe owner. He reorganized the way in which the order interacted with the community so that he could use the order to respond both to the changing business climate in the area[27] and to meet the needs of those women disaffected with their families because of the increased restrictions these families had placed on the women's ability to control their own bodies.

By using the Yewe order in this way, Quist, as an ethnic outsider, gained tremendous support from and gave great assistance to Anlo women (no matter their ethnic identity). This, in turn, had profound consequences for the norms that governed Anlo gender and ethnic relations. Acceptance of Quist as a leading figure in nineteenth-century Anlo society significantly altered the boundaries that had previously defined "we" and "they" in pre-colonial Anlo. The notion that wealth alone (along with a shorter period of residency) could define a person or group as an integral and central member of Anlo society joined earlier emphases on connections to the ancestral homeland, time of arrival and contributions to the welfare of the polity.

That many women joined Yewe to defy the norms governing gender relations contributed to the tendency for other young men and women to

see Toyin Falola and Paul E. Lovejoy, *Pawnship in Africa: Debt Bondage in Historical Perspective* (Boulder, CO, 1994).
25. See Greene, Field Note 70: Interview with Mr Kwami Kpodo, 12 January 1988; and Field Note 92: Interview with Togbui Amegashi Afeku IV, 18 February 1988, Tema. See also SC 14/1, p. 208; and Anlo Traditional Council Minute Book No. 3: 14/4/6–32/7/87, pp. 14–37 (Anloga Traditional Council Office, Anloga, Ghana).
26. Richard Tetteh Torgby, "The Origin and Organisation of the Yewe Cult", B.A. long essay, Department for the Study of Religion, University of Ghana, Legon (1977), pp. 24, 31.
27. For more discussion of this, see Greene, *Gender, Ethnicity and Social Change*, pp. 97–98.

establish their own unions (concubinage) without the benefit of direct parental involvement, a formal marriage ceremony or association with the Yewe order. This, in turn, had a major impact on the gendered manner in which families managed the marriages of their youth. Parental authority declined. Young men, but especially young women, reasserted their right to pick their mates.[28] In making such choices, young women not only successfully challenged the norms that governed gender relations in nineteenth-century Anlo, they also challenged the prevailing norms the defined ethnic outsiders like the Quist family as different, potentially dangerous and to be avoided and/or marginalized in all matters that affected the interest of ethnic insider families and the polity. This was the case because of the intimate connections that existed between ethnic and gender relations in Anlo.

CONCLUSION

This discussion of gender and ethnic relations among the Anlo-Ewe illustrates the importance of analyzing, as interconnected phenomena, shifts in the ways gender relations operated within the family and changes in the boundaries that the Anlo constructed to separate the ethnic "we" from the ethnic "they". When refugees flooded into the Anlo area and remained to compete with the earlier residents for access to the limited arable land in the district, the earlier residents not only redefined the boundaries that defined ethnic insiders and outsiders to limit the abilities of the newcomers to influence the affairs of the polity, they also altered the gendered manner in which they handled the marital affairs of their young. In response to these exclusionary practices, those marginalized because of their outsider status adopted for different reasons the same gendered marital practices introduced by the ethnic insiders. Those most affected by these changes – the young women in both ethnic insider and outsider families – then reacted to demands that they and not their brothers sacrifice their interests for the sake of their families by joining religious orders organized by a number of ethnic outsiders. In coming together in the context of these new religious groups, those stigmatized by their ethnic and gender identities were able to ameliorate their marginal status while also having a profound impact on the way the Anlo defined the boundaries that separated "we" from "they" and managed the marital affairs of their young.

Only by analyzing the interconnections between gender and ethnic relations is it possible to understand the extent to which social relations involving one set of defined identities is necessarily connected to other identities and social relations. For pre-colonial African history, such an analysis also helps avoid the all-too-common tendency to portray both "oppressor" and "oppressed" in one-dimensional terms where, for example,

28. Binetsch, "Beantwortung mehrerer", p. 46.

men are simply misogynists and women simply marginal to the political and social affairs of the entire society. Avoiding such simplistic portrayals is especially important within the field of pre-colonial African history because African men and women have been steeped for far too long in the racist imagery that continues to influence the way others see Africa, Africans and African culture. By analyzing gender and ethnicity together within the same study as inextricably connected phenomena, one can more accurately represent the histories of African peoples in all their complexities.

International Review of Social History 44 (1999), Supplement, pp. 33–52
© 1999 Internationaal Instituut voor Sociale Geschiedenis

Narratives Serially Constructed and Lived: Ethnicity in Cross-Gender Strikes 1887–1903*

ILEEN A. DEVAULT

On 1 August 1893, already feeling the pinch of economic downturn, management at the Pray, Small & Co. shoe factory in Auburn, Maine, posted new wages for its employees.[1] Twelve days later, facing their first lower pay checks, female stitchers in the factory walked off their jobs. The union which represented the stitchers declared the shop non-union a week later and called for all of its members to join the stitchers' strike. Only about a dozen male workers answered this call, as the two most highly-skilled groups of male workers, the lasters and the shoe cutters, remained on the job. These workers belonged to their own separate unions, which had either already agreed to the new wage list (the cutters) or were in the middle of negotiations over it with the company (the lasters). It took the cutters another week before they decided to join the stitchers' action; it would take the lasters a month and a half and a citywide expansion of the strike to make the same decision.

Once the lasters joined the strike, however, their employers lost no time in bringing in recent immigrants from Armenia to replace the striking lasters. Strikers similarly lost no time in their response, firing off both letters to their congressmen and bricks and stones at the hapless Armenians. The strikers, who had appeared to be almost hopelessly divided by gender and skill at the beginning of August, found themselves in early October united as "honest American workmen" [sic] against "the pauper labor of Europe".[2]

The Auburn strike highlights both the gender and the ethnic identifications of these members of the working class and encourages us to begin to think about the complex relationships among class, gender, and ethnicity. How did the Auburn workers view their participation in the strike of 1893? Did the stitchers view themselves as women, as well as workers? How self-conscious was the identification of the cutters and lasters as men and male breadwinners? Did the introduction of Armenian strikebreakers congeal the strikers' identities as "Yankees" or simply as non-Armenians? How can the

* My thanks to the editors of this supplement, Eileen Boris and Angélique Janssens, as well as to Jeanne Boydston, Marjorie DeVault, Lori Ginzberg, Michael Lounsbury, and Roey Thorpe for their comments.
1. Unless otherwise noted, the story of this strike comes from coverage in the *Lewiston Evening Journal* (hereafter cited as *LEJ*), the *Boston Globe*, and the *Shoe and Leather Reporter*, vol. 56 (hereafter cited as *SLR*).
2. *SLR*, 5 October 1893 (vol. 56, no. 14), p. 798.

historian begin to untangle these conflicting possible identifications, all brought to surface in this ultimate expression of class – the strike?

Unfortunately, available sources do not permit complete answers to any of these questions. Newspaper accounts of the strike provide only snippets of the strikers' own words, combined with incomplete coverage of their actions. At best, both the newspapers and the scattered extant union reports only provide observers' views and opinions of the strike, its events, and its participants. These and other sources, however, do present some sense of the actions taken by some strikers and they facilitate understanding the identities assigned to the strikers by others and against which the strikers would develop their own consciousnesses.

Even without such problematic sources, the historian is left with only the sketchiest of answers to questions of intent and cognizance. Use of the Sartrian concept of *seriality* can begin to overcome this problem and start to untangle the knotty problems of workers' identifications and conscious-ness.[3] This essay will argue that class, gender, and ethnicity are "serial" in two senses of that term. One is Sartre's philosophical sense of such categories as *serial*, of individuals' consciousness of belonging to such categories in effect waiting to be ignited by external events and then acted upon by the individuals in question. The other is the more ordinary sense of events being serial, of their occurring one after another – in other words, the standard understanding of historical narrative. My goal is to overlay these two senses of the ways in which individuals' identifications are serial.

For Sartre, a *series* was a collection of individuals defined as such by their basic orientation toward and relationship to material structures. (His illustration begins with individuals waiting for a bus in the morning.) From outside the *series*, observers may see these individuals as having certain characteristics in common, but the members of the *series* do not necessarily see themselves as having anything in common. Their commonality only exists in relation to the bus and its route. If something happens (such as the bus passing them by) to make them aware of themselves and each other as having something in common (they may all be late for work now), they may acknowledge their commonality, for example, through conversation. At this point, Sartre argues that the *series* becomes a *group*. In this way, any individual is, at any given time, a member of many different *series*, a poten-tial member of many different *groups*. It is only when these individuals begin to take action (perhaps combining to take a taxi to work) that their *group* becomes a *fused group*. If this *group* were to organize a boycott of the

3. See Iris M. Young, "Gender as Seriality: Thinking about Women as a Social Collective", *Signs*, 19 (1994); Sonya Rose, "Class Formation and the Quintessential Worker", in John Hall (ed.), *Reworking Class* (Ithaca, NY, 1997); and Jean-Paul Sartre, *Critique of Dialectical Reason* (London, 1976), esp. vol. I, book I, ch. 4 and book 2, chs 1, 2, 6, and 7. In what follows, when I refer to Sartre's use of terms such as "*serial*", I will put them in italics. When this word, or others appear not italicized, then I am using them in their ordinary English usage.

bus, they would become a *pledged group*. Sartre, whose interest was in discussing the significance of a "working class", then considers the ways in which these *fused* and *pledged groups* might be formalized as *institutions*. (His analysis, formulated in the 1950s, focused particularly on what he called *ossified institutions*, a clear reference to the bureaucratized unions of the 1940s and '50s.)

Iris Young has argued that Sartre's concept of *seriality* provides us with a useful way of thinking about women, allowing us to account for women whose experiences may vary widely depending on their race, ethnicity, social class, and other factors. As Young puts it, "Gender, like class, is a vast, multifaceted, layered, complex, and overlapping set of structures and objects. *Women* are the individuals who are positioned as feminine by the activities surrounding those structures and objects."[4] The many structures determining the *series* of women include the socially constructed sexual division of labor in the workforce. Race and nationality could also be seen as a form of *seriality*, though Young does not discuss the ways in which these might function.

Like Young, I borrow freely these useful concepts from Sartre's work. For my purposes, the use of Sartre's concept of *seriality* translates into the following pattern: a strike begins at the moment when individual workers (in the *series*, "workers in X plant") come together and recognize that they have interests, needs, or desires in common which are in opposition to those of their employer (thereby forming a *group*). They collectively stop work (becoming a *fused group*). At this point, some of these workers may form a union (a *pledged group*) or attempt to utilize an existing union (an *institution*) in order to sustain their struggle. The moment of a strike's inception – that moment when workers as a collective put down their tools and stop working – demonstrates the coalescence of the *series* into the *group* which we can recognize as exhibiting incipient working-class identity. This moment of incipient class crystallization, however, is difficult to sustain. Individual workers' identifications with other *series* to which they belong often rise to the surface, especially during extended strikes. Gender, ethnicity, race, religion, and family status are only a few of the possible examples of the social markers of such *series*. Some of these markers subsequently become encoded in workers' union organizations, or *institutions*.[5]

While my focus on strike activities leads to a certain privileging of class over other categories, here my interest is not so much in the strike itself as an expression of class but in the ways in which a strike situation heightens

4. Young, "Gender as Seriality", p. 728.
5. The further comprehension of such an encoding of genders into unions belonging to the early AFL is the goal of my larger study, tentatively titled *United Apart: Sex, Gender, and the Rise of Craft Unionism* (forthcoming, Cornell University Press). See also my essay, "'To Sit Among Men': Skill, Gender, and Craft Unionism in the Early American Federation of Labor", in Eric Arnesen, Julia Greene, and Bruce Laurie (eds), *Labor Histories: Class, Politics, and the Working-Class Experience* (Chicago, IL, 1998).

and highlights the many points of tension and division which normally operate below the surface of workers' daily lives. Rick Fantasia has examined contemporary strikes in a similar manner, calling on Lloyd Warner's discussion of the strike as a crisis in which people have to make fundamental decisions about their lives and livelihoods.[6] Strikes not only highlight the class or economic components of workers' lives, but also bring to the surface the fracture lines disrupting so-called "pure" class consciousness. My concern lies in the ways in which a strike serially leads workers to confront the significance of different *series* to which they may belong.

Thinking about workers' identifications in this serial/*serial* way does away with questions of whether any one of the categories (i.e., class, race, gender, ethnicity) is dominant over the others. Instead, the use of Sartre's concept underscores that every individual at every moment holds within herself a simultaneous range of possible identities. Which of these identities will enter the consciousness of this individual and therefore inform her actions at any particular point in time depends on her role in the ongoing historical narrative, or serial.

This way of conceptualizing the issue keeps alive the basic concepts of historical materialism. Workers do not act randomly; their actions in fact grow out of the material circumstances of their lives. (In this case, those material circumstances arise at the conjuncture of their positions within given workplace and family divisions of labor.) At the same time, using Sartre's concept of a *series* keeps alive the idea of individual workers' agency as well, since the worker retains the ability to decide whether or not to act out of any given *serial* membership at any moment. It is only within the actual twists and turns of the historical narrative that we can begin to understand the shifting contingencies of specific situations. In turn, these contingencies endow historical actors with the power of agency. The strike stories narrated below show the operation of the complexities possible in the interaction of historical narrative, historical materialism, and individuals' agency.

All of the strikes under consideration involve workforces divided deeply and fundamentally by sex. As we will see, all the industries involved depended on relatively elaborate sexual divisions of labor.[7] Because of this, gender was a frequent social marker around which *group* consciousness developed within the class-driven dynamics of these strikes. Yet gender and ethnicity, as *series*, both coexist and serially surmount one another. What follows presents four stories of strikes in which gender and ethnicity are interwoven in different ways. The strike of shoe workers in Auburn, Maine, illustrates the ways in which incipient gender divisions could be overcome

---

6. See Rick Fantasia, *Cultures of Solidarity: Consciousness, Action, and Contemporary American Workers* (Berkeley, CA, 1988), p. 16.
7. *United Apart* examines strikes in four broad industries: boots and shoes, clothing, textiles, and tobacco products. All but tobacco products are represented in the narratives given in this paper.

by the introduction of strikebreakers defined as an ethnic "other". The next strike, that of New Jersey thread workers, exemplifies the reinforcement of deep gender divisions by equally deep ethnic divisions among the workers. A strike of Baltimore garment workers demonstrates the ways in which ethnic ties among workers could overcome gender divisions, an outcome cemented by the presence of an ethnic "other" in the industry. Finally, a strike of Wilkes–Barre, Pennsylvania, lace workers reveals how both gender and ethnic divisions could be muted by workers' family positions and community relationships.

In all of these strikes, workers' multiple positions in relation to material structures both limit and expand their agency within their particular historical narrative. As we have already begun to note in the Auburn strike, different patterns of gender and ethnicity are not necessarily mutually exclusive. Rather, as the strike narratives proceed, we see how these different interactions of gender and ethnicity can be realized both *serially* and serially, in sequence. Following these types of interactions through historical narrative avoids static categories and allows us to witness instead the flux and contingency of actors' identifications along lines of class, gender, and ethnicity.

I

With this in mind, then, let us return to the Auburn strike, this time in a bit more detail. The workforce at Pray, Small & Co., like that at other shoe factories throughout New England, was highly segregated by sex. Male "cutters" cut out the leather pieces for the shoes; female "stitchers" used specialized sewing machines to sew the pieces together, make buttonholes in them, and add decorative stitching; male "lasters" shaped the leather upper to the sole in order to size the shoe; and male "bottomers" did the final fastening together of the shoe. By the 1890s the long history of the sexual division of labor in shoe production ensured that the workplaces of New England shoe workers as well as their unions were stratified by sex.[8]

For almost two weeks after the posting of new wages on 1 August, Pray, Small's female stitchers presumably discussed the proposed changes. It is easy to imagine the groans at the initial announcement of wage cuts, followed by increasingly animated discussion of the burdens the cuts would place on them and their families. Here we see the stitchers initially acting out of their sense of membership in a *series*, that of stitchers at Pray, Small. On Saturday 12 August they walked off their jobs, refusing to work for the lower wages. The union representing the stitchers, Local 12 of the Boot and

8. See Mary Blewett, *Men, Women, and Work: Class, Gender, and Protest in the New England Shoe Industry, 1780–1910* (Urbana, IL, 1988), for a full description of the production process, its changing sexual division of labor, and the unions involved in nineteenth-century shoe production.

Shoe Workers' International Union (BSWIU), then convened meetings of both the striking stitchers and of the non-striking male workers in the factory. For the first week of the strike, male workers continued at their jobs even though only a handful of women remained in the stitching room. Without the labor of the stitchers, however, shoes remained unfinished. As negotiations with the company ground to a halt, the shoe workers' union declared the shop non-union and announced that all workers would join the stitchers' strike. Now some male workers, too, would be acting out of their membership in a larger *series*, that of Pray, Small employees.

Though more workers joined the strike on Monday 21 August, neither the lasters belonging to the Lasters' Protective Union (LPU) nor the shoe cutters of the Boot & Shoe Cutters' Union (BSCU), responded to strikers' appeals for solidarity. The cutters already had reached agreement with Pray, Small on the new wages, and the lasters were still negotiating with the company. For both these groups of skilled male workers, their membership in their own *series* of skilled workers still outweighed their identities as members of the *series*, Pray, Small employees. This soon changed for the cutters, however, who, despite their prior agreement with management on wages, on Friday 25 August "packed their traps and left the shop". Firm officials rightly "supposed [that the cutters' walkout] was because of the trouble in the stitching room".[9] Cutters now joined the *group* of strikers at Pray, Small.

The following Monday, 28 August, the Auburn Manufacturers' Association, with which Pray, Small, and Co.'s management had been conferring throughout the past two weeks, escalated the stakes. The seven shoe companies belonging to the association told their cutters and stitchers that they would not be needed after the following Saturday. By this action, the shoe companies announced their "intention [...] to run free shops in the future", in other words, not to recognize union contracts.[10] This action by the manufacturers made all Auburn's shoe workers aware of their status as members of the *series*, shoe workers. In the light of the manufacturers' actions, Auburn shoe workers held a mass meeting, featuring a two-hour-long speech by Henry J. Skeffington, national secretary of the BSWIU. The meeting ended with an "enthusiastic" vote for arbitration of the current dispute.[11] Virtually all of Auburn's shoe workers could now see themselves as and act out of their membership in a common *series*.

The following Monday was Labor Day and Auburn shoe workers participated in both city and state parades. In both, they acknowledged the industry's division of labor and their own understanding of the different *series* they belonged to, as cutters, lasters, and other male shoe workers each marched separately, while "lady" shoe workers rode in carriages.

9. *LEJ*, 25 August 1893, p. 7.
10. *SLR*, 31 August 1893 (vol. 56.9), p. 493.
11. *LEJ*, 29 August 1893, p. 5.

After Labor Day, the seven shoe employers of the Auburn Association announced that all of their workers – except lasters – would now sign "individual contracts", and agreements with the workers' unions would no longer be recognized. Manufacturers gave workers until noon on Tuesday September 19 to sign the individual contracts.

The workers responded by declaring through their unions (BSWIU Local 12 and BSCU Local 164) that:

> Believing in our right to organize for our mutual benefit, and having taken the solemn obligations of our respective unions, we firmly declare that we will fight this issue to the bitter end, at all times ready to hold to our agreements, submit to arbitration all difficulties arising between our employers and ourselves, and that is what we most desire to do on the question of adjusting prices in the stitching room the Pray, Small Company.[12]

All the female stitchers and most of the town's male shoe workers were now united in their fight against the employers.

Auburn lasters, in the meantime, had thus far declined to join the job actions, identifying themselves more as members of their *pledged group*, their union, than as members of the larger *series* of shoe workers in general. Just before Labor Day, union lasters at the Pray, Small Company had agreed to the company's proposed wages for the next year. By the following week, these same lasters also had no reason to work in the Association shops due to their reduced workforces. On Saturday 22 September one of the shops told their lasters to return to work. The lasters refused, calling it "an unreasonable demand [...] done simply as a test". Declaring that "for them to last shoes which are turned out by non-union men they would be false to their fellow workmen", the lasters met later that afternoon and voted to stop work and "remove their jacks from the shops" on Monday morning.[13]

At noon on Monday 25 September some 300 to 400 lasters gathered at the Lasters' Union Hall in Auburn. After an hour and a half of discussion and debate, they "came out and marched in squads to their respective shops after their kits". Other shoe workers cheered the lasters' decision, and an officer of the BSWIU asserted that: "We have feared that the lasters were going to let us fight on single handed. Their action has given us both strength and courage."[14] The manufacturers retorted that the lasters had now broken their contract. The lasters responded that they had not broken their contract and "that the manufacturers intended to haul them over the coals from the very beginning. 'Their aim was to break our union along with the rest', said a prominent member of the Lasters' Union."[15]

The action of the lasters signaled a new phase of the strike. The most

12. *LEJ*, 16 September 1893, p. 16.
13. *LEJ*, 23 September 1893, p. 7; *Boston Globe*, 24 September 1893, p. 7.
14. *LEJ*, 25 September 1893, p. 7.
15. *LEJ*, 26 September 1893, p. 7.

skilled male workers in the shoe shops, the lasters had remained carefully aloof up to this point. Their decision to walk out meant that any continuing work in the shops ground to a halt, whatever the employers might say. Finally, the lasters acknowledged their membership in the larger *series* of Auburn shoeworkers, and thus joined the strikers. The manufacturers, for their part, vowed to continue production. The *Shoe and Leather Reporter* now prophesied a "long and bitter" conflict and reported that "the manufacturers feel that they must carry their point or there will be no peace for them in the future".[16]

Less than a week after the lasters entered into the fray, reports reached strikers that the shoe companies were planning to bring in immigrant labor – either Italian or Armenian – to replace the now-striking lasters. When a dozen Armenian lasters arrived in town and began working in the factories on Saturday 30 September all hell broke loose. Ethnicity, as much as gender or strike status, became the basis for *series* identification. Non-immigrant strikebreakers brought into town that day were met by union members, who took them out to dinner and then to the local union hall. Armenians, on the other hand, were greeted by crowds of stone-throwing strikers and their supporters. Strikers accused Armenians of responding with firearms and knives. Over the following week, physical conflict between the Armenian strikebreakers (said to number two dozen by the week's end) and crowds including "hundreds of women and children" continued whenever the Armenians ventured outside of their hotels or boarding houses. For a brief time, ethnic identifications superseded all others, both among the self-styled "Yankee" strikers (many of whom were themselves immigrants from both French and British Canada) and among the Armenians, who were reminded of their membership in the two *series*, that of "Armenians" and that of "scabs", every time they poked their noses out of the door and were met with the shouts, bricks, and bats of the strikers. At this point, gender virtually disappears as a salient *series* of identity; both male and female strikers battled Armenian strikebreakers in Auburn's streets.

In addition to their direct action against the Armenian strikebreakers, the Auburn strikers and their unions appealed to their Congressional representatives for relief from immigrant competition. Union leader Skeffington accused Auburn manufacturers of trying "to fill the places of their Yankee employees with the imported offscouring of Europe". Within a week, Armenian communities in Massachusetts had become concerned enough about the situation to send representatives to Auburn to attempt to quiet down the situation. The goal of the Armenian "Hentchakist" (or "Hentsharkist") party of Lynn in doing this was clearly stated as being "to

16. *SLR*, 28 September 1893 (vol. 56, no. 13), p. 745.

assist the union with their utmost efforts".[17] One of the representatives sent was quoted by a Boston newspaper as saying that the approximately 7,000 Armenians in the US "believe in unions, and think their countrymen should keep away from places where strikes are on".[18]

The arrival of the Armenian Hentchakists seems to have quieted down the anti-Armenian hysteria in Auburn. By Sunday 8 October rumor had it that "the Armenian shoemakers were leaving the shops and going back where they came from". (Presumably in the US, not Armenia!)[19] By this time, too, strikers in Auburn had new worries with which to concern themselves. On 5 October the first of several injunctions was granted in the Supreme Court against leaders and activists of the shoe workers' unions. Though the strikers remained suspicious of the national origins of later strikebreakers, in general the legal battles now took precedence.

Once the injunctions moved the Auburn struggle from the streets into the courtroom, two things happened. First of all, the legal battles were taken over more and more by the national unions and their leaders. As control of events slipped out of local workers' hands, enthusiasm for the strike waned. Secondly, manufacturing began to resume, albeit slowly, in the city's shoe factories. By February 1894, though the strike was still officially in place, some 500 of the original 2,000 to 3,000 strikers had returned to work.[20] Many more workers had been replaced by this point, and most of the original strikers joined the swelling ranks of the unemployed at the beginning of the 1890s depression. The strike which women stitchers had begun so enthusiastically in August would dwindle away, remaining a reality only in the boycott lists of the AFL and in the continued unemployment of many of the strikers.[21]

II

The narrative of the Auburn strike suggests one role ethnicity might play in a strike situation. Other strikes give us different scenarios, and therefore

17. *LEJ*, 5 October 1893, p. 5. Spelling aside, this may be a reference to the Social-Democratic Hnchagian Party, founded in 1887. See Robert Mirak, *Torn Between Two Lands: Armenians in America, 1890 to World War I* (Cambridge, MA, 1983), pp. 88–89, 207–209.
18. *Boston Globe*, 7 October 1893, p. 7.
19. *Boston Globe*, 8 October 1893, p. 1.
20. Samuel Gompers to AFL Executive Council, 5 February 1894, in Stuart B. Kaufman and Peter J. Albert (eds), *The Samuel Gompers Papers vol. 3: Unrest and Depression, 1891–94* (Urbana, IL, 1989), p. 460. The *LEJ* reported Auburn shoe factories to be operating at two-thirds of their capacity as of early January, 1894. United States Bureau of Labor, *Tenth Annual Report of the Commissioner of Labor, vol. 1: Strikes and Lockouts* (Washington DC, 1896) (hereafter referred to as *Strikes and Lockouts*), reported 1,106 new workers in the factories as of 1 January 1894.
21. Pray, Small and Co. was still on the "We Don't Patronize" list in the *American Federationist*, vol. 2, no. 6, August 1895.

other serial/*serial* possibilities. A second strike narrative, that of male mule spinners and their female co-workers in New Jersey during the winter of 1890/91, highlights the ways in which ethnicity and gender could at times overlay and reinforce each other.[22] As in the boot and shoe industry, workers in thread factories such as Clark's ONT Thread Company of Newark and Kearney faced a sexual division of labor that made them highly interdependent. Female carders and framers prepared raw materials for spinning. Mule spinners and their assistants, all male, then worked the cotton into yarn. Female workers applied themselves to more mechanized ring spinning, turning the men's yarn into fine thread. Though the sexes worked in completely separate workrooms – and even buildings – within the factory complex, the labor of both sexes was required for the completion of the work. If one group stopped production, the other usually had to follow suit in short order.

Within this sexual division of labor, workers at the New Jersey thread mills found themselves divided along ethnic lines as well. While the male workers in the mills were mainly Protestants from "north country" England and Scotland, the young female workers were overwhelmingly Irish and first-generation Irish-American Catholics.[23] Furthermore, the history of the male mule spinners' union, the National Cotton Mule Spinners' Association (NCMSA), was also firmly tied to the migration of Lancashire immigrants to New England.[24] Both occupationally and organizationally, ethnicity and gender operated in tandem in the New Jersey mills. This dual functioning of *series* memberships plays a key role in our strike narrative, almost overdetermining that the proud mule spinners would make the condescending statements about and dismissive actions toward their female co-workers which occurred in the course of the strike.

Members of the *series*, mule spinners at the Clark thread mills, held a number of complaints against their employer by the winter of 1890/91. Their wages had decreased in recent months and they also decried abusive treatment by the mills' superintendent, Herbert Walmsley. On Saturday, 6 December 1890, Walmsley fired one of the company's older spinners. Forty of his fellow spinners in one of the mills left their work the following Monday in protest. In response, Walmsley "told the men that if they did not

22. Unless otherwise noted, this strike story is taken from the *New York Times* (hereafter cited as *NYT*) and the *Newark Daily Advertiser* (hereafter cited as *NDA*).
23. US Department of the Interior, Census Office, *Report on Population of the United States at the Eleventh Census: 1890, Pt. II* (Washington DC, 1897), pp. 698–699; *Fourth Annual Report of the Commissioner of Labor, 1888: Working Women in Large Cities* (Washington DC, 1889), pp. 236, 274–275. The statistics in these sources also indicate a large number of German male workers among the "cotton, woolen, and other textile mill operatives", but Clark's was known for hiring "Scotch or North country Englishmen". See *The New York Daily Graphic*, 25 January 1888, p. 617.
24. See Mary H. Blewett, "Deference and Defiance: Labor Politics and the Meaning of Masculinity in the Mid-Nineteenth-Century New England Textile Industry", *Gender & History*, 5 (1993), pp. 398–415.

like his management they could put on their coats and leave, and refused to treat with the men".[25] Spinners in the company's other two mills met and voted to quit work as well. By 1 p.m. all 120 spinners at Clark's chose not to return to their work. Since the spinners were no longer at work, a number of their co-workers – both male and female – also found themselves out of work.

On Tuesday, out of the mills' approximately 2,000 employees, 800 (reportedly all men) stayed away from work, closing the spinning departments of all three mills. At a meeting that morning, strikers "decided not to go back to work again till they [were] assured of satisfactory treatment".[26] At the end of the workday, mill management announced that all departments would close for an indefinite length of time. The *New York Times* reported that: "The 1,200 or 1,500 girls who were thrown out of employment at the time when they most need money, and when misery becomes more miserable without it, were disheartened by the turn of affairs, and some of them showed their disappointment in their tears."[27] For the women of the Clarks' mills, recognition of their *series* membership came with the hardship of unemployment.

The Clarks attempted to reopen their mills the following Tuesday, but none of their employees responded to the call to return to work. Some of the young women, however, were expected "to return to their benches" to finish work which they had left uncompleted at the time of the strike/ shutdown. One of the spinners told the *New York Times* that "his bell is constantly ringing to admit young girls who come to plead with him to make a speedy settlement of the troubles".[28]

On Saturday strikers arrived at the mill offices to collect their final pay checks. Eight men, local leaders of the spinners' union, were told that their services were no longer needed. Arguing that the firm was attempting to destroy their union, the fired men once again spoke out against "the most unjust and tyrannical oppression ever imposed upon us by one of the most obnoxious Superintendents ever imported from Russia or elsewhere to this beloved country of ours".[29] Though it is unclear whether Walmsley actually came from Russia, the use of this accusation, with its overtones of the known brutality of the Russian tsar, was a way for the spinners to reinforce their own ethnic heritage as "free Britons".

Following strict craft union principles, money from the spinners' national union would go *only* to the mule spinners and the boy piecers and creelers who worked under them. The strikers' acknowledgment of their fellow

25. *NYT*, 9 December 1890, p. 2.
26. *NYT*, 10 December 1890, p. 9.
27. *NYT*, 11 December 1890, p. 2.
28. *NYT*, 17 December 1890, p. 3.
29. *NDA*, 20 December 1890, p. 1.

workers combined a mix of solidarity, condescension, and indifference. "Of course," commented one spinner to the *New York Times*,

> [...] we fell [sic] with the 2,700 operatives who are not organized, and who will not receive any pecuniary assistance. We'll do what we can to help the boys and girls who have widowed mothers or others who cannot help themselves depending upon them by organizing entertainments. But the shut-down will not drive us from our purposes.[30]

As Christmas approached, efforts to solicit additional financial contributions for the strikers and their supporters increased. Women workers went door-to-door and one local saloon keeper offered to contribute all of his Christmas earnings to the relief fund. New York city and national unions were also approached for support. These various fund-raising efforts were soon embroiled in controversy, however, as out-of-work women claimed that they did not receive any of the funds from the various benefits. Late December Newark newspaper accounts repeatedly discussed the "considerable feeling among the thread mill girls" about the "efforts for relief made in their behalf by the public" and from which they received little benefit.[31]

The irony here is that the non-union funds appear to have been solicited largely by the women themselves or through appealing to the public's sympathy for the women. For example, in January, with the beginning of scab production in the mills, the New York Central Labor Union called for a boycott of the mills' products. The Executive Council of the AFL nationalized this boycott in early February, using Walmsley's abusive treatment of women workers as the most prominent example of the "system of tyranny and persecution" at Clarks' ONT Thread mills.[32]

At the end of December, the Clarks began to import yarn from their Scottish mills. They claimed that they did this because of the public outcry over the condition of the mills' women workers thrown out of work by the mule spinners' strike. As one newspaper reporter put it, "The girls wanted to stand by the spinners, but the wolf was growling outside the door, so they had to bury their wishes and return to work."[33] The women worked for three days on the imported yarn, but were told on New Year's Eve that the mills would close until the first Monday of the new year. Monday 5 January, described by a Newark reporter as "a cold bitter morning", witnessed a "touching scene" at the mill gates, as several hundred women

---

30. *NYT*, 11 December 1890, p. 2. This statement also implies that there were important divisions by age as well as by sex and ethnicity in the mills.
31. *NDA*, 27 December 1890, p. 1, and 26 December 1890, p. 1.
32. SG to AFL Executive Council, 4 February 1891, Samuel Gompers Letterbooks, microfilm reel 4, vol. 5, frame 408; SG to Henry A. Woods, Kearney, NJ, 5 February 1891, reel 4, vol. 5, frame 413. AFL's boycott circular found in *The Tailor*, 2.20 (April 1891), p. 6. Most of the comments about Walmsley's treatment of women referred back to an 1888 strike of women workers at the mills. See *The New York Daily Graphic*, 25 January 1888, p. 614.
33. *NYT*, 4 January 1891, p. 16.

workers gathered to plead for their jobs back. Many told observers that the "scanty assistance" received from the relief funds forced them to return to work, even if, as rumored, they would be working with imported strikebreakers.[34]

Through this first week of January, the Clarks did in fact begin to recruit strikebreakers aggressively. News reports said that the Clarks especially sought Canadian spinners from other textile centers. The company also began to stock the mills with food and sleeping supplies. Striking spinners scoffed at the idea of the mill hiring Canadian spinners, pointing out that "on a former occasion Superintendent Walmsley had said he would never again employ a down-east spinner, as there had always been trouble with those who came from Canada. He said that the Canadian spinners are not competent men and are little, if any, better than the piecers who are employed in the Clark mills."[35]

Despite strikers' disdain and picketers' efforts to prevent the introduction of strikebreakers, production resumed in some mill departments in January. The Clarks announced that once the initial spinning was underway, other workers would be reemployed and more departments would reopen. The introduction of strikebreakers escalated the strike, as mill management had apparently known that it would. The weekend before the mills reopened, the Clarks had requested further police protection for their property, though the mule spinners scoffed at the company's fears, stating that "they neither contemplate violence nor will countenance it if it be attempted".[36] Nevertheless, intermittent violence marked the strike throughout the rest of January and February.

Striking spinners continued to deny their participation in violent outbreaks, largely through claims to their heritage as responsible employees and union men. As the company intermittently opened various mill departments, female employees faced difficult decisions. Should they accept employment alongside strikebreakers in order to gain much-needed wages? Or should they support the striking mule spinners and refuse to work on "scab products"? Despite the fact that the mule spinners had shown little support for the women thus far, over the remaining months of the strike women workers in the mills decided to walk out from their jobs a surprising number of times. Though it is difficult to understand where the women's sense of solidarity came from, given the deep divide between them and the male strikers, at least some of it was rooted in the main focus of the male spinners' cause: the women's old nemesis, Herbert Walmsley. When it became clear in March that Walmsley would remain as the mills' superintendent, over 100 women decided to quit work, arguing that "their earnings

34. *NDA*, 5 January 1891, p. 1.
35. *Ibid.*
36. *NYT*, 12 January 1891, p. 2.

had been so miserably small since the strike as not to tempt them to handle material prepared for them by scab' hands [...]. [T]here was to be no escape from Walmsley, and they could not reconcile themselves to the idea of permanent servitude to such a boss."[37] The women's interests in the strike were therefore simultaneously financial, solidaristic, *and* selfish. The women workers' identifications as members of different *series* would lead them to alternately join the male spinners' strike and to resume work.

The strike at Clarks' mills ended officially in April, when Massachusetts state senator and long-time NCMSA leader, Robert Howard, negotiated with the Clarks the terms for the mule spinners' return to work. The *New York Times* reported that: "[E]ven Superintendent Walmsley has agreed to make things as comfortable as he can for [the men who are taken back]."[38] Just as the spinners' union had ignored the financial needs of the unorganized female workers throughout the strike, the strike's settlement ignored them as well. The women of the Clarks' mills would remain aware of their own *series* memberships if only because their co-workers refused to acknowledge their existence.

In this strike, gender and ethnicity were so closely identified with each other that it is virtually impossible to untangle the identifications out of which workers acted. It was apparently also impossible for the workers themselves to untangle these, as attempts to join together in any sort of class-based action failed repeatedly. With the mule spinners' union so deeply embedded in traditions of immigration from Scotland and northern England, the spinners repeatedly dismissed the concerns of the mostly Irish and Catholic female workers laid off by the cessation of production in the mills. The women workers' identifications as members of various *series* (women workers, laid-off workers, non-union members, Irish Catholics) came close to congealing into *group* identities at points, only to be ripped apart by the impact of financial need or the mule spinners' stronger organization.

III

Jewish garment workers in 1892 Baltimore, Maryland, generated yet another series of ethnic, gender, and class identifications.[39] Their strike demonstrates the ways in which cross-class ethnic ties could be torn asunder by cross-gender class consciousness, which was then further reinforced by the appearance of an ethnic "other". Institutional rivalries compound this story. The workers in this strike, mostly recent Jewish immigrants from Poland, labored in the sweatshops of Jewish coat tailors who contracted to supply

37. *NYT*, 12 March 1891, p. 1.
38. *NYT*, 19 April 1891, p. 8.
39. Unless otherwise noted, the story of this strike is taken from the *Baltimore Sun* (hereafter cited as *Sun*).

coats to various clothing wholesalers. As in the other strikes examined, the Baltimore garment workers' work process also entailed a definite sexual division of labor. Employed directly by the wholesalers, Lithuanian men worked as cutters. Coat pieces were then sent to individual shops for construction by the "Hebrew" workers there. As the Maryland Bureau of Industrial Statistics described it, "[i]n most of the coat tailors' shops the employees work in teams, comprising an operator, whose work is upon a sewing machine, a baster, a presser and several girls".[40]

The Polish Jews in the coat sweatshops had initially formed local assemblies of the Knights of Labor, but in 1891 switched their allegiance to the AFL's United Garment Workers of America (UGWA). In the late spring of 1892, these workers attempted to negotiate standard terms of employment with their bosses, eventually sparking a strike.

On 23 June the workers' union submitted a list of demands to their employers, asking for a uniform ten-hour day, regular payment of wages, signing of a union contract, and acceptance of a system of "walking delegates" allowed to enter each shop at regular intervals. At this point, the action against the "sweaters", as their bosses were called, was fairly disorganized. What historian Susan Glenn has called "the familial tone of the workroom life in these ghetto shops",[41] complicated presentation of the demands. Sharing religious, ethnic, and geographic ties with their immigrant employers inhibited workers from taking the firm action required so as to make their demands stick. The employers assured workers that they would discuss the demands at the end of the week. At this point, workers' identifications as union members battled with their membership in the *series*, Polish-immigrant Jews, a membership shared with employers.

The arrival in town of Henry Reichers, secretary of the UGW, began to change this paralysis. Since Reichers did not share workers' ethnic identification with the coat contractors, he moved to put the strike on more formal footing. Acting on Reichers' advice, members of the two union locals involved pre-empted their employers' offers of negotiations and voted to strike as of Thursday 30 June. Almost a thousand workers walked out that day against some thirty-four contractors. During the first few days of the strike, contractors mainly seemed panicked over what they interpreted as demands for higher wages and the abolition of piece work. Many argued that they could not sign a union contract, since they could not be sure of having consistent work throughout the year. The union also asked contractors to post a $500 bond to ensure that workers received their pay, and some of the contractors balked at that, possibly because they simply could not come up with the money.

40. Maryland, Bureau of Industrial Statistics, *Second Annual Report of the Bureau of Industrial Statistics of Maryland*, (Baltimore, MD, 1894), p. 81.
41. Susan A. Glenn, *Daughters of the Shtetl: Life and Labor in the Immigrant Generation* (Ithaca, NY, 1990), p. 134.

Over the next several weeks, a number of contractors gave in to the workers' demands, and by the end of the first full week of July over a third of the contractors had signed, providing work for some of the strikers. These expressed satisfaction with the new working conditions, and one even told the Baltimore newspaper "that the contractor for whom he worked had expressed regret that the system had not been adopted long ago".[42] Over the next few weeks some of the city's wholesale clothing houses also asked the contractors who worked for them to sign the union agreement.

At this point in the strike attempts were made to have the situation submitted to a bilateral committee for "arbitration". On 11 July the contractors' organization, the Monumental Tailors' Beneficial Association (MTBA), held a long discussion of arbitration and ultimately voted unanimously to attempt it. For the next six weeks strikers and contractors experimented with many different committee permutations for arbitration.

Though the local paper hardly mentions the women involved in this strike, they apparently took an active role. The "women's branch", Local 33, solicited financial support for the strike, and also received sisterly support from the "Women's Branch of the Garment Workers' Union in New York". The secretary of Local 33, "Miss Cilea Grott", told the *Sun* "that the woman workers were making a firm stand and were no less determined than the men".[43]

The union women's decision "not to work as finishers on garments made by non-union workmen" as well as the agreement by many of them "to remain on strike without drawing benefits from the union" paid off in the last week of July.[44] When the arbitration committee met on 27 July the contractors' representatives attempted to divide the strikers along gender lines, suggesting that women employees not be required to belong to the union. Male union representatives rejected this suggestion, arguing that "the girls had stood by them during the strike and the male members of the union would look after them".[45] Local 26's membership the next night ratified this immediate reaction from the UGW's all-male arbitration committee, when "the men [...] voted to stand by the girls".[46] Faced with this resolve, the contractors made no further efforts to divide the strikers by gender. In this case, ethnic ties shared among the workers operated against the contractors. Appealed to on the basis of their membership in gendered *series*, neither the men nor the women allowed themselves to be used against the other group.

Yet another development underscored how common ethnic bonds among the men and women on strike contributed to ensuring their continued

42. *Sun*, 9 July 1892, p. 8.
43. *Sun*, 16 July 1892, p. 8.
44. *Sun*, 20 July 1892, p. 8.
45. *Sun*, 28 July 1892, p. 8.
46. *Sun*, 29 July 1892, p. 8.

solidarity. At the July 11 meeting of the MTBA, local leaders of the Knights of Labor had spoken strongly in favor of arbitration. While this first participation in the strike by the Knights was positive, the Knights fairly quickly took a number of stands which transformed the strike into "a clean cut [fight] between the Federation and the Knights".[47] Already by 12 July the Knights' District Master Workman was claiming that all the clothing cutters in Baltimore belonged to the Clothing Cutters' and Trimmers' Assembly No. 7507, and using that information to urge the wholesalers to pressure contractors *not* to sign the UGW's agreement. Several divisions other than the organizational one made the continuing distinction between garment workers (in the UGW) and clothing cutters (in the Knights of Labor) especially salient. Clothing cutters worked in the shops of the contracting wholesalers, not in the sweatshops of the coat tailors. In addition, the cutters organized by the Knights in Baltimore were largely Lithuanians, so they did not share the ethnic bonds of the Polish–Jewish garment workers. These distinctions underlay the division of workers in the Baltimore industry into opposing union organizations. Later in the strike, the striking sweatshop operators would themselves join the Knights of Labor, forming the "Monumental Coat Contractors' Assembly" of that organization.

Over the ensuing months the conflicts brought to light by the original strikers in Baltimore would be played out on the organizational level, telling us much more about the dying Knights of Labor and the growing American Federation of Labor than about the identifications of the workers themselves. Before becoming bogged down in these organizational battles, though, the Baltimore strike demonstrated yet another way in which gender, ethnicity, and class might be played out in a volatile strike situation. While Baltimore garment workers refused to let their bosses divide them along gender lines, the organizations of the workers divided them along ethnic lines. The mixed responses of the boss "sweaters" to the strike demands may very well have resulted from conflicting ethnic and economic pulls on the coat tailors. While their common ethnicity encouraged some to sign the Garment Workers' agreement, economic necessity motivated others to do whatever was necessary to stay in the good favor of the wholesalers who kept them in business and with whom they had few ethnic ties.

IV

Ethnic discord might be expected in our final example since many ethnic as well as gender and organizational differences divided the workforce. But in this strike we find no discord whatsoever. The several hundred employees of the Wilkes–Barre, PA, Lace Manufacturing Company in 1902 belonged to five separate craft unions and encompassed (in descending order of

47. *Sun*, 16 August 1892, p. 8.

representation) workers of Irish, German, English, native-born American, Welsh, Scottish, Polish, Austrian, French, Swedish, Swiss, Danish, British-Canadian, French-Canadian, and Hungarian descent.[48] Here, too, a sexual division of labor ensured that occupational distinctions separated most men and women at the workplace. Though this strike, too, ultimately ended in failure (workers returning to work on management's terms), it illustrates the type of situation in which incipient ethnic rivalries could be overcome by shared family ties with larger contextual events.

The famous anthracite coal strike of 1902 was just over a month old when it propelled men and women employed by the Wilkes–Barre Lace Company into a strike of their own.[49] In the midst of the fiercely-fought coal strike, the lace strike began when members of the lace workers' unions approached five female workers who had relatives still at work in local coal mines. The lace workers gave these co-workers a choice of either quitting their jobs or having their relatives quit working in the mines. When the women refused – or were unable – to do either, the lace unions approached mill management and asked that they be fired. On Tuesday 17 June mill manager J. W. Doran announced that he would not fire the girls. In response, the lace workers' unions voted to strike. At a joint meeting of the Cotton Workers' Union #8957, Lace Finishers' #8948, Lace Menders' #8151, Brass Bobbin Workers' #8628, and Lace Weavers' Branch No. 2, workers voted to remain on strike until the issue was resolved.

The family ties of the lace workers appear to have both initiated their strike and overcome their ethnic differences. Almost a third (thirty-two per cent) of the lace workers lived with at least one coal mine worker in their household. Women were more likely than men were to live with a coal miner; forty-one per cent of the women and only eighteen per cent of the men did. Younger lace workers were also more likely to reside with coal miners than were older lace workers. For example, forty-four per cent of women between fifteen and nineteen years old and twenty-nine per cent of men in that age group lived with a miner. Not surprisingly, most of the miners were the fathers or brothers of these lace workers, which helps explain why the lace workers would have found it difficult to convince the miners in their families to change their strategies regarding the coal strike.[50] Ethnic differences in the presence or absence of miners in lace workers'

---

48. Unless otherwise noted, the story of this strike is taken from the *American Wool & Cotton Reporter*, vol. 16, and the *Wilkes–Barre Times* (hereafter cited as *WBT*). Information on the workers' ethnicity and households comes from the 1900 Manuscript Census for Wilkes–Barre, PA. The list of ethnicities includes both immigrants from the country indicated and those who could be identified as having parents or grandparents from the given country.
49. R. Fillipelli (ed.), *Labor Conflict in the United States: An Encyclopedia* (New York and London, 1990), pp. 17–19.
50. Of the women who lived with miners, forty-seven per cent lived with a coal-mining brother and fifty-seven per cent had coal-mining fathers.

households appear to have been insignificant. The lace workers' comprehension of coal miners' solidarity and the symbolic reach of that solidarity into their own work lives therefore grew out of very personal familial ties.

Lace mill management must have found it difficult to understand why their workers felt so strongly about an issue which seemingly had nothing to do with their own work. At the same time, the workers' demand that the "girls" be fired went against all concepts of management's right to make hiring and firing decisions. The result appears to have been to create two unmoveable parties to the situation. Lace workers would not end their support of the coal strike; management would not give up their workplace control. The third party to the situation, the workers' national union, had its own views of the strike. One can only imagine the consternation of the executive board of the "National Amalgamated Association of Lace Workers" when they heard of the Wilkes–Barre strike. The board, based in Philadelphia, disapproved of the Wilkes–Barre strike, believing in both arbitration and prior strike approval by the board.

The resulting mixed feelings of the executive board were apparently communicated when manager Doran met with the board on July 5 in a conference which officially ended without any agreement. Within a week, mill management announced that they would reopen the mills, reserving for themselves the right to "employ or discharge" employees and to make decisions on promotions and mill rules. They further required that workers acknowledge overseers' judgements on the allotment of work and submit any complaints only to the mill management. Striking mill workers met over the weekend, voted not to accept management's conditions, and therefore did not return to work the following Monday. Without workers, production could not resume. As the Wilkes–Barre paper put it, "It is now likely that this fight between the management and the strikers will be one to a finish."[51]

Almost a month later, a conference between Doran and a committee of the strikers settled the strike. At this point, strikers agreed to virtually all of Doran's conditions, with the addition of an arbitration procedure, as urged by the union's national executive board. On Monday 11 August work resumed in the mill. The Wilkes–Barre paper reported that "Apparently the strikers were pleased that the difficulty is settled and naturally all were in good humor."[52]

The brief narrative of this strike provides few of the identification shifts seen in previous strikes. Despite the consternation of the workers' national union, the Wilkes–Barre lace workers remained unwavering in their identification as supporters of the coal miners' strike. Membership in neither their ethnic nor their gender *series* rose to supplant this identification. Instead,

51. *WBT*, 15 July 1902, p. 8.
52. *WBT*, 11 August 1902, p. 6.

workers' familial connections to the massive 1902 anthracite coal strike remained paramount throughout the lace strike. *Series* identification arose more from workers' experiences beyond their workplace than from those within the workplace.

V

The strikes narrated in this paper have illustrated different ways in which individuals' recognition of ethnic identity could interact with their recognition of gender and class identities. In each strike workers' identities developed along with the serial narrative of the particular strike situation. The use of Sartre's concept of the *series* helps us think about the many possible variations of class, ethnicity, and gender. Though Sartre planned to use his concept of *series* as a way to examine peoples' class identities, my employment of the concept broadens it to include other categories of identification as well. Using the concept this broadly highlights the importance of three key issues: historical narrative, historical materialism, and the agency of individuals and groups within both of those. In each of the strikes retold here, individuals act out of identities formed by both specific material circumstances and specific events. By thinking of these identities as representative of memberships in different *series* we keep alive the possibilities of change inherent in individuals' lives. Each individual has at her disposal an array of experiences from which she can and must construct her own responses to the events in which she finds herself. Thinking of these experiences as the formative materials of membership in different *series* aids the historian in thinking about class, gender, ethnicity, race, and other categories less as one-time choices of identity made by individuals and more as part of an array of choices out of which individuals act.

The shoe workers of Auburn, Maine, the thread workers of Newark and Kearney, the Baltimore garment workers, and the Wilkes–Barre lace workers all brought a range of options with them into their workplaces and therefore into their strikes. At times viewing themselves as women or men, skilled workers or unskilled workers, members of one ethnic group or another, members of families, or simply as strikers, workers in these strikes (just as workers in contemporary strikes) highlight the interactions of ethnicity, gender, and class. They remind us that the members of the working class are always also members of many other *series*, any one of which may reinforce or undermine their class identity and consciousness during the course of living, that is, of creating historical narrative.

International Review of Social History 44 (1999), Supplement, pp. 53–75
© 1999 Internationaal Instituut voor Sociale Geschiedenis

Competing Inequalities: The Struggle Over Reserved Legislative Seats for Women in India*

Laura Dudley Jenkins

Introduction of the Women's Reservation Bill was stalled in Lok Sabha on Monday amid unprecedented scenes of snatching of papers from the Speaker and the law minister and the virtual coming to blows of members [...]. As the shell shocked minister stood rooted to the spot, the member tore the papers with relish and flung them in the air provoking members from the treasury benches to storm the well. By this time, the well of the Lok Sabha looked like a veritable battle field with members from both sides preparing for a scuffle as the Speaker adjourned the House for the day.[1]

What caused such a commotion in the lower house of India's Parliament in July 1998? The Women's Reservation Bill was an attempt to reserve thirty-three per cent of seats in Parliament and state assemblies for women. In a society characterized by many forms of stratification, demands for sub-reservations within the category of "women" for other disadvantaged groups have repeatedly squelched the bill's progress. Defining which social categories should be eligible for such reservations leads to heated disputes because these questions involve both emotional commitments to group identities and material calculations of group interests.

"Reservations" in India are affirmative action policies for disadvantaged groups, allocating government jobs, and, in some cases, university admissions and legislative seats to such groups. The groups currently benefiting from reservations include the lowest castes, officially dubbed "scheduled castes" (SCs), and geographically isolated groups known as "scheduled tribes" (STs). Those receiving more limited benefits, which vary from state to state, include women and an intermediate category of certain lower-caste or lower-class groups called the "other backward classes" (OBCs).[2] (The

* This article is based on my research in India as a Fulbright–Hays Scholar and in the United States as a United States Institute of Peace Scholar and MacArthur Scholar at the University of Wisconsin–Madison. The title is a tribute to, and a twist on, the title of Marc Galanter's classic work on compensatory discrimination in India, *Competing Equalities*. My thanks to Robert E. Frykenberg and Barbara Ramusack for encouraging me to historicize my political science and to Sushma Sharma, Kristy Bright and Tapati Bharadwaj for their assistance and support. Thanks also to all the women who invited me to join them at a New Delhi rally, inspiring me to study the issue of reservations for women in Parliament.

1. "RJD–SP Stall Introduction of Women's Quota Bill", *Times of India*, 14 July 1998.
2. For a more detailed description of these policies in comparison with other "affirmative action policies", see Laura D. Jenkins, "Preferential Policies for Disadvantaged Ethnic Groups: Employment and Education", in Crawford Young (ed.), *Ethnic Diversity and Public Policy: A Comparative Inquiry* (London, 1998).

OBCs are generally better off than the "untouchable" SCs). Neither OBCs nor women currently have reserved seats in Parliament. An irony of these policies to help disadvantaged groups in Indian society is that competition over the allocation of benefits often divides groups that might otherwise work together to fight inequality. A case in point is the recent downfall of the parliamentary reservation proposal for women due to demands for a sub-quotas within the category of women for "other backward classes" (OBCs) and Muslims, a religious minority group. Each category is arguably made up of victims of historical discrimination and inequality; yet claims and counterclaims for reservations on the basis of sex, caste, class and religion have resulted in political gridlock. The politics of competing inequalities divides oppressed groups, which, if consolidated, have the potential to be numerically and politically dominant.

The issue of reserved legislative seats for women in India has reappeared, without resolution, at different historical moments. The following discussion includes three such moments: the debates over constitutional reforms in the last years of the British *Raj*, the disagreements over a major government report on the status of women in 1974, and the contemporary demand for the Women's Reservation Bill in the 1990s. These disputes over women's reservations challenge current theories about identity politics, specifically theories of "post-materialism" and "new social movements". By linking benefits to certain identities, the issue of women's reservations throws into question assumptions that identity politics can be characterized as "post-material". A lack of class-based movements does not necessarily mark a post-material shift. As class-based movements, policies and analyses become scarcer, we need to develop new frameworks to recognize the material dimensions of identities other than "class". To do this, we can productively consider the long struggle over women's reservations in India, which demonstrates that the intersection between interests and identities – whether based on gender, class or religion – is nothing new. After elaborating on how India's "competing inequalities" challenge current theories, this article will focus on pre- and post-Independence debates about reservations for women in order to draw conclusions about the need to "complicate the categories" of gender, class and religious identities.

MATERIAL GIRLS: GENDER AND IDENTITY IN A MATERIAL WORLD

The decline of socialist governments and class-based movements has sparked a search for new theoretical frameworks. At the same time, ethnic, gender and other "identity"-based movements are becoming more prevalent. These historical trends have contributed to literatures on "new social movements" and "post-material" politics. Scholars studying "new social movements", at first primarily in Europe, argue that social movements have shifted away from class-based issues toward post-material issues and identity politics. According to Larana, Johnston, and Gusfield,

> [...] there is a tendency for the social base of new social movements to transcend class structure. The background of participants find their most frequent structural roots in rather different social statuses such as youth, gender, sexual orientation, or professions that do not correspond with structural explanations.[3]

Advocates of "post-material" explanations, again originally focusing on Europe, argue that a post-material value shift has resulted in the decline in class-based voting and rise of new social movements, such as women's or environmental movements, which cut across traditional classes by mobilizing around other forms of collective identity and interests.[4]

Although injecting a needed dose of culture into analyses too often driven by economic explanations, the new social movements literature often swings too far in the other direction. Advocates have argued, for example, that new social movements around collective identities are "essentially cultural in nature".[5] The division between European "new social movements" and American "resource mobilization" approaches to social movements has contributed to the failure to synthesize. cultural and economic analyses. Resource mobilization theorists emphasize the material incentives, opportunities and strategies of rational actors at a given moment to explain the rise of social movements. The new social movements literature's focus on collective identities constrasts with the American approach, governed by a rational action paradigm inspired by economics. Neither approach adequately addresses class, and, even if paying lip service to both economic and cultural factors, neither framework effectively incorporates both.[6] It is time to turn to different regions and new approaches.

The study of non-Western societies complicates conclusions that we are entering a post-class phase of history, let alone a post-material phase.

---

3. Enrique Laraña, Hank Johnston, and Joseph R. Gusfield, *New Social Movements: From Ideology to Identity* (Philadelphia, PA, 1994), p. 6.

4. Ronald Inglehart, *Culture Shift in Advanced Industrial Society* (Princeton, NJ, 1990).

5. Kenneth D. Wald, James W. Button and Barbara A. Rienzo, "The Politics of Gay Rights in American Communities: Explaining Antidiscrimination Ordinances and Policies", *American Journal of Political Science*, 40 (1996), p. 1169.

6. An example of classic "resource mobilization" scholarship is Craig J. Jenkins, *The Politics of Insurgency: The Farm Worker Movement in the 1960s* (New York, 1985). Doug McAdam's "political process" model builds on this tradition. See Doug McAdam, *Political Process and the Development of Black Insurgency 1930–1970* (Chicago, IL, 1982). Some have called for a bridge between the European and American approaches: Bert Klandermans and Sidney Tarrow, "Mobilization into Social Movements: Synthesizing European and American Approaches", in Bert Klandermans, Hanspeter Kriesi and Sidney Tarrow (eds), *From Structure to Action: Comparing Social Movements Across Cultures* (Greenwich, CT, 1988). Subsequent work creatively engaging in such a synthesis has, nevertheless, tended to remain primarily in one camp, as in Sidney Tarrow's tendency to reduce culture to a "cultural tool chest" exploited by political entrepreneurs: Sidney Tarrow, *Power in Movement: Social Movements, Collective Action and Politics* (Cambridge, 1994).

Research on women and on non-Western societies pose the greatest challenges to assumptions about "post-materialism" and "new social movements". Feminist scholars have rightly pointed out that most women's movements, whether in Western or non-Western societies, cannot be accurately characterized as "post-material" movements, due to their involvement in issues of wages and work, or, in many cases, subsistence and survival. The notion of "new social movements" has been used in political analyses of the developing world, most often Latin America but also India. Analysis of "new social movements" in India demonstrates that identity-based movements are neither completely "new" nor "post-material" in these contexts.[7] Since many scholars of post-materialism and new social movements make no claim that these theories hold true in the developing world, this article will not try to debunk them through examples from India. Rather, due to the failure of European and American approaches to adequately synthesize cultural and economic factors or address the intersections of class, gender and other forms of identity, this article draws on India to illustrate the continuing salience of all these forms of identity and the danger of dichotomizing "material" politics, too often simply equated with class, and "post-material" politics, too often equated with gender and ethnicity. Even scholars focusing on the Western world are becoming uncomfortable with the artificial division between the politics of recognition (of different identities) and the politics of redistribution (of material resources).[8] The following analysis of "competing inequalities", based on rival demands for both group recognition and power redistribution, presents an alternative to post-materialism for scholars of both Western and non-Western societies.

India is a particularly rich case in this regard due to its extreme cultural diversity and material disparities. Solidarities are constantly emerging and shifting on the basis of both the emotional pull of certain identities and rational calculations of interests. People have multilayered identities, which can include gender, class, caste, race, religion, ethnicity as well as many others, but material considerations may highlight one facet of identity. As Madhu Kishwar, an Indian feminist, writes, "A group or person may begin to assert a particular identity with greater vigour if it provides greater access to power and opportunities."[9] For example, Indian women at various times have asserted their identity as women in order to demand reserved legislative

7. Gail Omvedt, *Reinventing Revolution: New Social Movements and the Socialist Tradition in India* (Armonk and London, 1993). See also Arturo Escobar and Sonia E. Alvarez (eds), *The Making of Social Movements in Latin America: Identity, Strategy and Democracy* (Boulder, CO, 1992) and Alfred Stepan (ed.), *Democratizing Brazil: Problems of Transition and Consolidation* (New York, 1989).
8. Catherine Hoskins and Shirin M. Rai, "Gender, Class and Representation: India and the European Union", *European Journal of Women's Studies*, 5 (1998), pp. 345–365. See in particular their discussion of Iris Marian Young's work on "unruly categories".
9. Madhu Kishwar, "Who Am I? Living Identities vs. Acquired Ones", *Manushi*, 94 (1996), p. 6.

seats. The political power associated with these seats has important material dimensions, including the opportunity to have a say in the distribution of state resources. Women in elected office are in a position to try to "improve their access to the resources that count, from education and credit to the ownership of land and housing".[10]

This current demand for women's reservations does not differentiate between privileged women and OBC or Muslim women. Although "women" do not constitute a universal category, for political purposes women sometimes choose to "act as if such a category indeed exists, precisely for the reason that the world continues to behave and treat women as though one does".[11] In India, the category of woman is riddled by class, caste, religious, and countless other cultural divisions. The current dilemma facing the Indian women demanding reserved seats in Parliament is that such a demand may not adequately recognize these other categories; on the other hand, opening the Pandora's box of sub-quotas has mired the Women's Reservation Bill in endless debates over which groups of women should receive their own categories of reservations.

The following discussion focuses on the overlapping, and yet competing, categories of women, OBCs, and Muslims. Some clarification of these categories, particularly the OBCs, is in order. The women in India who have been most actively demanding the right for parliamentary reservations have been largely although not exclusively from upper-class Hindu backgrounds. The "other backward classes" are an official category in India, made up of groups – "other" than the scheduled castes and scheduled tribes – recognized as eligible for preferential policies in the Indian constitution. Each state draws up lists of groups that qualify as OBCs. They are generally lists of Hindu lower castes which are not as low as the "untouchable" scheduled castes, as well as some low-caste-like groups within other religions. The use of the term "classes" in this context means that the distinction between "caste" and "class" has become subject to legal as well as sociological debate in India.[12] Suffice it to say that caste and class have some sociological similarities, both referring to groups within a status hierarchy, often involving occupational distinctions. A "caste" or *jati* distinction is more likely to be based on religious ideology and the notion of status being determined at birth. Classes on the other hand could, in theory, encompass many different *jatis* and other groups. The term class, as in the official term "backward classes", is used not just as a euphemism for caste but also serves as a more inclusive term than caste. For example, disadvantaged groups of Muslims

10. Jane S. Jaquette, "Women in Power: from Tokenism to Critical Mass", *Foreign Policy*, 108 (1997), pp. 23–27.
11. Rosalind O'Hanlon and David Washbrook, "After Orientalism: Culture, Criticism, and Politics in the Third World", *Comparative Studies in Society and History*, 34 (1992), p. 154.
12. A.M. Shah, "The Judicial and Sociological View of the Other Backward Classes", in M.N. Srinivas (ed.), *Caste: Its Twentieth Century Avatar* (New Delhi, 1996), pp. 174–194.

can be included on OBC lists. Some states have reserved jobs and university admissions for OBCs since long before Independence, yet national reservations of central government jobs have only recently been extended to this group in the last decade. This controversial policy precedent and the growing political power of the OBCs spurs demands for reserved seats for OBC women in Parliament. Some argue that the OBCs may be forming a lower- to middle-"class" challenge to established power hierarchies, but the OBCs are still quite regionally-based and divided.[13] The following references to "class" must be considered in light of these complex relationships between class and caste. Muslims in India are a socio-economically disadvantaged group, particularly since partition, when much of the Muslim elite had the resources to go to Pakistan, leaving a smaller and even more disadvantaged religious minority in India. Although Muslims had special rights under the British, only those Muslim communities classified as "backwards" currently benefit from national level reservations. Neither women, OBCs, or Muslims currently get reserved seats in Parliament.[14]

How do India's gender-, class- and religion-based demands for reservations pose an alternative to the theories of "post-material" identity politics and new social movements? These literatures assume that the decline of class-based politics equals "post-materialist" politics, thus ignoring the economic aspects of gender identity, to say nothing of the cultural aspects of class identity. The link between group benefits and all kinds of identities in India belies this false dichotomy between class versus other, purportedly post-material, identities. India's complex intersections of identities, resulting in competing arguments that some groups are more *un*equal than others,' demonstrate the need to "complicate the categories" not only in social analysis but also social policy.

"MINOR MINORITIES": CONTESTED CATEGORIES AND WOMEN'S RESERVATIONS IN HISTORICAL PERSPECTIVE

The demand for women's reservations in legislative bodies is not new; neither is the controversy over the appropriate categories to use when allocating reservations. Pre-Independence precedents touch on similar issues to those being raised today. Legislative reservations for women were under discussion during debates in the 1920s and 1930s over constitutional reforms for India. At that point, too, the category of women took a back seat to other categories, such as religion and caste, in the eyes of British officials in

13. Francine R. Frankel, "Middle Classes and Castes in India's Politics: Prospects for Political Accommodation", in Atul Kohli (ed.), *India's Democracy: An Analysis of Changing State-Society Relations* (Princeton, NJ, 1988), pp. 225–261.

14. For a detailed discussion of these categories and reservation policies for them see Marc Galanter, *Competing Equalities: Law and the Backward Classes in India* (Delhi, 1991).

London and New Delhi. One went so far as to place "female suffrage and legislative seats in the category of minor minorities" (religious communities such as Muslims and Sikhs and caste groups such as the so-called "untouchables" were considered the major minorities).[15] A classic example of competing inequalities is this division of "minorities" against themselves.

In the last decades of colonial rule, Britain granted Indians limited rights to serve as representatives in legislative bodies. In part an effort to neutralize nationalists and expand the "circle of collaborators", such policies also contributed to "divide and rule" tactics by giving special electoral rights to certain groups.[16] These policies include the 1909 Indian Councils Act (based on the Minto–Morely Report), the 1919 Government of India Act (based on the Montagu–Chelmsford Proposals), and the 1935 Government of India Act. This period also saw the first attempts at forming "All-India" women's associations, such as the Women's India Association (WIA) in 1917, followed by the All India Women's Conference (AIWC) and the National Council of Women in India (NCWI). These major women's associations tried to influence the new policies by passing resolutions, sending delegates to conferences, submitting memoranda and letters, and lobbying various decision makers. Their primary agenda was gaining the right to vote for Indian women, but they became involved in the issue of reserved seats for women in legislatures. Ironically, although these major Indian women's organizations came down against such reservations, they were granted to them in 1935.

At that point some "major minorities" had already received reserved seats, as well as separate electorates, meaning only members of the community in question could vote for candidates for their reserved seats. Muslims received separate electorates under the Government of India Act of 1909. The Government of India Acts of 1919 and 1935 granted Muslims, Sikhs, and Christians separate electorates. "Depressed classes" (lower-caste groups) were provided a few nominated seats in 1919, more in 1925, and even more elected seats in 1932.[17] These proliferating categories, nationalists argued, facilitated continuing British control.

Concerned about divisions within the nationalist movement, the Indian National Congress (the leading nationalist organization) objected to special electoral rights for any of these groups. The major women's organizations, in turn, came to oppose similar proposals for women. Women associated with other political organizations held a different position. Muslim activist Begum Shah Nawaz, for one, agreed with the Muslim League's support for reserved seats and special constituencies for Muslims. She also supported

---

15. Barbara Ramusack, "Cultural Missionaries, Maternal Imperialists, Feminist Allies: British Women Activists in India, 1865–1945", *Women's Studies International Forum*, 13 (1990), p. 316.
16. Janaki Nair, *Women and Law in Colonial India* (New Delhi, 1996), p. 122.
17. Galanter, *Competing Equalities*; Thomas R. Metcalf, *Ideologies of the Raj* (Delhi, 1995).

reservations for women. When the Congress boycotted the first roundtable conference on constitutional reform in 1930, Nawaz and another non-Congress female delegate, Mrs. Subbarayan, submitted a memorandum in favour of reserved seats for women, arguing that "we regard the phrase 'a fair field and no favour' at the present time as an illusory one".[18] The major women's associations denounced them.

When the Congress decided to participate in the second roundtable conference on constitutional reform in 1931, a very different women's delegation introduced a joint memorandum of the AIWC, NCWI and WIA. This stated that "to seek any form of preferential treatment would be to violate the integrity of the universal demand of Indian women for absolute equality of political status".[19] Initially the WIA supported reservations for women as a "transitional necessity" but subsequently it signed onto the joint resolution, an example of a nationalist agenda superseding concerns specific to some women.[20] The WIA's Muthulakshmi Reddi subsequently wrote in opposition to reservations even for lower castes (who had been granted reservations as "depressed classes") in Indian society, for the sake of a "common platform": the "only way to bring the Brahmans, the women and the pariahs together on a common platform is by enfranchising the women and the depressed classes on equal terms with others".[21] Thus Congress and the major women's associations opposed reservation policies that would recognize distinct social categories within the Indian "nation", whether those categories were based on religion, gender, class or caste.

Ignoring the stance of the major Indian women's organizations, the Government of India Act of 1935 granted women forty-one reserved seats in the provincial legislatures, as well as limited reservations in a central legislature.[22] This puzzling decision may be due to the influence of Eleanor Rathbone and other British advocates for the rights of Indian women, or it may be an example of the British taking their commitment to group-based policies to its logical end. In any event, despite their dim view of such a "minor minority", the British added women to the list of groups with special electoral rights. Yet, their overriding concern with the major minorities

18. Gail Pearson, "Reserved Seats – Women and the Vote in Bombay", in J. Krishnamurty (ed.), *Women in Colonial India: Essays on Survival, Work and the State* (Delhi, 1989), p. 205.
19. Pearson, "Reserved Seats – Women and the Vote", p. 207.
20. *Ibid.*, p. 206. On the relationship between the nationalist and women's movements in India, see also Nair, *Women and Law in Colonial India*, and Partha Chatterjee, "The Nationalist Resolution of the Women's Question", in Kumkum Sangari and Sudesh Vaid (eds), *Recasting Women: Essays in Indian Colonial History* (New Brunswick, NJ, 1989), pp. 233–253.
21. Pearson, "Reserved Seats – Women and the Vote", p. 208.
22. The proportion of women elected to the central legislature under this plan was only 3.4 per cent; Government of India, Ministry of Education and Social Welfare, Department of Social Welfare, *Towards Equality: Report of the Committee on the Status of Women* (New Delhi, 1974), p. 356.

affected even the women's reservations, which were subdivided on a religious basis, with certain women's seats reserved for Muslim women. This minute division of the electoral pie brought out tensions along both gender and religious lines. The major women's organizations, such as the AIWC, including its Muslim women members, protested that "the communal award will divide us, Indian women".[23] On the other hand, the prominent Muslim Begum Shah Nawaz continued her support of reserved seats for both Muslims and women. Some male members of "major" minorities, however, were rather disgruntled at having their quotas diluted by women. Muslim leaders in Punjab, for instance, were "angry that of the few seats for Muslims, one was reserved for a woman".[24] Muslim women in particular fell between the cracks of the "major" and "minor" minorities during this period prior to Independence and the partition of India and Pakistan; in addition to facing such resistance from Muslim men, some Muslim women were becoming estranged from the Hindu-dominated women's movement.[25]

When granted reservations despite their own protests, women's associations made the most of the situation. The AIWC initially considered refusing to participate in the new constitutional provisions, but eventually it officially resolved to take advantage of them. Various women's groups even lobbied for additional seats in their areas. In the 1937 elections fifty-six women became legislators, forty-one in reserved seats; ten were in unreserved seats and five in nominated seats. Most were relatively wealthy Congress candidates.

After Independence in 1947, the new government only retained the legislative reservations for the scheduled castes and scheduled tribes in the lower house of Parliament, the *Lok Sabha*, and the lower houses of the state legislatures, the *Vidhan Sabhas*.[26] The post-Independence constitution did not reserve any legislative seats for the other backward classes, religious minorities, or women. The constitution also outlawed separate electorates for national and state assemblies, so the general electorate voted for candidates for reserved seats.[27] Ironically, although the major women's organizations opposed women's reservations, and the reservations themselves were quite short-lived, they gave elite, nationalist women a foothold in Indian legislative life.

23. Pearson, "Reserved Seats – Women and the Vote", p. 210.
24. Geraldine Forbes, *Women in Modern India* (Cambridge, 1996), p. 196.
25. *Ibid.*, pp. 196–203.
26. Anglo-Indians also got a few nominated seats.
27. The Indian Constitution (1950) granted adult suffrage, so women were included in the electorate. Prior to this, the British Southborough Committee had left the issue of women's suffrage up to the provincial legislatures, after which "each of the Indian provincial legislatures voted to make it possible within a short span of time for women to be represented at par with men", writes Madhu Kishwar, "Women and Politics: Beyond Quotas", *Economic and Political Weekly*, 26 (1996), pp. 2867–2874.

COMMUNITIES AND CATEGORIES: *TOWARDS EQUALITY* AND THE RENEWED DEBATE OVER WOMEN'S RESERVATIONS

Independence brought a "lull" in feminist campaigns.[28] The Indian National Congress became the ruling Congress Party. It incorporated a number of feminists into the government. The 1950 constitution declared women to be equal and granted them the right to vote. But optimism about freedom and "modernization" in the early years of independence gradually waned as the status of women seemed to stagnate or even decline. In spite of dramatic exceptions, such as the election of Indira Gandhi as prime minister in 1966, most women did not achieve the equality formally granted to them. In the early seventies, the government of India did a comprehensive study of the status of Indian women. The resulting 1974 report of the Committee on the Status of Women in India, *Towards Equality*, must be considered in any discussion of women's reservations for two reasons. First, no other similarly comprehensive government report on women in India exists. Second, the issue that most divided the committee was legislative reservations for women.

With the Western feminist movement at its peak in the early seventies, the United Nations started to focus more on the status and development of women in low-income countries. Partly in response to this new UN agenda, the government of India in 1971 formed the Committee on the Status of Women in India in order to gather new data as well as compile and analyze existing information.[29] This report was released in time for the 1975 observance of the International Women's Year. In addition to the international push for reconsideration of women's status, Indian women began to push for change during the seventies. Both the report and the renewed activism brought the status of women back into national debate. The woman in charge of the report, political science professor Veena Mazumdar, was previously uninvolved in the women's movement. But she was so appalled by her findings that she became a leading figure in the "new wave" of Indian feminism.[30]

Towards Equality reported on women's demographic, sociocultural, legal, economic, and educational status, evaluated current programs and policies and made several recommendations. Although a government report, it was quite critical of the government. It addressed the economic plight of many

28. Radha Kumar, "From Chipko to Sati: The Contemporary Indian Women's Movement", in Amrita Basu (ed.), *The Challenges of Local Feminisms: Women's Movements in Global Perspective* (Boulder, CO, 1995), p. 60.
29. Elisabeth Bumiller, *May You Be the Mother of a Hundred Sons: A Journey Among the Women of India* (New York, 1990), p. 126. Another example of the rising UN interest in women's rights during the seventies is the 1979 Convention on the Elimination of All Forms of Discrimination Against Women.
30. Bumiller, *May You Be the Mother of a Hundred Sons*, pp. 125–127.

women since Independence and the reluctance of legislators to put constitutional ideals into practice. "Large sections of women have suffered a decline of economic status", it concluded. "Every legal measure designed to translate the constitutional norm of equality or special protection into actual practice has had to face tremendous resistance from the legislative and other elites."[31] Such findings set the stage for the debate in the committee over reserved seats for women in legislative bodies. Those in charge of the report, like Mazumdar, came from backgrounds far more privileged than those of most Indian women, yet the report attempted to reflect diverse viewpoints. The issue inspiring the most divergent viewpoints, necessitating the addition of several "notes of dissent" at the end, was legislative reservations for women.

Mazumdar and her committee, particularly those from the "pre-Independence generation", initially had no intention of considering the issue of legislative reservations for women. In the tradition of the nationalist women's organizations, they had "never been supporters of special representation or class representation in any form". They still associated such reservations with colonial strategies and "in academic discussions we had often criticized the system of reservations for scheduled castes and scheduled tribes as a legacy of the historical period which institutionalized the backwardness of certain sections of our population". The committee's initial interviews and surveys did not include any questions on the issue of reservations for women. "Only when the problem kept being posed repeatedly before us by various groups of women in the course of our discussions did we become aware that a problem like this was real", Mazumdar confessed.[32] By the release of the report, Mazumdar had embraced the concept of legislative reservations. She even personally espoused reservations in Parliament, going beyond the committee's recommendation to limit them to the municipal level. *Towards Equality* signalled a shift towards more open acceptance of reservations among some women, even those previously opposed to such measures. At the same time, the committee was very guarded in its limited endorsement and included many familiar arguments against reservations. Though summarizing arguments for reservations up to the level of Parliament, the committee as a whole concluded that they could not recommend such a step.

Major arguments against reservations for women continued to involve concerns about other unequal groups, namely religious minorities and lower classes and castes. Two types of arguments along these lines emerged in the debate over *Towards Equality*. One argument was that the inequalities faced by these other "communities" outweighed those faced by the "category" of women. This argument parallels the British distinction between major and

31. Government of India, *Towards Equality*, p. 301.
32. *Ibid.*, p. 355.

minor minorities and subsequent decisions to grant women's reservations at a later date than those for other groups, and then only within communal subdivisions. A second type of argument has precedents in the nationalist movement's anti-reservation stance. Concerns about national unity continued after Independence. This critique raised the spectre of national disintegration in the wake of such official distinctions between groups, be they religious-, class-, caste- or gender-based.

The report's conclusions draw on both types of arguments against reservations, prioritizing "communities" over "categories" and expressing concern about national integrity. In terms of communities, it considered fallacious "the entire argument for separate representation for women. Women's interests as such cannot be isolated from the economic, social and political interests of groups, strata and classes in the society."[33] This conclusion depended on a critique of the "category" of women, which in contrast to other groups, did not constitute "a community". The committee admitted, "Though they have some real problems of their own, they share with men the problems of their groups, locality and community. Women are not concentrated in certain areas confined to particular fields of activity. Under these circumstances, there can be no rational basis for reservation for women."[34] Although not using the word "caste", the committee contrasted the plight of women with the spacial and occupational segregation characterizing the caste system. Notably, the word "community" in the Indian context had become a common euphemism for castes and religious groups, reinforcing the committee's distinction between women as a category and other groups as communities.

The committee further included the national unity argument against reservations: "Such a system of special representation may precipitate similar demands from various other interests and communities and threaten national integration."[35] In spite of these concerns, it made some limited recommendations for reservations for women at the local level as a "transitional measure". This careful choice of phrase echoed the WIA's initial support of reservations for women in 1931 as a "transitional necessity", prior to their decision to join with the other two major women's organizations in opposition to reservations.

Even the recommendation of limited and local-level reservations sparked notes of dissent, appended to the report. Phulrenu Guha seconded the committee's discomfort with prioritizing the category of "women" over class divisions by arguing that "there is a possibility that reservation of seats will

33. *Ibid.*, p. 304. Examples in this report of the arguments for legislative reservations include the need for political empowerment of women to precede socio-economic empowerment in the Indian context, the need to compel political parties to shift strategies in candidate selection, and the value of "a body of spokesmen of the women's cause" in legislatures. See pp. 302–303.
34. *Ibid.*, p. 304.
35. *Ibid.*

only help women of a particular class who are already privileged. It should be our aim to see that the masses of women of all classes become equal partners with men in all senses in our society." Guha's dissent also embraced the national unity argument that "this type of reservation of seats might lead other communities/classes to argue for reservation of seats. This, to my mind, will encourage separatist tendencies and hamper national integration."[36]

In another note of dissent, Vina Mazumdar and Lotika Sarkar felt the report did not go far enough and advocated reservations at higher levels. They claimed that the number of women in Parliament was still less than five per cent, only marginally higher than the proportion elected in the central legislature after the 1935 Government of India Act. These dissenters discounted the "community versus category" critiques of women's reservations, arguing that helping women will help the women of various communities as well. "Larger numbers" of women in Parliament, they proposed, "will also help to break the somewhat exclusive class composition of this group".[37] Mazumdar and Sarkar also rebutted the national unity argument, or, as they described it, "the argument that special representation might precipitate fissiparous tendencies". Here they actually deployed the idea that women are a category and not a community to defend the notion of special reservation. Contrasting women with other minority groups, they argued that reservations for women could not create the "isolated pockets" feared by critics of reservations.[38]

Although the rhetoric shifted from a distinction between "major" and "minor" minorities to one between "communities" and mere "categories", the Committee on the Status of Women continued the tradition of ambivalence towards women as a unitary category for public policies. From the beginning the report noted that "the inequalities inherent in our traditional social structure, based on caste, community and class have a very significant influence on the status of women in different spheres".[39] One legacy of colonial policies was the continuing primacy of caste and religious communities as the groups needing special attention, even in the eyes of many members of the Committee on the Status of Women. This viewpoint countered demands for a special reservation for "women" as a group. Since Independence, fears that the nationalist movement might disintegrate had transformed into fears that the nation might disintegrate. This viewpoint countered demands for reservations in general. Both types of arguments, with their roots in the colonial era, limited the success of the continuing demands for women's reservations. Ironically, some low-caste organizations

36. *Ibid.*, p. 354. This quotation is from Phulrenu Guha's "Political Status: Note of Dissent".
37. *Ibid.*, p. 357. This quotation is from Lotika Sarkar and Vina Mazumdar's "Political Status: Note of Dissent".
38. *Ibid.*
39. *Ibid.*, p. 3.

in the seventies drew parallels between their oppression and women's, undeterred by the continuing official distinctions between communities and categories.[40] Yet the more frequent pattern of activism by women and other disadvantaged groups was a continuing division between urban elite organizations and rural, grassroots movements.

The proposal for local-level reservations for women eventually became part of the 73rd Constitutional Amendment Act – an attempt to revitalize the local government system known as *panchayati raj*. Initially introduced by prime minister Rajiv Gandhi in 1989, the amendment passed in 1993. The village *panchayats* or councils must reserve one third of their seats for women and also reserve seats for "scheduled castes and tribes" in proportion to their populations in that area; one third of SC and ST seats are reserved for SC and ST women.[41]

The support of Rajiv Gandhi and others from the Congress Party, like former government minister Margaret Alva, marked a further shift from the former abhorrence of reservations as a nationally divisive policy. Alva reintroduced the demand for reservations on all levels, including Parliament, in the 1980s when she was Minister for Women. She viewed the thirty-three per cent reserved seats for women in the *panchayats* as a stepping stone to reservations in Parliament. "Let us start with the *panchayats*", she declared. "Instead of taking on everybody, let's start with the *panchayats* and see how it runs, and then move upwards." Alva felt such gradualism would quell the doubts of those who believed that "you won't find women to contest, you know; they are not educated; they are not trained. How do they do it?"[42] Later Alva could point to the success of the initiative:

> In the course of the last three years, between '93 and '96, one million women have been elected to local bodies. Now one million [...] is more then the population of some countries. But one million women today are elected representatives in local bodies all over the country. Now just imagine if one million have been elected, at least five million have contested [...] five million women have gone through the political process.[43]

The adoption of this constitutional amendment, with the endorsement of major members of the Congress Party, signalled the increasing acceptability of women's reservations; yet numerous bills attempting to extend such reser-

40. Kumar, "From Chipko to Sati", p. 63.
41. Hoshiar Singh, "Constitutional Base for Panchayati Raj in India: The 73rd Amendment Act", *Asian Survey*, 34 (1994), pp. 824–825; P.M. Bakshi. *The Constitution of India: With Selective Comments by P.M. Bakshi* (Delhi, 1996), pp. 182–183.
42. Author's interview with Margaret Alva, former government minister, 19 December 1996, New Delhi. Alva was appointed to the upper house of Parliament by Indira Gandhi in 1974. She later was appointed by Rajiv Gandhi as head of the women's department within the Ministry of Human Resource Development. She has also served as Minister of State for Youth Affairs, Sports and Women.
43. Author's interview with Margaret Alva, 19 December 1996, New Delhi.

vations to the national level failed. The major arguments against these latest proposals repeated those of the past.

"ELECTED BODIES": WOMEN'S RESERVATIONS IN THE NINETIES

It's a step but it's not going to deal with all the problems that women face because, then again, politics is not only elected bodies. Politics is what's happening around you and how you're treated on the streets.
Feminist leader Brinda Karat, on reservations for women.[44]

How women are treated can vary due to class, caste or religion, but organizing a movement or a policy on the basis of such nuances is difficult. The 1990s brought several movements pushing for more equal representation into conflict with each other. The competing demands of women, OBCs, and Muslims for their own legislative reservations have led to political gridlock. In 1990, the Indian government granted reservations in central government jobs, though not in the legislature, to the OBCs. This recognition has given the previously more diffuse class- and caste-based critiques of women's reservations a political grounding. Like the 1998 scene in the Indian Parliament previously described, an earlier 1996 attempt to introduce a women's reservations bill succumbed to squabbling over recognition of the OBCs within the category of women.[45] Muslim demands for reservations have also competed with women's demands. The "competing inequalities" of gender, class, caste and religion have delayed a purely gender-based reservation scheme at the national level.

Key proponent of the women's reservation bill, Margaret Alva, argued for the legal recognition of women as a legitimate category for reservations. "Whether one is fighting for the scheduled castes, the backward classes, or the minorities – the largest group that is effected is women", she contended. "Women are the single largest group of backward citizens in the country."[46] Other women have been more critical, even while supporting the bill, as

---

44. Author's interview with Brinda Karat, women's movement leader (AIDWA), CPM (Communist Party-Marxist) political activist, 10 December 1996, New Delhi.
45. The Constitution (Eighty-First Amendment) Bill, 1996. See debates in the *Lok Sabha* of 13 September 1996, when MP Madhukar Sarpotdar argued as follows: "Would the skies have fallen on the nation if it [the Eighty-First Amendment Bill] had been kept pending or had been referred to a Select or Standing Committee and then, once and for all, a comprehensive Bill in this regard was brought forward? [...] It should have been brought after involving every section and after proper deliberations. Today the Scheduled Castes, the Scheduled Tribes have been involved but what about the people from the Other Backward Classes who have not been included in this bill?"
46. Congress MP and former government minister Margaret Alva, quoted in Meenakshi Nath, "Cutting Across Party Lines: Women Members of Parliament Explain Their Stand on Reservation Quotas", *Manushi*, 96 (1996), p. 11.

the views of leftist activist Brinda Karat and Hindu nationalist Uma Bharati indicate.

The major critiques of parliamentary reservations for women again distinguish between the claims of the "major minorities" or "communities" and those of women. "National unity" is less prominent than in previous debates. Some critics do not want to thwart the bill but to point out its limitations for backward classes and Muslims. Their concerns are reminiscent of *Towards Equality* and its recognition of diversity within the category of women. Other critiques come from incumbent politicians, who have suddenly raised similar objections in order to quash the bill on the floor – in spite of the decision of every major party to support the bill in their 1996 party platforms. Such tactics resemble group-based policies under the British, which strategically both divided and appeased various groups. By endorsing the bill in party platforms but failing to pass it out of a sudden concern for backwards citizens or Muslims, politicians court the women's vote, the backwards vote, the Muslim vote and simultaneously protect their own seats. Notably, any new reservations would unseat many incumbents.

Some of the more well-intentioned critics have analysed the condition of the backward women under the new local-level reservations in order to emphasize the limits of such policies. For example, although she holds that even lower-caste women have benefited a great deal from reservations in local councils, feminist and leftist (Communist Party of India-Marxist) activist Brinda Karat noted that reservations are not always enough to grant them access. She lamented the progress and predicaments of a subcategory of women, the scheduled castes:

> What we are finding is scheduled caste women who would never have been given an opportunity to come into [...] politics, are now coming in. Unfortunately, in many, many cases, they are, just as the scheduled caste men have been all along, just a rubber stamp [...] They are not allowed to participate [...] we had cases, where they hold the meeting deliberately in the house of an upper caste person, so the scheduled caste women, because of the social immobility, would censor herself [...] and so she will be sitting outside and they would send her the register and she would put her thumbprint on it. And so you see reservation on its own cannot be an instrument to remove this.[47]

Local-level reservations sparked some concern among even those supportive of such a measure, because these policies for "women" were blunt tools and not a panacea for the problems particular to the women of the lowest castes.[48] Another activist recognized the mixed success of the local-level

47. Author's interview with Brinda Karat, 10 December 1996, New Delhi.
48. Dana Dunn, "Gender Inequality in Education and Employment in the Scheduled Castes and Tribes of India", *Population Research and Policy Review*, 12 (1993), pp. 53–70. Likewise, in spite of policies aimed at the socioeconomic uplift of the scheduled castes and tribes, the women within these groups remain "doubly disadvantaged": "The multiplicity of social categories in India often

reservations but argued that if only a few of the elected women feel that they are an important part of the political process, that is an advance.[49]

Karat not only considers this diversity within women, but also the failure of many women's organizations to build bridges to other disadvantaged groups, a fact that exacerbates competing inequalities. Many women's organizations have not been terribly supportive of lower castes or of the extension of job reservations to OBCs. Having learned from minority women's critiques of the United States' women's movement, Karat's organization has promoted the notion that "sisterhood means you have to come out and openly support *dalit* [untouchable] women". But when OBCs were given reservations, there were "middle-class women in the streets of Delhi threatening to kill themselves and coming out with the most obscene signs" as well as "a section who preferred to remain silent". Only four or five national women's organizations defended OBCs' job reservations.[50] This backdrop increases the tensions between supporters of women's reservations and those of OBC reservations in legislatures.

Women's organizations have been ambivalent towards Muslim demands for reservations as well. Karat claims that Muslims are underrepresented in Parliament, but a Muslim reservation would do little for Muslim women without the women's reservation as well. "This is the only way that Muslim women are going to be able to come out into public life, because even if you have community representation, they will never allow Muslim women to come in and represent. No way."[51] Muslims, on the other hand, fear that a women's reservation would essentially be a Hindu women's reservation. Such qualms parallel Muslim fears in the 1930s that extending even the right to vote, let alone reserved seats, to women would increase the political power of the Hindu majority, due to the larger number of educated Hindu women. Thus Muslim resistance to some political rights for women is not just due to cultural conservatism but to electoral calculations. In recent years some Muslim groups have been demanding the reserved seats that they lost at Independence.[52] This demand also came up in the context of parliamentary debate over women's reservations.

Some women understand the logic behind the demands for reservations on a class or religious basis, but feel that women's reservations should come first. Feminist and Christian leader Jotsna Chatterjee admits that "we have

---

serves to obscure the status of women in the most disadvantaged segments of the population" (p. 66).

49. Author's interview with Vimla Farooqui of the National Forum for Indian Women (NFIW), Delhi, 2 December 1996.

50. Author's interview with Brinda Karat, 10 December 1996, New Delhi.

51. *Ibid.*

52. Theodore P. Wright, "A New Demand for Muslim Reservations in India", *Asian Survey*, 37 (1997), pp. 852–858.

no objection to the OBCs getting reservations", but first, women should be given thirty-three per cent reservation, and "automatically this will apply to every category". That would mean "that women will have to be given space in the scheduled caste, scheduled tribe section, and then if it is extended to the OBCs, it will have to be also given in the OBCs and also in the minorities".[53] Chatterjee represents a religious minority community, Christians, but since their educational and socioeconomic status tends to be higher than that of Muslims, Christians have not been inspired to lodge a similar demand for sub-reservations within women's reservations.

These activists remain supportive of women's reservations, although they recognize that this policy is a blunt tool which does not adequately address the doubly disadvantaged OBC or Muslim women. Politicians in parliamentary debates, however, may have raised concerns about Muslim and OBC women in order to defeat the Women's Reservation Bill. Alva has charged: "When it was introduced [...] there was hullabaloo in the House [...] No man has the courage to stand up in the House and say we don't want it, so they had to sabotage it. Now the only way they could sabotage it is to appeal to caste. Because caste cuts across women."[54] Some activists supportive of women's reservations describe this as a strategy to divide women on the basis of caste, class and creed, or as "splitting hairs" to divide and rule or at least maintain seats in Parliament.[55] One commentator memorably predicted that the Women's Reservation Bill "will be diluted and further diluted till you have a law that says you can have your one third reservation for women provided they have pink hair, are totally backward, completely unheard of in any political arena".[56]

An ambiguous example of this approach came from Uma Bharati, a Member of Parliament from the Bharatiya Janata Party (BJP). She herself is difficult to categorize, a female member of the backward classes in a party dominated by Hindu upper castes. Although her party platform supported the bill and she claimed to support it as well, she became a spokeswoman for the demand to amend the bill to include OBCs, an amendment that led to its downfall. Ironically, the BJP had vociferously decried the extension of reserved central government jobs to OBCs in 1990, a campaign that led to several self-immolations by upper-caste students. At that point the BJP, which is a nationalist organization promoting the idea of India as a Hindu nation, was quick to criticize the OBC reservations as divisive and a threat to national integrity. Although this sudden concern for OBCs in the context

53. Author's interview with Jotsna Chatterjee, women's movement leader and YWCA activist, New Delhi, 22 November 1996, New Delhi.
54. Author's interview with Margaret Alva, 19 December 1996, New Delhi.
55. Author's interview with activists, Miss Gangoli of the YWCA in Delhi, 3 December 1996, and Jotsna Chatterjee, 22 November 1996.
56. Maneka Gandhi, "And the One Who Differs [...] Maneka Gandhi on the Women's Reservation Bill", *Manushi*, 96 (1996), p. 18.

of the women's reservations bill seems suspicious, Uma Bharati's credentials to make such a proposal are hard to fault: "Since I am from the backward castes, I know from experience that women from the oppressed classes are the weakest of the weakest section of society."[57]

In short, the discourses of "communities" came up again in the debate over women's reservations in the nineties, at times in ways reminiscent of the British and at times in ways similar to the Committee on the Status of Women. National unity was a minor theme in this latest round. Even the BJP remained unusually silent about the threat such group-based policies posed for Hindus and national integrity, letting the Women's Reservation Bill fail largely due to squabbling over proposals to include OBCs. The competing inequalities at the basis of gender, class, caste and religious minority movements for reservations have not yet reached a detente.

CONCLUSIONS: COMPLICATING THE CATEGORIES

For women to get rights is not a very simple thing.
Vimla Farooqui, National Forum for Indian Women.[58]

The history of demands for women's reservations in India illustrates the many ways administrators, politicians and activists have socially constructed women's identities and interests. Like the British administrator who categorized women as "minor minorities" in comparison with caste and religious groups, after Independence the Committee on the Status of Women in India contrasted women as a "category" with "communities" based on caste or religion, which were still considered more legitimate political groupings. The extension of reservations to women in local level legislative bodies signaled a shift towards the acceptance of the category of "women" as a legitimate target of such public policies; yet the recent uproar in Parliament over the Women's Reservation Bill demonstrates that women's goals are still seen as competing with other groups rather than complementing them. Muslims fear Hindu women will dominate the reserved seats; lower classes and castes argue that privileged women will prevail. A few politicians see the parallels between different disadvantaged groups. For example, former prime minister V.P. Singh, who in 1990 expanded the scope of reservation policies to include OBCs, likewise argues that India "can't have social justice without justice to women".[59]

The history of debates over women's reservations, particularly the competition between various unequal groups, is a particularly rich example of the

---

57. BJP MP Uma Bharati, quoted in Meenakshi Nath, "Cutting Across Party Lines: Women Members of Parliament Explain Their Stand on Reservation Quotas", *Manushi*, 96 (1996), p. 11.
58. Author's interview with Vimla Farooqui, Delhi, 2 December 1996.
59. Author's interview with former prime minister of India, V.P. Singh, New Delhi, 20 November 1996.

complexity of overlapping identities and the tendency of material factors to bring different identities into relief at different historical points. This issue also demonstrates how "complicating the categories" leads to not only academic but practical challenges. The colonial categorizations of Indian society were both too complicated and not complicated enough. British attempts to simultaneously appease and divide the "major minorities" caused them to subsume vast diversity under the categories of a Hindu "majority" and Muslim "minority" as well as develop a similarly oversimplified yet divisive codification of the caste system. These primary categories were superimposed onto gender-based provisions.

This legacy effected the debate over women's reservations in the 1974 report, *Towards Equality*, which recommended only limited, local-level women's reservations, in large part due to overriding concerns about caste and religious communities. Two major concerns expressed in the report were the more legitimate claim of such "communities" for reservations, as opposed to the claim of women, who constitute a mere "category", and, conversely, the fear that any reservations – particularly for "communities" – could lead to the disintegration of India. The contemporary arguments against reservations for women continue these streams of historical arguments. The priority given to the category of women has fallen behind Muslims and backward classes on the one hand and the nation on the other. What makes the persistence of these same arguments remarkable is the very different motivations at play in the three time periods under consideration, ranging from a colonial power trying to maintain control of an unruly colony, to a government committee genuinely concerned about the plight of women, to policy makers hoping to retain their seats in Parliament.

Why is gender repeatedly singled out as a problematic category for group-based policies? Is there a sound basis for past distinctions between the category of gender and communities of religious minorities or lower castes? Do these latter communities more neatly coincide with class, legitimating their claims to special policies? Every sort of group in India has internal diversity. There are well-off Muslims and relatively "forward" backward classes; yet women have the most internal diversity, since they are a substantial part of all class groups. If the only purpose of the policies is to help redistribute power and resources to the poor, gender alone may not be an appropriate category; yet ignoring gender and using other categories can be equally problematic, since women within other disadvantaged categories are often the worst off.[60] Moreover, reservations are not simply a redistributive policy since they are also a means for group recognition and representation. For this purpose, women may be as relevant a group as any, even if they are

---

60. Dana Dunn, "Gender Inequality in Education and Employment of the Scheduled Castes and Scheduled Tribes of India", *Population Research and Policy Review*, 12 (1993), pp. 53–70.

scattered throughout the class hierarchy. As Benedict Anderson has famously pointed out, even people who may never meet can become "imagined communities".[61] On the other hand, the extremely diverse category of women is particularly prone to politically-motivated reimaginings. Thus politicians could appeal to half of the Indian electorate when promising parliamentary reservations for women, but in the later debates they could argue, for any other constituency, that those seats would be taken by the women of a rival group. Due in part to such political manipulations and to the nature of the category itself, women's organizations in India have not achieved unity, let alone a broader solidarity between women, Muslims and backward classes. Given the diversity within and between these groups, what could facilitate the formation of broader coalitions? One possibility is revising or complicating the categories of group based policies to discourage group-based competition.

Reservations, which tie material and political benefits to peoples' identification with certain social categories, are a recipe for explosive politics. Yet such targeted policies may be necessary to deal with inequalities. India is faced with the dilemma of a country with an incredibly complex patchwork of overlapping identities and at the same time profound inequalities and stratification on the basis of many of these identities. Group-based policies can alleviate this stratification, yet the best way to categorize society for this purpose is far from clear. Although India is an extreme case due to the sheer number of dimensions of cultural identity and the degree of stratification, the dilemma facing it is not unique to India. The biggest challenge to affirmative action policies today – in both Western and non-Western societies – is defining the boundaries of the beneficiary categories. In the United States, for example, race- and gender-based policies are under fire, and proposals incorporating class and multifaceted notions of "disadvantage" are proliferating.

India's much longer history of affirmative action is instructive in this regard. Although the category of "backward" citizens is proliferating perhaps too quickly, the "other backward classes" or OBC category is an interesting attempt to incorporate several different indicators of disadvantage. Trying to recognize the so-called "backward" within other broader categories such as women could avoid reifying the category of women and reach the most disadvantaged members of society. Yet the ongoing controversies over defining categories and subcategories may prevent any policy innovations at all. Given the complexity of Indian women's identities, policy makers and activists must walk the grey line between exploring more complex policies and courting political gridlock. Competing inequalities may impede the political unity of the disadvantaged; nevertheless, if policies to benefit

61. Benedict Anderson, *Imagined Communities* (London, 1991).

disadvantaged groups are passed despite the "hulabaloo in the House", these competing forces may also result in more nuanced policies.

It is not the purpose of this article to make policy recommendations or to advocate a position on women's reservations; yet a theoretical recognition of the complexity of social categories and the intertwined nature of identities and interests does have practical implications. When lines of social and material stratification coincide, group-based policies such as reservations may be necessary. Rather than reinforcing social categories, as many critics argue, judicious use of such policies may be the only way to combat extreme disadvantage. However, a side effect of such policies is the tendency, seen in these case studies, for disadvantaged groups such as women, backward classes and religious minorities to compete over group-based benefits rather than form coalitions. One promising policy approach for India, suggested recently in terms of employment and educational reservations, is to target not the standard major and minor minorities but to allocate benefits to those who break down such barriers.

One example is reservations for people in intercaste marriages. To avoid penalizing low-caste women who take on the official status of their higher-caste husbands, the Ministry of Welfare has recently considered reserving jobs for such mixed families. Former government minister Ram Vilas Paswan also has advocated a new reservation category for those who have intercaste marriages:

> In India you can change religion, you can change the party, you can become rich, rich can become poor, but you can't change your caste. So caste is just like a rock. So the only process where the caste system can be weakened is intercaste marriage [...]. If the reservation is made on that ground, intercaste marriage, then slowly, slowly caste system will be abolished. And if there is no caste then there will be no reservation on the basis of caste.[62]

In this way, material benefits become associated with those who do not fit into categories rather than with the reified categories of gender, caste, class or religion. Such innovations may be a promising way to alleviate the competing inequalities along these lines and to reflect in practice our academic attempts to "complicate the categories" of Indian society. By disconnecting material benefits from official gender, religious or class categories, such policies can facilitate a sense of shared interests rather than competition between disadvantaged groups, one step toward building coalitions.

Rather than entering a "post-material" age of identity politics, both the Western and non-Western worlds face increasingly complicated relationships between interests and identities. As critic Shane Phelan observes:

---

62. Author's interview with Ram Vilas Paswan, General Secretary of the SC/ST MPs Forum, Minister of Railways, MP from Bihar, Hindu *dalit* Leader, Delhi, 20 December 1996.

Interest talk may make sense if all the members of a group share every "relevant" social characteristic or submerge difference(s) among themselves, but this eventuality is increasingly unlikely. In modern societies, where overlapping social movements and identities are increasingly present, interest becomes as unstable as identity.[63]

In the theoretical speculations over what may be replacing "class" politics in Europe and the West, then, we should avoid drawing a false dichotomy between material and post-material politics, often equated with a shift from class-based movements to "new social movements" based on gender and other "identities". This tendency overshadows the fact that classes may share a sense of group identity, not just interests; likewise, groups based on gender, religion or caste may rally around shared interests, not just identities. This is true in the West as well, but becomes particularly apparent in case studies from a non-Western society like India. Moving away from the European and American approaches to these debates forces us to challenge the dichotomy between material and post-material politics, which is misleading even in Western cases and inapplicable to most non-Western cases. Moreover, women's movements in both Western and non-Western societies also pose a serious challenge to such dichotomies, since they are based not just on gender identities but also material questions ranging from access to food to access to political office. Theory built from a non-Western case such as India can produce a more nuanced alternative to the material versus post-material or class versus identity schisms in the literature.

---

63. Shane Phelan, "The Space of Justice", in Linda Nicholson and Steven Seidman (eds), *Social Postmodernism: Beyond Identity Politics* (New York, 1995), pp. 338–339.

International Review of Social History 44 (1999), Supplement, pp. 77–99
© 1999 Internationaal Instituut voor Sociale Geschiedenis

"The Black Man's Burden": African Americans, Imperialism, and Notions of Racial Manhood 1890–1910*

MICHELE MITCHELL

Take up the White Man's Burden –
Send forth the best ye breed –
Go bind your sons to exile
To serve your captives' need [...]
Comes now, to search your manhood
Through all the thankless years,
Cold-edged with dear-brought wisdom,
The judgment of your peers!
Rudyard Kipling, 1899[1]

Take up the Black Man's burden –
"Send forth the best ye breed",
To judge with righteous judgment
The Black Man's work and need [...]
Let the glory of your people
Be the making of great men,
The lifting of the lowly
To noble thought and aim [...]
J. Dallas Bowser, 1899[2]

In 1899, about fifteen years after the Conference of Berlin accelerated Europe's partitioning of Africa, African-American preacher Henry Blanton Parks fervently believed the fate of Africa would be determined during the twentieth century. Parks struggled long and hard as a young man to secure an education in Georgia and rise in the ranks of the African Methodist Episcopal (AME) Church; he earned a reputation for having an expansive outlook in the process. By the time he became Secretary of Home and Foreign Missions, Reverend Parks not only located Christian redemption of Africa within the promise of a new century, he authored a book to convince other African Americans that it was their duty to conquer the continent for God, for Africans, for themselves. In *Africa: The Problem of the New Century*, Parks contended that if the AME Church failed to secure a righteous "destiny [...] [for] the junior races of the world [...] [and] historic

* The author would like to thank Nancy MacLean, Tessie Liu, Nancy Hunt, and Eileen Boris for their comments on earlier versions of this article.
1. Rudyard Kipling, "The White Man's Burden", stanzas 1 and 7, reprinted in *Rudyard Kipling's Verse: Definitive Edition* (New York, 1940), pp. 321–323.
2. J. Dallas Bowser, "Take Up the Black Man's Burden", stanzas 1 and 6, Salt Lake City *Broad Ax*, 25 April 1899, p. 4.

Africa", the scramble for Africa would blight the continent with liquor, vice, and genocide. Africa's destiny was a signal issue for Parks, but so was the question of imperialism.[3]

Parks was hardly alone when he worried about the "native simplicity" of Africans being corrupted by Europeans – other African-American women and men pondered the ramifications of imperialism in Africa as well.[4] Some shared racist assumptions about "darkest Africa" commonly found in popular travelogues; others felt European forays into Africa would enlighten the continent.[5] Prominent newspaper editor T. Thomas Fortune railed against British, French, German and Belgian encroachment during the 1880s. By the 1895 Congress of Africa, however, Fortune projected European imperialism would, in time, have a beneficial outcome. Fortune conceded that while "laying the foundation of empires" occurred at the expense of "savage tribes", the "intermingling of so many race elements [would] work for national and spiritual and material strength in Africa".[6] In 1892, Ida Wells expressed tempered optimism as she uneasily acknowledged a European foothold in Africa. Wells nevertheless held fast to a belief that black Americans could prosper there since the continent had not been completely overrun by "rapacious" whites. S.H. Johnson was more pessimistic than either Wells or Fortune; Johnson maintained European ascendancy in Africa ominously signaled that whites would soon subjugate blacks across the continent. Whether these journalists believed Europeans would eventually succeed in wrenching all rights and land from Africans, Reverend Parks had a job to do. He needed to convince African Americans that Africa was theirs to save.[7]

3. H[enry] B[lanton] Parks, *Africa: The Problem of the New Century; The Part the African Methodist Episcopal Church is to Have in its Solution* (New York, 1899), pp. 5, 8–9, 20. For biographical information, see Horace Talbert, *The Sons of Allen* (Xenia, OH, 1906), pp. 212–214.
4. Overviews of Afro-American viewpoints on European campaigns in Africa include Sylvia Jacobs, *The African Nexus: Black American Perspectives on the European Partitioning of Africa, 1880–1920* (Westport, CT, 1981) and Elliott P. Skinner, *African-Americans and US Policy Toward Africa, 1850–1924: In Defense of Black Nationality* (Washington DC, 1992). For analysis of the AME Church and its complex relationship to Africa, see James T. Campbell, *Songs of Zion: The African Methodist Episcopal Church in the United States and South Africa* (New York, 1995).
5. See Walter L. Williams, "Black Journalism's Opinions About Africa During the Late Nineteenth Century", *Phylon: The Atlanta University Review of Race and Culture* , 34 (1973), pp. 224–235; *idem*, *Black Americans and the Evangelization of Africa, 1877–1900* (Madison, WI, 1982); Kevin Gaines, "Black Americans' Racial Uplift Ideology as 'Civilizing Mission': Pauline E. Hopkins on Race and Imperialism", in Amy Kaplan and Donald E. Pease (eds), *Cultures of United States Imperialism* (Durham, NC, 1993), pp. 433–455.
6. T. Thomas Fortune, "The Nationalization of Africa", in J.W.E. Bowen (ed.), *Africa and the American Negro: Addresses and Proceedings on the Congress of Africa* [...] (Atlanta, GA, 1896), pp. 199–204, esp. pp. 201, 203–204. Consult Jean M. Allman and David R. Roediger, "The Early Editorial Career of Timothy Thomas Fortune: Class, Nationalism and Consciousness of Africa", *Afro-Americans in New York Life and History*, 6 (1982), pp. 39–52 for analysis of Fortune's editorial writing.
7. Ida B. Wells, "Afro-Americans and Africa", *AME Church Review*, 9 (1892), pp. 40–44, esp. p. 41; S.H. Johnson, "Negro Emigration: A Correspondent Portrays the Situation and the Benefit

Henry Parks was able to do so by skillfully manipulating the language of empire. He proudly informed his black American readers that:

[...] the AME Church [is] confronted with responsibilities as [...] broad as the new American policy of empire [...]. [It] stands on the threshold of a policy of expansion [...]. Africa – the second largest continent in the world – is the new colonial possession of the Missionary Department of the AME Church[.]

Enlightening Africans with Christianity and progress was not "the white man's burden", Parks continued. Rather, race pride alone should convince African Americans that if spreading civilization involved bearing burdens, people of color should make sure imperialism was benevolent.[8]

Christian zeal clearly blinded Parks to the possibility that religious imperialism might be anything but benevolent in the eyes of prospective converts, but why was he so eager for black Americans to build their own empire in Africa? Why were the pages of *Africa: The Problem of the New Century* peppered with militaristic images of "warlike conquerors" and a "marching army" of civilization? And why, when soliciting donations, did Parks liken the financial needs of his "missionary campaign" to funding a war? Parks did so because he was a man of his era: he accepted contemporary notions that empire building required militaristic demonstrations of prowess. Thus, when Parks wrote the "conquest of the Cross" was far more potent than "conquest by war", he could actively suggest that the real men in Africa were not European soldiers or colonists, but black missionaries who would save the day for Africans and the race as a whole.[9]

Like many African-American texts written between 1890 and 1910, *Africa: The Problem of the New Century* made both subtle and blatant claims about imperialism, race, and manhood. Placed in its historical context, Parks's plea for Africa assumes significance for other reasons as well. First of all, it was produced during an era when racial oppression was at once extreme and common. Negotiating their lives around the realities of disfranchisement, lynching, and low status, few black American men fully exercised the prerogatives of manhood at the turn of the century. Parks could therefore appeal to black men by arguing that going to Africa was a decisive opportunity for them to create and belong to "a better manhood".[10] Such an appeal was most likely to resonate with men like Parks – ambitious strugglers within a cohort of aspiring class African Americans whose status was anything but secure.

Second, Parks' book appeared when Social Darwinism was tremendously

to Be Derived by Emigration", Indianapolis *Freeman*, 26 March 1892, p. 3; Parks, *Africa: The Problem of the New Century*, pp. 20–22.
8. Parks, *Africa: The Problem of the New Century*, pp. 29–30, 41.
9. *Ibid.*, pp. 7, 8–9, 20, 48.
10. *Ibid.*, p. 7.

popular in the United States.[11] Social Darwinism complimented gendered
notions of conquest implicit in imperialism as it provided a rationale for
subjugating people of color. By ranking racial "types" on a hierarchical scale
according to fitness, character, and culture, Social Darwinism promoted
notions that each race had its own domain and linked racial fitness to both
virility and whiteness. "Colored" races were less fit for civilization because
they were less manly; they were less manly because they were not white.[12]
Africa: The Problem of a New Century shared more than a few civilizationist,
social Darwinist assumptions: Parks categorized Africans and Afro-
Americans as two *distinct* races; blacks in the US were supposedly more
evolved due to constant contact with Anglo-Americans and acquisition of
modern tools of progress. In the process of outlining how the trappings of
civilization enabled Afro-Americans to inch further up the evolutionary
ladder, the author subverted a critical tenet of Social Darwinism by presenting Africans as inherently manly. Parks did not go as far as AME bishop
Henry McNeal Turner, a fiery orator and leading advocate of emigration
to Liberia, who claimed West Africans were *manlier* than blacks across the
Atlantic. Still, Parks insinuated that black Americans could bolster their
own racial manhood by working in tandem with Africans to "civilize" the
continent.[13] Henry Parks was influenced by Social Darwinism but he warped
it just enough to suit his own concepts of race, civilization, and manliness.

  Finally, when *Africa: The Problem of the New Century* appeared in 1899,
there was an ongoing, heated debate among African Americans over the
implications of the Spanish–American and Philippine–American Wars.
Whereas some African Americans were staunch anti-imperialists who
believed any form of imperialism had dire consequences for people of color,
many others welcomed US wars for empire. They did so, in part, because
gambits for empire involved attributes closely associated with masculinity:
if black men bravely participated in American war efforts they might succeed
in refuting long-standing charges that manliness was forever beyond their
grasp. While Parks was trying to enlist soldiers for God with the promise

11. Richard Hofstadter, *Social Darwinism in American Thought: 1860–1915* (New York, 1959);
August Meier, *Negro Thought in America, 1880–1915* (Ann Arbor, MI, 1966); J. Edward Chamberlin
and Sander L. Gilman (eds), *Degeneration: The Dark Side of Progress* (New York, 1985).
12. For commentary on gendered subtexts of imperialism, race, Social Darwinism and civilization
in *fin de siècle* thought, consult Gail Bederman, *Manliness and Civilization: A Cultural History of
Gender and Race in the United States, 1880–1917* (Chicago, IL, 1995) and Jan Breman (ed.), *Imperial
Monkey Business: Racial Supremacy in Social Darwinist Theory and Colonial Practice* (Amsterdam,
1990).
13. Parks, *Africa: The Problem of the New Century*, pp. 8–9, 22, 40–51, 43. For observations by
Turner, see Edwin S. Redkey (ed.), *Respect Black: The Writings and Speeches of Henry McNeal
Turner* (New York, 1971), pp. 124, 159. Analysis of civilizationist suppositions within Afro-
American appropriations of Social Darwinism may be found in Gaines, "Black Americans' Racial
Uplift Ideology as 'Civilizing Mission'", pp. 433–455, esp. p. 438, and Williams, "Black Journal-
ism's Opinions About Africa During the Late Nineteenth Century", p. 230.

that the AME's work in Africa was akin to "the new American policy of empire", US expansionism presented its own opportunities.

This article explores gendered notions among black people in *fin de siècle* United States by highlighting concepts of race and manhood within Afro-American discourse. The connection between US imperialism and imperialism in Africa within this discourse is particularly important. US imperialism initially seemed to afford black men a rare chance to prove themselves better men than their white contemporaries. After these hopes proved illusory, Africa appeared to be one of few fields where black Americans could flex muscle, build nations, and demonstrate virility by fending off white-skinned intruders. Whereas US imperialism potentially bolstered masculinity within the race, the prospect of a black American reclamation of Africa proved just as, if not more, promising.

Significantly, the majority of extant Afro-American commentary on race and empire was produced by ambitious men within the aspiring and elite classes.[14] These men were most likely to view imperialism as an opportunity to improve their station and fortify black manhood: like Henry Parks, many aspiring and elite black men overcame formidable obstacles to achieve and acquire. Given steady disfranchisement, escalating racial violence, and the unstable economy at the century's end, aspiring and elite men were likely to feel that their hard-won gains were slipping away; ironically, such men usually offered little explicit commentary about class when commenting on imperialism. Even aspiring and elite men hostile to expansionism relied upon a trope of manhood constructed around race, as did men who believed class mobility could be best achieved outside US borders. Class informed rather than defined Afro-American discourse on imperialism in that anxieties over class were articulated through racialized language about manhood. If there was relative silence concerning class, there were other important silences as well. Since the push for empire was primarily gendered as a struggle over manhood, it is not surprising that aspiring and elite black women, while not altogether silent on imperialism, focused their energies on domestic reform and the sexual politics of respectability during this

14. Although this essay deals with the industrial age, applying standard class labels – "working class", "bourgeois", "owning class" – to African Americans who lived between 1890 and 1910 would obscure the specific circumstances of a people barely a generation removed from slavery. Since over seventy per cent of African Americans still resided in the rural south by 1900 and approximately ninety per cent were workers, I use slightly different terminology. "Working poor" refers to people who struggled to survive – sharecroppers, domestics, underemployed seasonal laborers. "Aspiring class" refers to workers – from seamstresses to skilled tradesmen to teachers to small proprietors – able to save a little money. These women and men were concerned with appearing "respectable"; many had normal school education or were self-educated and some worked multiple jobs in order to attain class mobility. "Elite" refers to college-educated professionals, many of whom were prominent in national organizations, owned well-appointed homes, and had successful businesses.

period.[15] As for working poor women and men, many wrote impassioned letters about emigrating to Africa, but relatively few recorded their views on empire.

At no time between 1890 and 1910 were all US blacks of one mind about imperialism, but by 1910 greater numbers of African Americans were against both US imperialism and European imperialism in Africa. However, at times, anti-imperialist blacks all but suggested that some form of civilizing conquest was necessary if Africa ever hoped to keep apace with Europe, North America, and Asia in the march of progress. Existing literature has certainly accounted for the complex relationship between African Americans and imperialism; indeed, it has even commented on the ambivalence of black soldiers who participated in wars for empire.[16] Still, interpreting how African Americans responded to imperialism and understanding what came to be known as the "black man's burden" during the late nineteenth and early twentieth centuries requires analysis of racialized ideas concerning manhood and sexuality.

MASTER CONTINENTS, MILITANTS, AND MANLINESS: RACE AND GENDER IN AFRO-AMERICAN DISCOURSE ON EMPIRE

In the rapidly industrializing and newly reconstructed United States, gender informed how black Americans organized households, established institutions, and negotiated work arrangements. After reconstruction, gender assumed special significance for African Americans due to persistent arguments that blacks were "feminine" compared to "masculine" Anglo-Saxons; black women were frequently derided in popular discourse as aggressive, immoral, and slovenly while black men were either demonized as oversexed brutes or satirized as servile – and impotent – "uncles".[17] Most black

15. For analysis of black women's political activism during these years, see Evelyn Brooks Higginbotham, *Righteous Discontent: The Women's Movement in the Black Baptist Church, 1880–1920* (Cambridge, MA, 1993), Glenda Elizabeth Gilmore, *Gender & Jim Crow: Women and the Politics of White Supremacy in North Carolina, 1896–1920* (Chapel Hill, NC, 1996), Stephanie J. Shaw, *What a Woman Ought to Be and To Do* (Chicago, IL, 1996), and Deborah Gray White, *Too Heavy a Load: Black Women in Defense of Themselves, 1894–1994* (New York, 1999).
16. See, for example, Willard B. Gatewood, Jr, "Negro Troops in Florida, 1898", *Florida Historical Quarterly*, 49 (1970), pp. 1–15; *idem*, "Black Americans and the Quest for Empire, 1898–1903", *Journal of Southern History*, 38 (1972), pp. 545–66; *idem*, *Black Americans and the White Man's Burden, 1898–1903* (Urbana, IL, 1975); Richard E. Welch, Jr, *Response to Imperialism: The United States and the Philippine–American War, 1899–1902* (Chapel Hill, NC, 1979), pp. 101–116; Kevin Gaines and Penny von Eschen, "Ambivalent Warriors: African Americans, US Expansion, and the Legacies of 1898", *Culture Front*, 8 (1998), pp. 63–64, 73–75.
17. George M. Fredrickson, *The Black Image in the White Mind: The Debate on Afro-American Character and Destiny, 1817–1914* (New York, 1971), pp. 97–129, *passim*; James Oliver Horton, "Freedom's Yoke: Gender Conventions Among Antebellum Free Blacks", *Feminist Studies*, 12 (1986), pp. 51–76, esp. p. 53.

Americans resisted such racist characterizations: they responded to attacks on their collective character by emphasizing respectable femininity in women and uncompromised manliness in men and the race as a whole. As much as African Americans were concerned about the impact stereotypes and racial oppression had on black women, the possibility that the race was losing its "manhood stamina" within the United States was a specific anxiety.[18] Exclusionary practices left many black men chronically underemployed during the 1890s while civil rights were tenuous and under attack. Moreover, attempts by black men to seize prerogatives of manhood – particularly the franchise – often resulted in retributive mob violence at the hands of white men; conflagrations in Wilmington, North Carolina (1898) and Atlanta, Georgia (1906) were both sparked by conflicts between black and white men over political rights. White vigilantism exacted certain and brutal tolls on black women and children, and black women were indeed lynched, but mob violence was perceived as having the greatest impact on masculinity and black male bodies.[19] As an angry Henry Turner put it, such oppression was "so repugnant to the instincts of respected manhood" that black Americans were at risk of either "transmit[ting] [...] servility to their posterity" or, even worse, "*unracing* themselves".[20]

To further compound matters, black men's sexuality was relatively circumscribed in comparison to white men who routinely enjoyed consensual and coerced sexual intercourse with women of color. As much as it is an anemic historiographical truism that black men bitterly resented not being able to protect "their women", black men were certainly incensed by the racialized, sexual double standard that prevailed throughout most regions of the United States.[21] For Afro-American men in the late nineteenth century, then, asserting a claim to "manliness" was a potent means of countering restrictions in their daily lives.

A range of post-Reconstruction African-American discourse was therefore gendered and sexualized; it overwhelmingly emphasized the "manhood" of the race. Of course, "manliness" and "manhood" were frequently used by black and white Americans as generic terms including women.[22] But again,

18. [Quotation from Ida B. Wells], *Voice of Missions* , June 1894, p. 2.
19. Elsa Barkley Brown offers powerful commentary on past and present tendencies to view lynching as a "masculine experience". See Brown, "Imaging Lynching: African American Women, Communities of Struggle, and Collective Memory" in Geneva Smitherman (ed.), *African-American Women Speak Out on Anita Hill–Clarence Thomas* (Detroit, MI, 1995), pp. 100–124, esp. 101–102.
20. Henry McNeal Turner, "Essay: The American Negro and the Fatherland", in Bowen, *Africa and the American*, pp. 195–198, esp. p. 197. (Italics in original.)
21. See Reverend Emanuel K. Love, "Oration Delivered on Emancipation Day" (2 January, 1888), Daniel A.P. Murray Pamphlet Collection, Library of Congress, Washington DC; Wesley J. Gaines, *The Negro and the White Man* (Philadelphia, PA, 1897); Jack Thorne [David Bryant Fulton], *A Plea for Social Justice for the Negro Woman* (New York, 1912).
22. Norman Vance, *The Sinews of the Spirit: The Ideal of Christian Manliness in Victorian Literature and Religious Thought* (Cambridge, 1985), p. 1.

due to the particularly low status of black American men, Afro-American emphasis on manhood and masculinity was often a strategy to confer dignity and power upon men who were, in reality, accorded little respect or dominion.[23] Black commentary on racial oppression in the US south reflects this strategy: in 1890, for example, an article by obscure author Lucy Norman insisted mob violence could never diminish black manhood. In contrast, the much better known Bishop Turner was so outraged over conditions in the south, he observed with no small amount of disgust that *"there is no manhood future in the United States for the Negro* [...] he can never be a *man* – full, symmetrical and undwarfed". Black men could not be masculine men, Turner contended, until they went to a country where their manhood was universally recognized and respected.[24]

For many black men and women that country was Liberia. Whereas emancipated slaves and free blacks emigrated to Liberia throughout the nineteenth century, it was not until the 1890s that scores of working-poor and aspiring-class black Americans viewed removal to Liberia as a means of gaining access to opportunities and alleviating immiseration.[25] Black women and men across the United States formed their own "exodus associations" and "independent orders", while many others turned to the American Colonization Society, an agency with strong – if problematic – ties to Liberia. Letters claiming "thousands" wanted to emigrate poured into the society: in one such letter, grassroots organizer Mary Jackson declared that Liberia seemed nothing less than "the place for the best advantage of the Negro".[26]

Liberia was especially attractive to aspiring-class men. Lewis Lee looked forward to building a "Negro nation" where he, as a thirty-four-year-old farmer, could freely "exercise [...] privlege" [sic]. John Lewis – a molder forced to wait at tables due to discriminatory practices in the skilled trades – felt that since whites would "not let the Negroe [sic] advance beyond a prescribed limit", he had nothing to loose by emigrating. Twenty-six-year-old R.A. Wright was also unable to follow his chosen profession. A lawyer by training, Wright taught in a school and longed to live where both his

23. See David Leverenz's discussion of Frederick Douglass in *Manhood and the American Renaissance* (Ithaca, NY, 1989), pp. 108–134.
24. Lucy V. Norman, "Can a Colored Man Be a Man in the South?", *Christian Recorder*, 3 July 1890, p. 2; Turner, "Essay: The American Negro and the Fatherland", pp. 195–198, esp. p. 195; (italics in original.)
25. Edwin S. Redkey, *Black Exodus: Black Nationalist and Back-to-Africa Movements, 1890–1910* (New Haven, CT, 1969), pp. 1–23, *passim*. For representative primary evidence, see I.W. Penn to William Coppinger, 10 April 1891, American Colonization Society Papers, Library of Congress, Washington DC [hereafter, *ACSP*], container 280, vol. 283.
26. See, for example, *African Repository*, 43 (1887), pp. 49–51 and *African Repository*, 46 (1890), pp. 49–51; Mary E. Jackson to Coppinger, 20 May 1891, *ACSP*, container 280, vol. 283. For evidence of independent black emigration societies, see Mary E. Jackson to Coppinger, 16 June 1891, *ACSP*, container 280, vol. 283.

ambition and manhood would go unrestrained. "There are several reasons why I desire to go", Wright confessed, "chiefly among them [is] I desire to go where a man of color can, if he will, be a man in the true sense of the word." Lee, Lewis, and Wright were frustrated in their separate quests for mobility yet none discussed their frustration in terms of class. Black men did, however, express anxieties over the sexual proclivities of white men. A group of prospective emigrants in Arkansas wrote that two factors shaped their desire to leave the US: their inability to vote and the frequent murders of black men whose wives were then seized, terrorized, and assaulted by white mobs. Along similar lines, Tennessee resident James Dubose ruefully observed that white male access to black women made it impossible for a black man "to be a man in any Southern state".[27]

Emigration was rather controversial nonetheless. In contrast to aspiring and working poor folk who found emigration appealing, elite or otherwise privileged black Americans were more likely to warn against viewing Africa – especially Liberia – as a refuge or proving ground. Charles Taylor, a vocal black Democrat who served as US Consul-General to Liberia during the Cleveland administration, acidly referred to Liberia as "an independent farce" where Americo-Liberians "convert[ed] nobody [...] and g[o]t rich off of the natives". Taylor even went so far as to imply that in Liberia masculine power was routinely outstripped by feminine force. Without outwardly claiming men became eunuchs in Liberia, Taylor more than insinuated women were the manly ones among the Americo-Liberian populace.[28]

Like Charles Taylor, Amanda Berry Devine Smith also spent time in Liberia; the laundress-turned-evangelist did mission work there from 1882 to 1890. Smith included trenchant opinions on the merits of Liberia as a colonial enterprise in her 1893 autobiography and she described Afro-American emigration to the coastal republic in detail.[29] Much of what Smith wrote was less than flattering, including her description of a major gathering during late 1886 or early 1887 when a group of Americo-Liberians welcomed a contingent of approximately one hundred South Carolinians to their settlement. Sister Smith took umbrage when women were barred from attending and she resisted in dramatic fashion. Literally carrying her own chair into the proceedings, Smith ignored reproachful glances and seated herself in a conspicuous spot. The self-described "privileged character" then witnessed a parade of men spouting lofty rhetoric: when "[a]ll the prominent men of the place" reassured newcomers Liberia was a "free

27. Lewis Lee to J. Ormond Wilson, 23 October 1894, *ACSP*, container 286, vol. 291; John Lewis to Wilson, 31 January 1893, *ACSP*, container 288, vol. 294; R.A. Wright to Wilson, 26 February 1894, *ACSP*, container 286, vol. 291; F.M. Gilmore to Coppinger, 15 April 1891, *ACSP*, container 280, vol. 283; James Dubose to Coppinger, 12 February 1891, *ACSP*, container 279, vol. 282.
28. C.H.J. Taylor, *Whites and Blacks, or The Question Settled* (Atlanta, GA, 1889), pp. 33–34, 37, 39.
29. Amanda Smith, *An Autobiography: The Story of the Lord's Dealings with Mrs. Amanda Smith, the Colored Evangelist* (Chicago, IL, 1893).

country where they [...] could be *men*", Smith was troubled by her sense that manliness was being predicated upon anti-white sentiment.[30]

Despite her impatience with the exclusionary practices and hubris of some Americo-Liberian and Afro-American men, Smith supported emigration – but only conditionally. In her eyes, only the poorest of the southern poor crossed the ocean and she despaired too many were illiterate, ill-prepared, and ignorant of what it meant to start anew in another country. Because Smith witnessed extreme privation in Liberia her assessment of emigration only grew harsher with time. By 1895, she dismissed emigration as "an enterprise [...] detrimental in every possible way to our people".[31]

Levi Coppin, prominent editor of the *AME Church Review* who later served as a bishop in South Africa, attacked emigration on a different level:

> [...] those who favor the scheme of emigration [...] ask significantly if we would rather stay here and be menials than go back to Africa and be men[...]. [T]he argument is misleading [...]. [W]hen the American Negro [...] goes to Africa in search of an asylum, it will be well for him to remember that the man from whom he flees has gone on before [...] and planted himself.

According to Coppin, leaving the US was futile given the probability that Europeans in Africa would assume onerous, oppressive roles. If black men really wanted to showcase their manly resolve and virile constitutions, they should remain in the United States to "secure [...] the manhood and independence that we seek".[32] Negative press was effective in deterring emigration and news about Europeans in Africa weakened the resolve of a few hopeful emigrants.[33] Prospective emigrants might have been disinclined to compete with Europeans yet Americo-Liberians contended that anyone could succeed in Liberia as long as they possessed "self-dependence and [...] manhood". In 1894, one recent transplant, *Christian Recorder* correspondent A.L. Ridgel, proudly reported that the "*master* continent" of Africa held wonderful "prospect[s], especially for the Afro-American".[34]

Ironically, European activity on the continent led Afro-Americans to underscore ways in which imperialism allowed men of African descent to demonstrate masculine prowess. AME bishop and former Ohio legislator Benjamin Arnett, for one, believed African Americans and Africans should join forces in redeeming Africa by defending the continent in a manly fashion.[35] John H. Smyth, a Howard-trained lawyer who completed a long,

30. Smith, *Autobiography*, pp. 331–465; esp. pp. 414–417; (italics in original).
31. *Ibid.*, pp. 451–463; "Amanda Smith's Letter", *Voice of Missions*, July 1895, p. 2.
32. Levi J. Coppin, "Editorial: What Shall We Do?", *AME Church Review*, 10 (1894), pp. 549–557, esp. pp. 551–552.
33. See, for example, J.H. Harris to Coppinger, 5 August 1891, *ACSP*, container 281, vol. 284.
34. "Made a Fortune in Liberia", *Liberia Bulletin*, 9 (1896), pp. 84–86; A.L. Ridgel to Wilson, *ACSP*, 1 June 1894, container 286, vol. 291, reel 143; (emphasis in original).
35. Benjamin W. Arnett, "Africa and the Descendants of Africa: A Response in Behalf of Africa", *AME Church Review*, 11 (1894), pp. 231–238. esp. p. 233.

tumultuous stint in Liberia as Consul-General during the 1870s and 1880s, contended black manhood would always prove more formidable than European power.[36] Following the defeat of Italian forces in Ethiopia in 1896,[37] Sarah Dudley Pettey – who served as General Secretary of the AME Zion's Woman's Home and Foreign Missionary Society – declared the Ethiopians' victory as nothing less than the "the uprising of an oppressed race daring to assert manhood."[38] Although Pettey's tone was clearly celebratory when she rhapsodized that virility would restore the race's "ancient glory", neither Pettey, Arnett, nor Smyth suggested African or African-American men were superior to white men. Rather, during the mid-1890s, the majority of African-American observations about race, manhood, and imperialism in Africa were basic affirmations that Africans and African Americans possessed manliness.

That would change by the end of the decade as US imperialism spread to Hawaii, Puerto Rico, Wake Island, Guam, and Samoa. In particular, the 1898 entry of the US in the War for Cuban Independence – commonly referred to as the Spanish–American War – forged salient connections between race, manhood, and empire for African Americans. Just as the feats of black Union soldiers made the Civil War a "watershed for black manhood", black men's exploits in Cuba transformed 1898 into a similarly definitive moment.[39] As one race paper put it, if black men heartily joined the American show of force against Spain, they would, at last, be "treated as men among men". The Washington *Colored American* even declared the Spanish–American War an arena where "the Negro's manhood [would be] placed directly in evidence" alongside white soldiers. Black participation was controversial among African Americans, nonetheless, and black journalists were no exception: one editor argued that any black man who served a racist nation in a segregated army sorely needed "a few grains of self-respect".[40]

With the realities of segregation and terrorism on the home front, US imperialism was an uneasy vehicle for black manhood. A speech delivered by Nannie Helen Burroughs in mid-1898 cogently expressed the predicament facing black men – whether to fight for a country that routinely denied their humanity. Although black manliness was systematically

36. J.H. Smyth, "The African in Africa and the African in America", in Bowen, *Africa and the American Negro*, pp. 69–83, esp. pp. 74, 77.
37. Interestingly, V.G. Kiernan points out that "a large part of the army defeated at Adowa in 1896 was composed of men from [...] Afric[a]". See Kiernan, "Colonial Africa and its Armies", in Harvey J. Kaye (ed.), *Imperialism and Its Contradictions* (New York, 1995), pp. 77–96, esp. p. 83.
38. Sarah Dudley [Mrs C.C.] Pettey, *A.M.E.Z. Church Quarterly*, 7 (1897), p. 30.
39. Jim Cullen, "'I's a Man Now': Gender and African-American Men", in Catherine Clinton and Nina Silber (eds), *Divided Houses: Gender and the Civil War* (New York, 1992), pp. 76–91, esp. p. 77; Gaines and von Eschen, "Ambivalent Warriors", p. 64.
40. Parsons *Weekly Blade*, 9 July 1898; Washington *Colored American*, 30 April 1898; Coffeyville *American*, 7 May 1898, all quoted in George P. Marks (ed.), *The Black Press Views American Imperialism, 1898–1900* (New York, 1971), pp. 70, 53.

trampled upon by lynching and disfranchisement in the United States, Burroughs argued that no African-American man could afford to shrink from duty only to "sulk in his tent" at home. To "sulk", she implied, was to make the race vulnerable to further assault.[41] African Americans were acutely aware of their liminal status in the US, then, but the war with Spain still became a tremendous source of race pride. Black soldiers even found their experiences in Cuba so exhilarating they wrote home that Spanish combatants found them more ferocious than white enlistees. In late July 1898, for example, Sergeant M.W. Saddler of the Twenty-Fifth Infantry sent a dramatic dispatch from Santiago:

> Our men began to fall, many of them never to rise again, but [...] so effective was our fire that the Spaniards became unnerved and began over-shooting us. When they saw we were "colored soldiers" they knew their doom was sealed [...]. [The] coolness and bravery that characterized our fathers in the 60s have been handed down to their sons of the 90s. If any one doubts the fitness of a colored soldier [...] [the] Spaniards call us "Negretter Sol[d]ados" and say there is no use shooting at us, for steel and powder will not stop us.[42]

The manly derring-do of "Negretter Sol[d]ados" stirred up commentary earlier that month when black cavalrymen reportedly rescued Teddy Roosevelt's heralded Rough Riders at San Juan Hill. The Rough Riders were not damsels in distress, but in the eyes of many Afro-Americans, they would have perished had it not been for gallant black rescuers.

After he initially praised efforts of black cavalrymen, Theodore Roosevelt vehemently refuted notions that the Tenth Cavalry "saved the Rough Riders from annihilation". Some white soldiers, however, willingly conceded that during the charge up San Juan Hill – an iconic event that literary historian Amy Kaplan rightfully refers to as "a battle showcasing American masculinity" – black men proved themselves superior fighters.[43] Kenneth Robinson, a wounded Rough Rider, not only claimed black men saved his unit, he quipped "without any disregard to my own regiment [...] the whitest men in this fight have been the black ones".[44] If a white soldier could

---

41. Washington *Bee*, 21 May 1898, p. 5. This notice about Burroughs' speech, "Should the Negro Take Part in the Spanish-American Trouble?", is a summary and thus the text quoted above might not be her actual wording.
42. Willard B. Gatewood, Jr (ed.), *"Smoked Yankees" and the Struggle for Empire: Letters from Negro Soldiers, 1898–1902* (Urbana, IL, 1971), pp. 55–57.
43. Booker T. Washington *et al.*, *A New Negro for a New Century* (Chicago, IL, 1900), pp. 40–41; Amy Kaplan, "Black and Blue on San Juan Hill", in Kaplan and Pease, *Cultures of United States Imperialism*, pp. 219–236, esp. p. 226.
44. W.H. Crogman, "The Negro Soldier in the Cuban Insurrection and Spanish-American War", in J.L. Nichols and William H. Crogman (eds), *Progress of a Race or the Remarkable Advancement of the American Negro* [...], revised and enlarged (Naperville, IL, 1925), pp. 131–145, esp. pp. 137–138. For additional commentary that black troops "saved" the Rough Riders, see Herschel V. Cashin *et al.*, *Under Fire with the Tenth US Cavalry* (New York, 1899).

go on public record lauding black heroism, then the widely reported bravery of black soldiers in Cuba did not pass unnoticed among African Americans on the home front. Women in Brooklyn distributed materials regaling black troops; Stella Brazley's "The Colored Boys in Blue" praised "scions of a warlike race" whose feats "[r]enew[ed] the prestige" of African-American people. Katherine Davis Chapman Tillman rewrote the last stanza of one of her previously published poems to memorialize those who "charged with such good will [a]nd saved the Rough Riders at San Juan Hill".⁴⁵ Other black Americans argued that man for man, black soldiers were literally superior specimens of physical manhood who were immune to both tropical diseases and bullets.⁴⁶ During the Spanish–American War, the mixture of race, manhood, and imperialism became powerfully suggestive as a number of commentators other than Kenneth Robinson dubbed black soldiers "the whitest men" in the war.

The Philippine–American War was a slightly different matter. Black Americans, for the most part, felt a racial affinity with both Cuban rebels and Philippine insurrectionists. The major difference, of course, was that black Americans and Cubans were allied in the struggle against Spain whereas in the Philippines, Afro-American soldiers would be fighting against Filipinos. The *Colored American* concluded that whereas Afro-Americans were bound to side with Filipinos due to "racial sympathies", they could not afford to forsake the United States. The Kansas City *American Citizen* unequivocally disagreed: black American soldiers should not fight other "negroes", the paper flatly stated, only to "fall [...] prey to southern hell hounds and civilized American cannibals" upon their return stateside. Other African-American newspapers summarily condemned imperialism as a coercive means to "blight the manhood of the darker races".⁴⁷ Even Sergeant Saddler, who once brimmed with enthusiasm over his exploits in Cuba, conceded it was difficult to relish a fight against "men of our own hue and

45. Theophilus G. Steward, *The Colored Regulars in the United States Army* (Philadelphia, PA, 1904), illustration between pp. 230–231; Katherine Davis Chapman Tillman, "A Tribute to Negro Regiments", and "The Black Boys in Blue", in Claudia Tate (ed.), *The Works of Katherine Davis Chapman Tillman* (New York, 1991), pp. 146, 188–189; Stella A.E. Brazley, "The Colored Boys in Blue", in W. Hilary Coston, *The Spanish-American War Volunteer* (Middletown, PA, 1899), p. 81. See also Lena Mason, "A Negro In It", in D.W. Culp (ed.), *Twentieth Century Negro Literature or, A Cyclopedia of Thought on the Vital Topics Relating to the American Negro* (Naperville, IL, 1902), p. 447. For a decidedly anti-war poem, see Frances E.W. Harper, "Do Not Cheer, Men Are Dying", Richmond *Planet*, 3 December 1898.
46. Crogman, "The Negro Soldier in the Cuban Insurrection and Spanish-American War", *Progress of a Race*, pp. 135–144; "W.A.B.", "The Rough Rider 'Remarks'", *World*, 22 August 1898, in *Under Fire with the Tenth US Cavalry*, pp. 277–279; Miles V. Lynk, *The Black Troopers, or The Daring Heroism of The Negro Soldiers in the Spanish-American War* (Jackson, TN, 1899), pp. 18, 69–70. See also Gatewood, *"Smoked Yankees"*, p. 11.
47. Washington, *Colored American*, ca. 1899, quoted in Gatewood, *"Smoked Yankees"*, p. 237; Kansas City *American Citizen*, 28 April 1899 and Helena *Reporter*, 1 February 1900, both quoted in Marks, *The Black Press Views American Imperialism*, pp. 124–125, 167.

color" in the Philippines.[48] In other words, when it came to the Philippine–American War, the question of allegiance – and imperialism – was rather tricky.

Both torn loyalties and domestic factors fueled black anti-imperialism by 1899. Whereas participation in the Spanish–American War filled African Americans with the hope that their display of patriotism at home and courage abroad would reduce racial oppression within US borders, the war "in fact accelerated the decline, the loss of civility, the increase in bloodshed, the white arrogance [as it] [...] enlist[ed] the North as an even more active partner in the subjugation of black Americans".[49] Not only did the Spanish–American war mend fissures caused by the American Civil War, black veterans returning from Cuban battlefields often faced intense resentment and violence. When black cavalrymen who served in Cuba were stationed in Huntsville, Alabama, during late 1898, they proudly possessed "enough manhood to resent any insult cast upon them" by local whites. As a result, two black soldiers were gunned down in the street – reportedly by another African American – after a local white resident "put out a reward for every black tenth Cavalrym[a]n" assassinated.[50] Thus, by the time black soldiers were deployed for the Philippine–American War in 1899, an appreciable number of black veterans chose to re-enlist rather than stay in the south.[51] An undeniable tide of racial violence – such as the infamous Wilmington massacre which claimed eleven black lives and effected countless more – certainly influenced many black men to enlist or re-enlist; that same racial violence piqued black anti-imperialism during the brief interwar period.

But if black anti-imperialism was both perceptible and on the rise, some African Americans still believed the race would benefit by going to the Philippines as colonists. Black settlement of the Philippines was a popular enough notion that by 1903, President Theodore Roosevelt dispatched T. Thomas Fortune on an expedition to explore the feasibility of mass black emigration to Hawaii, Puerto Rico, and, in particular, the Philippines. Approximately four hundred black Americans settled on the islands during and after the Philippine–American War; most were, at least by Fortune's judgment, fairly prosperous. Fortune was so impressed he fully endorsed black emigration to the Philippines. He also concluded that only Afro-American labor could tame the islands' terrain into a profitable colony:

> [I]t is written on the wall that ultimately, if the American flag remains in the Philippines, the Afro-Americans will have to be drafted to hold it up [...] for the

48. Gatewood, "*Smoked Yankees*", pp. 247–249.
49. Edward L. Ayers, *The Promise of the New South: Life after Reconstruction* (New York, 1992), p. 333.
50. Gatewood, "*Smoked Yankees*", pp. 88–89, 85.
51. Kaplan, "Black and Blue on San Juan Hill", p. 235.

white American does not find either the climate or the people and their ways to his liking [...] this is no sufficient anchorage [...] in the successful colonization of [a] country [.]

Fortune was so swept up in romantic ideas about empire that in the northern section of Luzon, he posed for formal portraits donning a field costume and hat which bore more than a passing resemblance to outfits worn by black cavalrymen who saved the day at San Juan Hill.[52]

Yet when African Americans looked to the Philippines – or Liberia for that matter – as a refuge from oppression, colonizationist impulses made them potential oppressors as well. Race man that he was, Fortune apparently saw little inherent contradiction in blacks being either colonists or imperialists. Since African Americans were denied "manhood and citizen rights" in the US, Fortune swiftly rationalized that the race deserved an opportunity to colonize territories recently acquired by the United States so they, too, could "enjoy life, liberty and the pursuit of happiness".[53] Fortune's view of the Philippines was not unlike Henry Parks's vision of Africa; for both men, it was possible if not preferable for African Americans to tame new frontiers and attain the heights of manhood beyond American borders.

Tom Fortune and Henry Parks deemed the possibility of black Americans acquiring their own empires as a literal opportunity for racial redemption. Other black Americans approached empire in a literary sense, producing a small wave of historical romances between 1899 and 1910: Pauline Hopkins published the serialized, Pan-Africanist *Of One Blood* (1902/3); Charles Fowler offered a sweeping tale of slavery, the Civil War, Reconstruction, and the Spanish–American War in *Historical Romance of the American Negro* (1902); John Wesley Grant's *Out of the Darkness* (1909) was an unwieldy epic of the "diabolism and destiny" facing a colonized colored race in the post-Reconstruction south. Baptist minister Sutton Griggs was especially prolific, expounding on race and empire in no less than three novels: *Imperium in Imperio* (1899), *Unfettered* (1902), and *The Hindered Hand* (1905).[54]

Both *Unfettered* and *Imperium in Imperio* contained their share of curious commentary. Part analysis of US incursion in the Philippines, *Unfettered* included a lengthy appendix entitled "Dorlan's Plan" that heartily endorsed

---

52. T. Thomas Fortune, "The Filipino: A Social Study in Three Parts", *Voice of the Negro*, 1 (1904), pp. 93–99, esp. pp. 96–97.

53. Fortune, "The Filipino: Some Incidents of a Trip Through the Island of Luzon", *Voice of the Negro*, 1 (1904), pp. 240–246, esp. p. 246.

54. Pauline Hopkins, *Of One Blood: or, the Hidden Self*, in Hazel V. Carby (ed.), *The Magazine Novels of Pauline Hopkins* (New York, 1988), pp. 441–621; Charles H. Fowler, *Historical Romance of the American Negro* (Baltimore, MD, 1902); J[ohn] W[esley] Grant, *Out of the Darkness; or, Diabolism and Destiny* (Nashville, TN, 1909); Sutton E. Griggs, *Imperium in Imperio* (Cincinnati, OH, 1899); Griggs, *Unfettered: A Novel; with Dorlan's Plan* (Nashville, TN, 1902); Griggs, *The Hindered Hand* (Nashville, TN, 1905).

"Americanization of the globe" and encouraged African Americans to chan-
nel their energies into the Philippines, Hawaii, Cuba, Puerto Rico, and
Africa.[55] *Imperium* explored the possibility of a black empire within the US;
the text praised racial purity, invoked Social Darwinist thought, and cursed
black disfranchisement. Above all, *Imperium* was suffused with muscular
rhetoric which boldly proclaimed "the cringing, fawning, sniffling, cowardly
Negro [...] [has] disappeared, and a new Negro, self-respecting, fearless, and
determined in the assertion of his rights [is] at hand".[56]

In *Imperium*, both protagonists are "fine specimens of physical manhood"
who are forced, over the course of the novel, to compromise their manliness.
Belton Piedmont, the "black" hero, is forced to masquerade as a woman
while the threat of racial extinction prevents mulatto Bernard Belgrave from
consummating his love affair with a devoted race woman.[57] Bernard's
intended, Viola, commits suicide; her suicide letter invokes Social Darwinist
concepts about sexuality, racial competition, and processes of extermination:

> [J]ust two years prior to my meeting you, a book entitled "White Supremacy and
> Negro Sub-ordination"[...] came into my possession [...] That book proved to me
> that the intermingling of the races in sexual relationship was sapping the vitality
> of the Negro race and, in fact, was slowly but surely exterminating the race [...] I
> looked out upon our strong, tender hearted, manly race being swept from the face
> of the earth by immorality, and [...] [m]y first step was to solemnly pledge to God
> to never marry a mulatto man.

Viola then bids her lover adieu by begging him to do everything he can to
preserve the race, up to and including emigration.[58]

After each ultramasculine protagonist suffers his share of travails, they are
reunited in a secret organization – or *imperium* – which plots to establish a
black empire. However, Belton and Bernard's plans for establishing a manly
black nation go awry: one is killed, the other loses his grip on reality.
Imperium forcefully asserted that denial of black manhood in the United
States inevitably led to death or insanity. As an historical romance, moreover, *Imperium* used plot devices similar to those in historical romances
produced by white Americans; the genre, as a whole, "spli[t] the subjects of
imperial power into gendered positions". *Imperium in Imperio*'s deployment
of manhood placed it firmly within a mainstream literary genre.[59]

55. Griggs, *Unfettered*, pp. 256–257, 275.
56. Griggs, *Imperium*, p. 62.
57. *Ibid.*, pp. 132–135, 173–174.
58. *Ibid.*, pp. 173–175. The work referred to in the suicide letter is J.H. Van Evrie, MD, *White
Supremacy and Black Subordination, or, Negroes a Subordinate Race, And (So-Called) Slavery its
Normal Condition* (New York, 1868), esp. pp. 149–167.
59. Amy Kaplan, "Romancing the Empire: The Embodiment of American Masculinity in the
Popular Historical Novel of the 1890s", *American Literary History*, 2 (1990), pp. 659–690, esp.
p. 672. For commentary on historical romances written by African Americans, see James Robert
Payne, "Afro-American Literature of the Spanish-American War", *Melus*, 10 (1983), pp. 19–32, esp.
pp. 27–29.

Literary commentary on masculinity and empire provided a unique opportunity for African-American writers to advance highly politicized rebuttals to popular stereotypes about black manhood. In this regard, a short story by poet and magazine publisher James McGirt was singularly notable. McGirt's "In Love as in War" (1907) was set during the Philippine–American War and told the tale of a Filipina princess, Quinaldo, who chooses an African-American sergeant to be her lover over an aristocratic Anglo-American lieutenant from Louisiana. Throughout the story, Quinaldo – a name that intentionally evoked Emilio Aguinaldo, leader of Philippine insurgents – swoons whenever she is in close proximity to the virile "Sarge". Their courtship is heated, yet chaste, with Quinaldo and Sarge's mutual desire reaching climax through his tales of conquest:

> They talked over many matters in swift succession, as though they wanted to crowd a lifetime in a few hours [...]. He then entertained her with stories of his hair-breadth escapes and his daring encounters with the Indians, as well as in the Spanish-American war [...]. The princess found herself at times moving, as though she herself were facing the enemy[.]
>
> When he had described these things to her until she could stand it no longer, she clapped her hands and exclaimed, "Brave! wonderfully brave!"

In contrast to Sarge's calm bravery, the white officer is a red-faced blue-blood, both "defeated and enraged" by the black enlisted man's edge with Quinaldo.[60]

Vaughn is ineffectual – if not effete – whereas Sarge is so manly he arouses passion in every Filipina who espies his glorious physique.[61] Here, the Philippines, as represented in the feminine forms of Quinaldo and other women, are more than willing to be possessed by black male bodies. The Philippines could not only be conquered, McGirt suggested, the territory was also a suitable "wife" capable of sustaining the material and sexual needs of any worthy *black* American man. Put another way, McGirt scripted an alternative to contemporary dynamics of power between black and white men in the American south and he used sexuality in an imperial setting to do so.

The sad reality was that whether black soldiers were conquerors on the battlefield or in the boudoir, participation in US military efforts abroad did little to change racial dynamics at home. Again, after 1898, outbreaks of racial violence involving returning black veterans and highly-publicized racial incidents between black and white soldiers in the Philippines – not to mention reports that some black soldiers defected and joined Filipino insurgents – influenced growing numbers of African Americans to argue

---

60. James E. McGirt, "In Love as in War", in McGirt, *Triumphs of Ephraim* (Philadelphia, PA, 1907), pp. 63–76, esp. p. 71. Background on the Philippine–American War may be found in Welch, *Response to Imperialism*.
61. McGirt, "In Love as in War", p. 75.

Michele Mitchell

black soldiers should not help white Americans defeat other people of color. To add insult to injury, black soldiers proved their mettle in Cuba and the Philippines only to have their manhood compromised upon their return to the States.

This sense of futility led members of the National Afro-American Council to inject a noticeably anti-imperialist tone into the Council's 1899 meeting. Two black anti-imperialist leagues were formed that year – the league in Chicago even called itself the "Black Man's Burden Society".[62] Black anti-imperialism was anything but universal after 1899, however. Classics professor W.S. Scarborough probably spoke for some aspiring and elite men when, in 1901, he maintained Afro-American colonization of "our new possessions" remained the one viable opportunity for "black manhood [to] stand erect and unhindered, and [...] enlarge respect for itself".[63]

Still, how do we account for Henry Parks's call for what was tantamount to Afro-American imperialism in Africa? Some black Americans – due to conviction that "progress" in Africa benefited Africans and African Americans alike – believed imperialism contained a civilizing component and thus provided race men and women with unparalleled international opportunities. *Alexander's Magazine*, for example, actively promoted Afro-American "development" of Liberia through columns written by Walter F. Walker, vice-president of the Liberian Development Association. *Alexander's* editorial stance remained constant until August 1908: the magazine's enthusiasm toward emigration cooled due to a disastrous trip Walker made to Liberia, not because of a mounting sense that Afro-American colonizers might become little more than dark-skinned imperialists.[64]

If emigrationism did not automatically imbue those looking toward Africa with anti-imperialist ideas, Pan-Africanism enabled blacks in the US and the Caribbean to oppose American and European imperialism as they sought active roles in determining Africa's destiny. In 1900, Trinidad's Henry Sylvester Williams organized the first major Pan-African conference in London to mobilize people of African descent against imperialism and colonialism. African-American writer and educator Anna Julia Cooper attended the conference, as did W.E.B. Du Bois; both chafed at the notion that imperialism enabled either civilization or progress.[65]

62. Kelly Miller, "Immortal Doctrines of Liberty Ably Set Out by a Colored Man; The Effect of Imperialism Upon the Negro Race", Springfield *Republican*, 7 September 1900, reprinted in Philip S. Foner and Richard C. Winchester (eds), *The Anti-Imperialist Reader: A Documentary History of Anti-Imperialism in the United States. Volume 1: From the Mexican War to the Election of 1900* (New York, 1984), pp. 176–180, esp. p. 180. See also Gatewood, "Black Americans and the Quest for Empire, 1898–1903", p. 559.

63. W.S. Scarborough, "The Negro and Our New Possessions", *Forum*, 31 (1901), pp. 341–349, esp. p. 347.

64. Walter F. Walker, "News about Liberia and Africa Generally", *Alexander's Magazine*, 5 (January 1908), p. 67; Walker, *Alexander's Magazine*, 6 (August 1908), pp. 162–166.

65. Carby, "Introduction", *The Magazine Novels of Pauline Hopkins*, p. xlv; Gaines, "Black Americans' Racial Uplift Ideology as 'Civilizing Mission'", p. 436. Insight on Du Bois' anti-imperialism

Given the rather blunt, conquest-hungry language in *Africa: The Problem of the New Century*, it might be difficult if not specious to situate Parks within such a Pan-Africanist camp. Parks dedicated his book to all people of African descent working "hand in hand for mutual good" and he clearly believed racial affinity should compel black Americans to act as counteragents of European imperialism.[66] His evocation of imperial conquest in the name of racial salvation was consistent with viewpoints of black Americans – such as Pauline Hopkins – who simultaneously expressed Pan-African and civilizationist ideas. Still, it is less useful to label Parks a "Pan-Africanist" than it is to assume he could point to Europeans in Africa as justification to fortify black American presence on the continent. As historian Kevin Gaines points out, it was not necessarily a contradiction for women and men like Hopkins and Parks to embrace imperialism as a providential opportunity for their own uplift work.[67]

Understanding Parks's motives, then, requires situating him within the larger context of the complex, conflicting ways African Americans analyzed imperialism and its impact on people of color. For all the reasons why blacks in the US opposed certain forms of imperialism, anti-imperialist African Americans could and did advocate imperial roles for themselves. Again, Afro-American commentary about Africa became decidedly more anti-imperialist after 1900 but that anti-imperialism was largely directed at white colonists. In 1909, for example, the *Colored American Magazine* condemned European "lust" for Africa only to call for African Americans to assume a greater role in Liberia. As *Colored American* contributor I. De H. Crooke put it, "Africa for the Africans" was a hollow cry unless black Americans "colonize[d] and appropriate[d]" resources and territories in Africa. As late as 1913, a familiar argument resurfaced as one race paper chastised black men for not being as aggressive as white men in taking full advantage of the continent: if black men were ever going to thrive as men, if US imperialism was a poor means of fostering Afro-American manhood, then black men needed an *African* outlet for their masculinity.[68]

Such a seeming contradiction might have resulted from any number of political realities, motives, or ideas. One explanation rests in Liberia's peculiar situation: the country had long been a virtual ward of the United States; given the succession of black consul-generals appointed to Liberia by the

is offered in Helene Christol, "Du Bois and Expansionism: A Black Man's View of Empire", in Serge Ricard and Helene Christol (eds), *Anglo-Saxonism in US Foreign Policy: The Diplomacy of Imperialism, 1899–1919* (Aix-en-Provence, 1991), pp. 49–63.
66. Curiously, the full quotation from the title page reads "[t]wo races hand in hand for mutual good"; Parks, *Africa: The Problem of the New Century*, title page.
67. Gaines, "Black Americans' Racial Uplift Ideology as 'Civilizing Mission'", pp. 437 and 440.
68. I. De H. Crooke, "Africa for Africans", *Colored American*, 15 (1909), pp. 101–102; "The Grab for Liberia and Her Needs", *Colored American*, 17 (1909), pp. 118–122; New York *Age*, 13 March 1913 and 13 November 1913, Tuskegee Institute News Clipping File, series 1, main file, reel 2, frames 13 and 333.

US government, some African Americans likely expected that an "American" role in Africa would, in reality, be carried out by blacks.[69] Moreover, the predominance of racialized theories such as Social Darwinism enabled aspiring class and elite black Americans to abhor "white" imperialist domination in Africa while embracing a claim for themselves. With popular African-American attitudes that the race was duty-bound to save Africans from European oppression, given a desire to confer "progress" on the continent by "civilizing" and Christianizing Africans, then perhaps Parks's manifesto was something other than rank justification of imperialism. Although it might be tempting to dismiss Parks as a confused crank or self-hating Samaritan, such dismissal would tell us little about Parks or the moment in which he lived. Parks's argument exemplifies tensions felt by many black American men who abhorred racial oppression, harbored an allegiance to Africa, and yet desperately wanted to exercise the prerogatives of manhood denied them in the United States. Parks's quest for conquest was, in all likelihood, buttressed by the aura of triumphant black veterans – men who suggested certain aspects of imperial endeavor could actually bolster feelings of virility in men in color. Even as growing numbers of African Americans came to view imperialism as threatening the integrity of people of color around the globe, visions of a potential role in Africa enabled aspiring class and elite black Americans to create new, racialized notions of manhood. In other words, Henry Parks embodied the contradictions and tensions inherent in what many of his contemporaries tellingly labeled the "black man's burden".

BURDENS OF GENDER, BURDENS OF RACE:
PRELIMINARY CONCLUSIONS ON AFRICAN
AMERICANS AND "HYPERMASCULINITY" IN
TURN-OF-THE-CENTURY US CULTURE

The very notion of a "black man's burden" facilitates analysis of gender and race between 1890 and 1910 at the same time it illuminates why black Americans held myriad opinions about the impact of imperialism on the race's manhood. Rudyard Kipling might have been commemorating war in the Philippines when he wrote "The White Man's Burden", but his phrase was widely appropriated. White Americans typically used the notion of a racialized, gendered burden to describe white responsibility toward "the Negro Problem".[70] Black Americans often placed the burden squarely on the shoulders of men of color: as H.T. Johnson wryly retorted, "Pile on the

69. Skinner, *African-Americans and US Policy Toward Africa*, pp. 13–16.
70. See, for example, B.F. Riley, *The White Man's Burden* (Birmingham, AL, 1910), title page. Anne McClintock points out that the concept of a "white man's burden" could be crassly commercial: Pears' Soap used the phrase as advertising copy. See McClintock, *Imperial Leather: Race, Gender and Sexuality in the Colonial Conquest* (New York, 1995), pp. 32–33.

Black Man's Burden; His wail with laughter drown; You've sealed the Red Man's problem; and now take up the Brown". Black journalist John E. Bruce – an eventual associate of Marcus Garvey whose Universal Negro Improvement Association promoted its own vision of a black empire in Africa – likewise considered white imperial paternalism as simultaneously ludicrous and tragic: "It is to laugh – to read of the white man's burden [...]. The white man's burden, self-imposed, will break his back if he is not soon relieved of it. He is the biggest joke in the world today, posing as a *superman.*" Howard University professor Kelly Miller shared Bruce's contempt for "the white man's burden", but Miller caustically wondered whether black Americans would "stultify" and "humiliate" the race by supporting imperialism. For Miller, the racial hatred and fear that legitimated segregation and justified lynching were the same as the rationale behind imperial aggression.[71]

Just as Miller condemned the racism implicit in imperialist ideologies and Bruce belittled white men for attempting to be global conquerors, some black Americans subverted the very notion that the burden was heaviest for any group of men, black or white. "The Black Woman's Burden", for example, appeared in the pages of *Voice of the Negro* and bemoaned sexual victimization of African-American women by white – and black – lechers. Similarly, in his take on the ever-appropriated concept, Du Bois addressed the sexual subjugation of colonized women by asserting women's bodies bore the brunt of "drunken orgies of war". In 1906, a year before his elegy "The Burden of Black Women" was published, Du Bois was less poetic about sex on the imperial front: in an Atlanta University publication, he maintained "a curious commentary on imperialism" was unfolding due to white soldiers in "foreign service" who spread syphilis and gonorrhea wherever they went.[73] Frances Ellen Harper's "The Burdens of All" went further still – it declared imperialism created havoc for all humanity.[73]

US and European imperialism affected a vast range of people and African Americans clearly understood this. However, given the ways in which racialized and gendered concepts informed notions of war and colonial conquest in the US between 1890 and 1910, most black American commentators stressed imperialism's impact on black men. It is no coincidence that the

---

71. H.T. Johnson, "The Black Man's Burden", Salt Lake City *Broad Ax*, 15 April 1899, p. 4; John E. Bruce, "The White Man's Burden", reprinted in Peter Gilbert (ed.), *The Selected Writings of John Edward Bruce: Militant Black Journalist* (New York, 1971), pp. 97–98, esp. p. 97; Miller, "Immortal Doctrines of Liberty Ably Set Out by a Colored Man", pp. 176–180.
72. Daniel Webster Davis, "The Black Woman's Burden", *Voice of the Negro*, 1 (1904), p. 308; W.E.B. Du Bois, "The Burden of Black Women", reprinted in David Levering Lewis (ed.), *W.E.B. Du Bois: A Reader* (New York, 1995), pp. 291–293; W.E.B. Du Bois (ed.), *The Health and Physique of the Negro American* (Atlanta, GA, 1906), p. 69.
73. Frances Ellen Watkins Harper, "The Burdens of All" (ca. 1900), in Frances Smith Foster (ed.), *A Brighter Coming Day: A Frances Ellen Watkins Harper Reader* (New York, 1990), p. 390.

overwhelming majority of these commentators were aspiring-class and elite men: their class status was precarious and they viewed empire as playing a decisive role in stabilizing – or destabilizing – their position vis-à-vis other Americans. However, instead of discussing their situation using class language, these men invoked racialized notions about manhood to express their anxieties.

While many black Americans between 1890 and 1910 believed campaigns for empire compromised people of color as a whole, imperialism was also construed as a site for a highly racialized and masculinized struggle of the fittest.[74] Imperial efforts in Africa, Cuba, and the Philippines were thus seen as having the potential to serve as figurative and literal fronts where black men could prove their manhood or openly compete with white men. For Kelly Miller and other African Americans, imperialism was little more than a rigged contest where black men would inevitably lose. Henry Parks and J. Dallas Bowser saw things in a different light: they viewed the "black man's burden" as a necessary step in racial redemption, as an inevitable by-product of globalized racial combat, and as a morally superior version of imperialism.[75]

The push for empire combined gender and race in provocative ways for Americans who were only decades away from being subjugated and enslaved themselves. Just as race was used at the turn of the century to "remake manhood",[76] imperialism remade and reinforced a gendered racial identity for black American men. Participation in US imperial wars was undoubtedly fraught with contradictions for black American men, but as Dennis Morgan has argued, "of all the sites where masculinities are constructed, reproduced, and deployed, those associated with war and the military are some of the most direct".[77] By participating in imperial endeavors as militants and missionaries, African-American men could forge masculine identities, which were, for the most part, beyond their reach in quotidian life. In a sense, staking a claim to manhood was an attempt to realize social mobility for working poor, aspiring, and elite black men alike.

Finally, in order to understand why many Afro-Americans embraced imperial roles for themselves in Africa as they became increasingly hostile

74. Bederman, *Manliness and Civilization*, p. 171.
75. For further commentary on Afro-American reworkings of Kipling, see Gatewood, *Black Americans and the White Man's Burden*, pp. 183–186.
76. Bederman, *Manliness and Civilization*, p. 5.
77. Dennis H.J. Morgan, "Theatre of War: Combat, the Military, and Masculinities", in Harry Brod and Michael Kaufman (eds), *Theorizing Masculinities* (Thousand Oaks, CA, c. 1994), p. 165. Relevant texts include: Mark C. Carnes and Clyde Griffen (eds), *Meanings for Manhood: Constructions of Masculinities in Victorian America* (Chicago, IL, 1990); Jeff Hearn and David Morgan (eds), *Men, Masculinities, and Social Theory* (London, 1990); Michael Kimmel, *Manhood in America: A Cultural History* (New York, 1996); Harry Stecopoulos and Michael Uebel (eds), *Race and the Subject of Masculinities* (Durham, NC, 1997); Darlene Clark and Earnestine Jenkins (eds), *A Question of Manhood: A Reader in US Black Men's History and Masculinity* (Bloomington, IN, 1999).

to US and European imperialism, it is useful to return to the US context. Both Clyde Griffen and Gail Bederman consider the period between 1890 and 1910 an era of "hypermasculinity" in the United States; Kristin Hoganson further contends that what Richard Hofstader has referred to as a "'psychic crisis'" in the US during the 1890s was, in fact, a "crisis of manhood".[78] If this was the case, imagine the predicament of African-American men. Not only were they emasculated beings according to mainstream discourse, but political disfranchisement, racial violence, and proscribed economic status often prevented them from asserting public claims to manhood; if economic downturns caused "fears of [...] dependency" among white men, those fears were all the more palpable for African-American men.[79] Without question, black men possessed integrity, agency, and virility, yet it must have been all but impossible for them to act in the same "hypermasculine" ways as their white contemporaries. In fact, the 1890s "hypermasculinity" might explain why aspiring and elite African-American men discussed imperialism in the ways that they did: class was hardly an inconsequential matter, but it seems that imperialism's obsession with race – combined with the era's hypermasculinity – led many aspiring and elite men to eschew class politics for a racialized politics of manhood. For all of its contradictions and compromises, imperialism was certainly a problematic arena, but it was nevertheless an arena in which some black men believed they could develop a manhood of their own making.

78. Clyde Griffen, "Reconstructing Masculinity from the Evangelical Revival to the Waning of Progressivism: A Speculative Synthesis", in Carnes and Griffen, *Meanings for Manhood* , pp. 183–204, esp. p. 199; Bederman, *Manliness and Civilization*, pp. 170–215; Kristin Hoganson, *Fighting for American Manhood: How Gender Politics Provoked the Spanish-American and Philippine-American Wars* (New Haven, CT, 1998), pp. 11–12.
79. Hoganson, *Fighting for American Manhood*, p. 12.

International Review of Social History 44 (1999), Supplement, pp. 101–122
© 1999 Internationaal Instituut voor Sociale Geschiedenis

Sex Workers or Citizens? Prostitution and the Shaping of "Settler" Society in Australia*

RAELENE FRANCES

INTRODUCTION

The history of prostitution, defined as the commercial exchange of sexual services, provides a fertile ground for the study of the intersections between gender, race and class. Obviously, the sale of sexual labour has implications for constructions of gender, although the specific implications may change with time. Commercial sex offers particularly sharp insights into the ways in which gender considerations intersect with class and race because of the physical intimacy and potential for procreation involved in the sex act. Prostitution literally forces societies to come face to face with their assumptions about and attitudes to class and race hierarchies and relationships. The Australian case is especially useful for studying these relationships because of the imbalance in the ratio of men to women which has characterized colonial society generally and certain types of communities in particular, and the ways in which this imbalance affected some classes and ethnic groups more than others. Colonial Australia also provides a complex tapestry of ethnic/racial issues because it included divisions not just between "white" settlers and indigenous Aborigines, but also between both of these groups and various groups of immigrant, "coloured" workers. In the twentieth century, when demographic patterns became more balanced in gender terms and more homogenous in racial terms, the international sex industry continued to be important because it played a part in Australia's quest for recognition as an independent member of the community of "civilized", white, nations. Finally, the process of reassessing Australia's place in the world was intimately connected to a reassessment of Australia's domestic policies, both in relation to prostitution generally and to the sexual exploitation of Aboriginal women.

Prostitution has thus played a singular role in the establishment and development of white society in Australia. From the outset, the sexual availability of certain classes of women was seen by governments as an important element in the maintenance of civil and social order. And in every case, the choice of which women should fill the role of public prostitute and which men they should service was intimately connected to official visions of a society constructed in relation to a particular configuration of class, race

* My thanks to the editors, Bruce Scates and Ann McGrath for comments on an earlier version of this article. I am also indebted to Michèle Langfield and Alison Holland for particularly helpful references and suggestions.

and gender factors. However, the precise relationship of these three factors varied considerably across time, particularly as a result of shifting racial attitudes and changing demographic structures. This article will chart the broad chronology of these developments from first white settlement in 1788 to the beginning of World War Two. However, the focus of the paper will be on the first three decades of the twentieth century because this period has been the least studied. I argue that the treatment of prostitutes and prostitution in Australia reflected changing priorities and objectives in government policy. Specifically, that Australian governments used immigration controls originally designed to ensure a racially "white Australia" to exclude "white" women whose sexuality was seen to pose a more subtle threat to the young white nation. Moreover, the case of prositution and immigration control provides insight into the shifting dynamics operating at both an international and Australian level to reshape the racial, class and gender characteristics of settler society in Australia.

PROSTITUTION IN CONVICT SOCIETY: IMPERIAL WHOREMASTERS?

The first white settlements were penal colonies where men outnumbered women by an average of six to one. Feminist historians such as Ann Summers have argued that convict women in these settlements were in a state of "enforced whoredom", with young women transported for relatively trivial offences in order to provide sexual partners for male convicts, their overseers and guards. British authorities hoped thereby to minimize the incidence of sodomy amongst convict men and also to reduce their inclination for rebellion. Prostitution was thus tolerated, even encouraged, as an antidote to more serious social and civil disorders.[1]

The founding Governor, Arthur Phillip, had a vision for the new society in New South Wales which was carefully constructed with regard to racial, gender and class hierarchies. Convict men would be provided with access to convict women in order to satisfy their lusts, which, he presumed, were more urgent and dangerous than the lusts of gentlemen. The more virtuous amongst the women, he hoped, might be inclined to form attachments to individual men and marry them. Phillip also believed that Aboriginal women might, in time, marry and live with convict men. For that other class of single men, the soldiers garrisoned to secure order, he envisaged importing Polynesian women whom they would marry. Thus, the original white settlement in Australia was founded on a vision which included a careful hierarchy, with Aboriginal women on the same level as convicts; Polynesian women on a higher level than either Aborigines or convicts, of

1. Ann Summers, *Damned Whores and God's Police: The Colonization of Women in Australia* (Melbourne, VIC, 1975).

equal status to soldiers. Above them all, of course, were the gentlemen officers, who would bring wives of their own race and class with them.[2]

The reality turned out somewhat differently to this cosy scheme. The limited opportunities for women in other occupations, and the high demand for their sexual services, meant that there was indeed a high incidence of prostitution in convict society. And many convict women formed long-term attachments, including marriage, with convict men. However, Phillip's dreams of racial harmony evaporated in the first year of settlement. Rape was more characteristic of male convict interaction with Aboriginal women than cohabitation: the lower levels of white society had a rather different hierarchy in mind, with Aborigines decidedly below all whites, including convicts. The scheme to import Polynesian women from the islands never eventuated, as on reflection Phillip decided this would be cruel to the women.[3] Meanwhile, convict women did not respect the class boundaries of Phillip's scheme, forming *de facto* and legal marriages with men from all colonial classes, including officers and governors. Often skilled at making calculated decisions about their best financial advantage, many women seized the opportunity to secure a socially and financially advantageous marriage rather than take their chances in the labour market, including the sexual labour market. Class hierarchies which may have been enforceable in Britain were unable to withstand the pressures of a distant and demographically-skewed society. Likewise, racial hierarchies which seemed desirable from the comfortable distance of England could not withstand the realities of the violent racial interaction which characterized the early years of the colony.[4]

THE LATE COLONIAL PERIOD: PROSTITUTION IN THE "WORKERS' PARADISE"

Transportation of convicted felons to eastern Australia ceased in 1851. This coincided with the gold rushes which brought thousands of prospectors from all over the world keen to try their luck. The new wealth generated both by the gold that was found and the newly arrived colonists themselves produced a society which was anxious to forget its convict past and establish

2. Patricia Grimshaw, Marilyn Lake, Ann McGrath and Marian Quartly (eds), *Creating a Nation* (Melbourne, 1994), pp. 30–31.
3. Letter Governor Phillip to Lord Sydney, 15 May 1788, *Historical Records of Australia*, series 1, vol. 1, p. 23.
4. There is a very large literature on the fate of convict women. More recent work includes Deborah Oxley, *Convict Maids* (Melbourne, VIC, 1997); Joy Damousi, *Depraved and Disorderly* (Melbourne, VIC, 1997); Kay Daniels, *Convict Women* (Sydney, NSW, 1998); see also Marian Aveling, "Bending the Bars: Convict Women and the State", in Kay Saunders and Raymond Evans (eds), *Gender Relations in Australia: Domination and Negotiation* (Sydney, NSW, 1992), pp. 144–157. For Aboriginal women, see Mary Anne Jebb and Anna Haebich, "Across the Great Divide: Gender Relations on Australian Frontiers", in Saunders and Evans, *Gender Relations in Australia*, pp. 20–41.

a reputation as a free and democratic society – the so-called "workers' paradise". Once again, prostitution played an important part in this revised vision. However, that role was by no means uniform across time and space. The precise role prostitution played in any particular part of Australia depended on sex ratios in specific groups of colonial society and evolving racial attitudes. Where men continued to predominate, such as in newly-opened gold mining areas or amongst groups of immigrant workers, prostitution was practised openly and was tolerated by the state. Where the "frontier" phase of settlement had passed or where sex ratios had equalized, state tolerance declined and policing priorities became more responsive to social purity pressure groups. These latter groups argued from the perspective of Christian, family and feminist values for the curtailment of public displays of prostitution, or more extremely, its total repression.[5]

In old convict towns like Hobart, the eradication of visible prostitution was part of a self-conscious move to distance a newly free society from its convict past. Prostitute women bore the moral burden of the "convict stain", whether or not they had in fact been transported or convicted. As Kay Daniels and Mary Murnane have shown, prostitute women were also forced to carry a greater burden – the responsibility for the health of visiting British sailors. The British Navy pressured local authorities in Tasmania to pass legislation similar to the notorious British Contagious Diseases Acts of the 1860s, forcing suspect women to undergo medical examination for venereal disease and incarceration if found infected. As in Britain, class-based judgments about female sexuality were used to control the sexuality of urban unrespectable poor women, using supposedly public health measures.[6] In Western Australia, police, magistrates and government medical officers achieved a similar outcome by exploiting the flexibility inherent in the vagrancy laws.[7]

It was in northern Australia, however, that we see commercial sex more clearly tied up with issues of race/ethnicity as well as class. In the late nineteenth century, Aboriginal populations in northern Australia still outnumbered whites and were still undergoing a process of subjugation by violence, starvation and persuasion. The sexual exploitation of black women by white men was an intrinsic part of this process. The "economy of sex" which evolved around Aboriginal women became, in many cases, the only

5. There is no comprehensive history of prostitution in Australia. Kay Daniels's edited collection, *So Much Hard Work: Women and Prostitution in Australian History* (Melbourne, VIC, 1984), is a series of case studies rather than an overview.
6. Kay Daniels and Mary Murnane, "Prostitutes as 'Purveyors of Disease': Venereal Disease Legislation in Tasmania, 1868–1945", *Hecate*, 5 (1979), pp. 5–21; also Kay Daniels, "Prostitution in Tasmania during the Transition from Penal Settlement to a Civilised Society", in Daniels (ed.), *So Much Hard Work*, pp. 15–85.
7. Raelene Davidson, "'Dealing with the Social Evil': Prostitution and the Police in Perth and on the Eastern Goldfields 1895–1924", in Daniels (ed.), *So Much Hard Work*, pp. 162–191.

way in which remnant Aboriginal groups could survive after the arrival of white pastoralists and miners. White men's sexual access to black women became both a means to and a symbol of the dispossession and defeat of Aboriginal people.[8]

In the north, however, the "coloured problem" did not just apply to Aboriginal people. The racial situation was further complicated by the presence of large numbers of immigrant workers from South-East Asia, China, Japan and the Melanesian Islands. With the exception of the Japanese, the overwhelming majority of these workers were men. The arrival of these "coloured" workers coincided with a hardening of racial attitudes amongst white Australians, who eagerly embraced the scientific racism of Social Darwinism to justify white dominance. Racial theories such as Social Darwinism, based on the assumption of physically distinct races, focused popular and government attention on the implications of interracial sex for white settler society. As Raymond Evans' work on Queensland has shown, colonial politicians and bureaucrats were only too willing to tolerate or even encourage the presence of Japanese prostitutes precisely because they offered a racially acceptable solution to the problem of the sexual desires of a large non-white male workforce. According to this logic, if Japanese women did not perform this service, "coloured" workers would seek out the services of white prostitutes or rape white women, both outcomes clearly having the potential to undermine the "purity" of the white race by producing children of mixed racial parentage.[9] But there was more to contemporary white objections to miscegenation than racial interbreeding. As Philippa Levine has noted in the Indian context, the presence of European prostitutes in mixed-race colonies "challenged white supremacy in distinctive and critical ways, which reveal dramatically and vividly the importance of sexual politics in colonial rule [...] the symbolic servitude of a white woman to a black man would radically and fatally undermine the basis of colonial rule".[10]

From the late nineteenth century we also see an increasing elaboration of the concept of "whiteness". As Ruth Frankenberg has illustrated, "whiteness changes over time and space" and is also a relational category, "one that is coconstructed with a range of other racial and cultural categories, with class and with gender".[11] In late colonial Australia, people of non-Anglo-Saxon descent were increasingly distinguished from the "real" white Australians: those of British descent. In Western Australia, for example, governments

8. Jebb and Haebich, "Across the Great Divide". See also Deborah Bird Rose, *Hidden Histories* (Melbourne, VIC, and Canberra, CT, 1992).
9. Raymond Evans, "'Soiled Doves': Prostitution in Colonial Queensland", in Daniels (ed.), *So Much Hard Work*.
10. Philippa Levine, "Venereal Disease, Prostitution and the Politics of Empire: the Case of British India", *Journal of the History of Sexuality*, 4 (1994), p. 593.
11. Ruth Frankenberg, *White Women, Race Matters: the Social Construction of Whiteness* (Minneapolis, MN, 1993), p. 236.

and police encouraged the presence of "foreign" prostitutes, not just Japanese but also French and Italian. They did this partly for purely racial reasons: as in Queensland, such women protected white women (here defined in the narrower , British, sense) from contamination by "coloured" men, such as the Afghan camel-drivers. More importantly in this case, however, was the protection they gave to the popular white settler vision of itself as a society. The extent to which women had to resort to prostitution as a form of economic survival became an important gauge of the civilized and progressive standing of a society.[12] The visible presence of large numbers of "foreign" women, be they Japanese, Italian or French, thus allowed local commentators to congratulate themselves on the advanced status of Western Australia. In 1915 a West Australian politician, the Honourable R.H. Underwood, told the Legislative Assembly that:

> We can take credit, and I think should take credit to ourselves in WA for our social conditions when we reflect that the supply of prostitutes in this country has given out. Most honourable members know that prostitutes in WA are supplied chiefly from France, Japan, and Italy. As a matter of fact the Australian social system has kept the Australian women out of it.[13]

Again, the parallels with the Indian case are striking, where authorities comforted themselves with the thought that the growing number of European prostitutes were Catholics or Jews, not "English girls".[14]

Expressed another way, white commentators such as Underwood believed their society was superior to both Asian and continental European society partly because of Australia's allegedly superior, more egalitarian class structure. In a society which still had a preponderance of men over women, the existence of "foreign" prostitution was critical to the maintenance of this belief because it allowed contemporaries to turn a blind eye to the majority of the urban prostitute population – Australian-born women of British descent.[15] To contemplate the significance of the latter group of prostitutes would have been to admit that even if Australia was a paradise for (white) working men, it did not provide so well for white working women. The ethnic/racial dimensions of prostitution thus obscured the gender realities of late colonial settler society. Underwood's statement also suggests how the focus on some forms of racial/ethnic difference could deflect attention from other, equally fundamental racial divisions. The "Australian women"

---

12. Raelene Frances, "Australian Prostitution in International Context", *Australian Historical Studies*, 106 (1996), pp, 127–141.
13. Hon. R.H. Underwood, *Western Australian Parliamentary Debates: Legislative Assembly*, 51 (7 September 1915), p. 637.
14. Levine, "Venereal Disease, Prostitution and the Politics of Empire", p. 593.
15. Raelene Davidson, "'As Good a Bloody Woman as Any Other Bloody Woman': Prostitutes in Western Australia, 1895–1939", in Patricia Crawford (ed.), *Exploring Women's Past* (Sydney, NSW, 1985).

identified by Underwood were by implication all white women. Aboriginal women were thus effectively rendered invisible and irrelevant to his conception of Australian society. Racial/ethnic divisions reinforced class and gender divisions, but different kinds of racial/ethnic divisions were also mutually reinforcing.

THE TWENTIETH CENTURY: ACHIEVING AND MAINTAINING A WHITE AUSTRALIA

The six Australian colonies joined together in 1901 to form a federated Commonwealth of Australia. The first Act of the new federal parliament was the 1901 Immigration Restriction Act. It was to provide the cornerstone of the new nation, a nation founded above all on the idea of a "white Australia". While Social Darwinist and eugenicist ideas achieved wide currency throughout Western societies in the late nineteenth and early twentieth centuries, in Australia they assumed a particular importance. The idea of "survival of the fittest" when applied to human "races" justified the dispossession and apparent demise of Australia's original inhabitants. Scientific racism had an added significance, though, because of Australia's history as an outpost of European civilization in Asia: ever-conscious of the "teeming hordes" of "coloured aliens" directly to the north, white Australians, who, by 1901, numbered around four million, had become increasingly nervous about the presence of Asians within their borders and increasingly determined to expel them. Expulsion seemed the most effective way of stemming the tide of "Asiatics" who threatened to swamp the relatively small numbers of white Australians. White Australians were also hostile to a mixed-race society because they feared that Asian values and practices would undermine what they saw as a superior Australian way of life. The labour movement, in particular, feared that cheaper Asian labour would undermine the conditions of Australian workers. Anti-Asian sentiment also had more overtly racist elements, with allegations that the Chinese (almost all of whom were men) debauched innocent white girls, engaged in sodomy and other vices, such as opium smoking and gambling.[16] Those who drafted the constitution and sat in the parliaments of the newly-federated Commonwealth had a (although admittedly imprecise and contested) view of Australia as an homogenous white society, based firmly on British institutions and peoples, but incorporating the democratic, egalitarian aspects of a new society. Until late in the nineteenth century, class could cancel out colour but not gender as a qualification for citizenship, so that, for example, male

---

16. A.T. Yarwood, *Attitudes to Non-European Immigration* (Sydney, NSW, 1968); *idem, Asian Migration to Australia: the Background to Exclusion 1896–1913* (Sydney, NSW, 1964). See also A.T. Yarwood and M.J. Knowling, *Race Relations in Australia* (Sydney, NSW, 1982) and Andrew Markus, *Australian Race Relations* (Sydney, NSW, 1994).

Aboriginal and Chinese property owners could qualify for the vote in colonial legislatures. By the early twentieth century racial background assumed greater significance than either class or gender. White people of all classes, both male and female, had privileged rights as citizens, while non-whites, whether indigenous Aborigines or immigrants, were either excluded completely or relegated to the status of second-class citizens.[17] Immigration control played a critical part in establishing and maintaining this hierarchy.

The federation of the Australian colonies also coincided with the advent of two new, albeit related, forces in Australian and international politics. Although some Australian colonies had already given women the right to vote in parliamentary elections, the Commonwealth Constitution gave all white women the right to vote for its parliaments. Feminist politics therefore assumed a newfound importance in the twentieth century. Secondly, the first decade of the twentieth century saw the establishment of an international movement concerned to abolish the sexual traffic in women and girls. Both these forces were to have an impact on the way in which immigration laws were enforced in Australia, giving a new, sexualized and gendered meaning to what began as a policy of racial exclusion.

To understand this process, however, we need to understand how the Immigration Restriction Act operated. The history of the Immigration Restriction Act has to date focused, not surprisingly, on the racial aspects of this so-called "white Australia policy".[18] My task here is to explore this history from a different angle, to examine how issues of gender, sexuality and class intersected with racial concerns in deciding who would be excluded from Australia. In so doing, I argue that the connections between race, class and gender outlined above for the colonial period were just as relevant for the early twentieth century, although the precise permutations changed over time.

Although popularly understood both within and outside Australia as a policy of racial exclusion, the Immigration Restriction Act was not framed in racial terms. On the contrary, there was no specific mention of racial attributes in the selection of immigrants, the primary mechanism for exclusion being a dictation test in a European language. The notorious dictation test was originally used in late nineteenth-century Natal to keep Asians from British colonies out of British African colonies. It was seized upon in the newly-federated Australian Commonwealth as a way of keeping out so-called "coloured" races without (it was hoped) giving obvious offence

17. For an excellent account of this process, see Patricia Grimshaw and Katherine Ellinghaus, "White Women, Aboriginal Women and the Vote in Western Australia", in *Studies in Western Australian History*, forthcoming women's suffrage centenary special issue.
18. *Ibid.*, fn. 14. Also, Myra Willard, *History of the White Australia Policy* (London, 1923); A.C. Palfreeman, *The Administration of the White Australia Policy* (Sydney NSW, 1967); Sean Brawley, *The White Peril: Foreign Relations and Asian Immigration to Australasia and North America 1919–78* (Kensington, NSW, 1995).

to other citizens of the British Empire or her allies in Asia. Those excluded were expected to believe that it was not the colour of their skin but their spelling that Australia found objectionable. The test was used in the twentieth century to exclude not just "coloureds" but also others considered subversive to Australia's political institutions. The case of the Communist Egon Kisch, excluded in 1934 after failing a test in Gaelic, is well-known.[19] Less well-known is the use made of this dictation test to exclude persons of suspect sexuality.

The tardiness of historians in recognizing this aspect of the "white Australia policy" is surprising, given the publicity to such deportations in the 1920s and 1930s. Several sensational cases involving French and Italian nationals in the late 1920s and early 1930s were widely reported in the popular press. On each occasion, the processes of exclusion were made only too transparent. For example, *Smith's Weekly* in April 1929 carried a report of a French woman of ill-repute who had married an "ex-digger" (that is, a returned Australian soldier) to escape deportation, but who had subsequently returned to her former acquaintances. "She was hailed before the customs office charged with being a prohibited immigrant. A dictation test in German was applied, and, failing to pass it, she was sentenced to six months imprisonment and deportation."[20] Four days later the *Sun* (Sydney) reported the deportation of one of her associates after failing to pass a dictation test in English. The article made it clear why he was being deported, reporting the item with a bold caption: "WHITE SLAVERY INQUIRY". The *Sun Pictorial* carried a version of the same story under the heading: "WEALTHY FRENCHMAN AND DICTATION TEST – MIGRATION CHARGE."[21] The public was left in no doubt as to the connection between dictation tests, deportations and allegations of white slavery/prostitution. Indeed, the Crown prosecutor was reported by the *Sun* as saying: "The Crown could deport anyone it chose, but wanted to show the court and the public that proceedings had been taken on proper grounds." To add weight to its action, the court and the press were informed that the government had only acted after receiving "a communication from the White Slavery Committee of the League of Nations".[22] Earlier cases made the same connection. In July 1928, the Melbourne *Argus* reported that two French women, residents of Perth, were to be deported after failing to pass the language test in English. "The police alleged that they kept a house of ill-fame."[23] The Melbourne *Age* went into more detail, reporting how the women had lived in Egypt before coming to Australia with £2,000 which

19. The most recent account of this episode is in Stuart Macintyre, *The Reds: The Communist Party of Australia from Origins to Illegality* (Sydney, NSW, 1998), pp. 270–273.
20. *Smith's Weekly*, 20 April 1929.
21. *Sun Pictorial*, 20 April 1929.
22. *Sun*, 24 April 1929.
23. *Argus*, 13 July 1928.

they invested in a house in Roe Street, Perth. As most Australians were aware, Roe Street was a notorious red-light district, while European women who lived in Egypt were immediately suspect.[24] The ʌdelaide *Advertiser's* report of the court case included the defence offered by the two sisters concerned. They argued that the Immigration Act should not have been applied to them as they had made it clear by their investments that they intended to settle in Australia permanently. As such they were "citizens", not "immigrants". The Chief Justice was unconvinced, pointing out that the dictation test could be administered any time within the first three years after arrival. "Persons who entered Australia could do so only subject to Australia's terms, and, so to speak, were here for the first three years on approval."[25] Clearly, Australia did not approve of prostitutes and therefore had the right to deport them. The Australian authorities, it is implied, were behaving in the best interests of Australia. Furthermore, the references to the League of Nations suggested that Australia was carrying out broader agendas as part of its responsibilities as a member of the community of (civilized) nations. What is clear from all of these cases is the importance of an association with prostitution as a criterion for exclusion, regardless of the wealth or property of the individual concerned. Nor were women the only targets of these deportations: men believed to be involved as procurers or associates of prostitutes were also excluded. This case also demonstrates that it was not only the right to citizenship that was contested in this period: clearly the nature of commercial sex was also open to different interpretations and representations. While the government and press were keen to use "white slave" terminology, the situation of the women and their male companions, as reported both by the police and by themselves in evidence, suggests that the relationship was a far cry from the popular idea of white slavery. The women concerned were neither young nor inexperienced, nor did they appear to be vulnerable to the men with whom they associated. However, by evoking the discourse of white slavery, the government was able to secure greater legitimacy for its actions.

THE WHITE AUSTRALIA POLICY AND THE WHITE SLAVE TRAFFIC: THE EARLY TWENTIETH CENTURY

Given official attitudes to foreign sex workers and entrepreneurs in the colonial period outlined above, this about-face calls for some explanation.

24. *Age*, 13 July 1928.
25. *Advertiser*, 13 July 1928. The difference of opinion on the basis of citizenship perhaps reflects the distinction identified by Rogers Brubaker, that is, between *jus sanguinis* and *jus solis*, between a principle of descent and a principle of residence. While Germans, for instance, in the nineteenth century emphasized nationality and German descent as qualifications for citizenship, the French state remained much more open to the naturalization of residents who had planted themselves in

The decision to exclude so-called "white slavers" was clearly not based on any dramatic increase in the traffic in women. Police records and press reports from the colonial period show that contemporaries were aware that there was a more or less organized movement of sex workers to Australia from Japan via South East Asia on the one hand and from Europe via the Middle East on the other.[26] The change over the first decades of the twentieth century is only partly explained by the fact that Japanese women ceased to come to Australia after 1901. Equally important is the changing popular perception of this traffic which increasingly saw the international movement of prostitutes as a "white slave traffic", involving an element of coercion.

By the late 1890s there were already signs of this change in attitude. Obviously inspired by W.T. Stead's campaigns in England, stories began to appear in the press about "white slavers" who lured innocent young girls to the colonies and then forced them into a life of prostitution.[27] In the popular imagination, the white slave traffic increasingly came to refer to forced prostitution, through violence or deception. Arguably, these narratives of white slavery served a similar function to earlier captivity narratives in defining the emergent Australian nation.[28] Colonial captivity narratives tended to place white women as captives of "savage" indigenous people: the barbarous treatment received by such captured white women justified the violent dispossession of their captors by white men, and redefined the dispossessors as the rightful owners of the land. The rescue of captured white women symbolized the restoration of the white nation to its legitimate place. Historians have already noted how the fear of "miscegenation" between Asian men and white women was a prominent feature of the move to exclude all Asians from Australian colonies in the late nineteenth

French cultural soil. Rogers Brubaker, *Citizenship and Nationhood in France and Germany* (Cambridge, 1992). See also Charles Tilly, "Citizenship, Identity and Social History", *International Review of Social History*, 40 (1995), Supplement 3, pp. 8–10.

26. E.g. D.C. Sissons, "Karayuki-san: Japanese Prostitutes in Australia, 1887–1916", *Historical Studies* 17 (1977), pp. 323–341 and 474–488; Charles van Onselen, *Studies in the Social and Economic History of the Witwatersrand: New Babylon* (Harlow, 1982); Ronald Hyam, *Empire and Sexuality: The British Experience* (Manchester, 1990); Raelene Davidson, "Prostitution in Perth and Kalgoorlie and on the Eastern Goldfields, 1895–1939" (M.A. thesis, University of Western Australia, 1980).

27. Raelene Frances, "Australian Prostitution in International Context", *Australian Historical Studies*, 106 (1996), pp. 128–129.

28. Carroll Smith-Rosenberg, "Captured Subjects/Subject Others: Violently Engendering the New American", *Gender and History*, 5 (1993); see also June Namias, *White Captives: Gender and Ethnicity on the American Frontier* (Chapel Hill, NC, 1993). For Australian captivity narratives, see Kay Schaffer, *In the Wake of First Contact: the Eliza Fraser Stories* (Cambridge, 1995); Kate Darian-Smith, "'Rescuing' Barbara Thompson and Other White Women: Captivity Narratives on Australian Frontiers", in Kate Darian-Smith, Liz Guner and Sarah Nuttall (eds), *Text, Theory, Space: Land, Literature and History in South Africa and Australia* (London and New York, 1996), pp. 99–114; Kate Darian-Smith, *et.al.* (eds), *Captive Lives: Australian Captivity Narratives* (London, 1992).

century.[29] In the twentieth century, narratives of "white slavery" continued
to feature "lecherous Asiatics" as major villains responsible for the sexual
slavery of innocent white girls.[30] Late nineteenth-century narratives also frequently identified "continental" men as the debauchers and enslavers of
British women. These narratives had similar kinds of symbolic significance
to that attributed to the frontier captivity narrative: the innocent white
woman comes to stand for the white Australian nation, and her rescue from
her captors symbolizes Australia's reclaiming of a purer, British identity
from degenerate continental Europeans and Orientals. Such stories encouraged a narrow British identification of "white Australia" and harsher puni-
tive measures against "foreigners". The police were urged to take action
against the men who were seen as the main instigators of this trade, and
politicians were encouraged to change the law to make tougher penalties
for so-called "bludgers", or men who lived off the earnings of prostitutes.

A sensational case against an Italian procurer in 1902 marked a turning
point in official response to foreign sex workers and entrepreneurs.[31] At the
same time, this case attracted international scrutiny which encouraged the
Australian authorities to adopt a harder line against "white slavers". The
flow of information was thus not a one-way process: while Australian audi-
ences had eagerly devoured reports of the English Stead case, stories about
what was happening in Australia filtered back to England where they added
fuel to the growing international campaign against the "white slave traffic".

One example of this is a booklet entitled *The White Slave Market*. Written
around 1909 by a Mrs Archibald Mackinolty (Olive Christian Malvery) and
W.N. Willis, it advocated a series of legal reforms to deal with the traffic
in women:

> What we want to do is to get some laws passed in England and in our colonies
> and our dependencies, and especially in the East – laws such as now exist in
> Australia, which within a year killed the traffic in women. Two men were captured
> in Australia with a batch of girls whom they had brought over from Europe, and
> whom they took to a certain mining camp and sold to a bad life. The men were
> captured and imprisoned for ten years, and during that period they received several
> floggings at intervals. There has never been a case of white slave traffic in Australia
> since these cases were dealt with, and there never will be as long as it is known that
> to traffic in a girl means a flogging as well as ten years' rigorous imprisonment.[32]

29. A.T. Yarwood, *Attitudes to Non-European Immigration* (Sydney, NSW, 1968); Raymond
Evans, Kay Saunders and Kathryn Cronin, *Race Relations in Colonial Queensland 1975* (Brisbane,
QLD, 1993), Part III.
30. See, for example, the "drama in four parts", *The White Slave Traffic* by Kate Howard, written
in the 1920s, AA Series A1336/2, item 3432; also Frances, "Australian Prostitution", pp. 136–137.
31. *Sunday Times*, 24 August 1902.
32. Mrs Archibald Mackinolty (Olive Christian Malvery) and W.N. Willis, *The White Slave
Market*, colonial edition (London, n.d. ca. 1909), p. 94. This account exaggerates the sentences
meted out: the men concerned received only two years' hard labour.

The prosecution of Cozzi, the man referred to above, coincided with an increase in international concern about the traffic in women. The international movement arising from this concern had close connections with existing "abolitionist" groups who sought an end to all systems of state-regulated prostitution. The first international congress on the white slave traffic was held in London in 1899, and this was followed by the first international convention for the suppression of the white slave traffic in Paris in 1904. The Commonwealth government overcame the initial reservations of several of the states and followed Britain's lead in ratifying the terms of this agreement in 1906. Another international convention was signed in 1910 and Australia adhered to this also in 1914.[33] Australian feminists were active in this campaign at both a local and international level. Being amongst the few enfranchised women in the world at the time, Australian feminists felt a responsibility to take a leading role in the international battle to improve women's status. Indeed, Millicent Garrett Fawcett, in her capacity as First Vice-President of the International Woman Suffrage Alliance, wrote to the Australian prime minister in 1913 to urge the Australian government to conduct an inquiry into the white slave traffic. In support of her case she wrote:

> It was pointed out by many delegates [to the Seventh Congress of the International Woman Suffrage Alliance] from countries where women have the vote, that one of the first uses to which women have put their newly acquired political power, was to strengthen the law for the prevention of commercialized vice and for the protection of the young of both sexes. A delegate from Australia informed the Congress that the existence of women voters in Australia had enabled the women of the Commonwealth to insist upon a vigorous and impartial administration of the laws for the repression of the White Slave Trade and kindred evils, with such satisfactory results that commercialized vice had been very greatly diminished in Australia.[34]

The delegates to this congress resolved to urge their own governments to "institute an international enquiry into the extent and causes of commercialized vice" and to "institute a national enquiry along the same lines". The Commonwealth government was not prepared to take any action, believing it had already done everything within its powers under the Immigration Restriction Act. The prime minister suggested the matter would be more appropriately dealt with by the state governments.[35] However, Australian authorities were not convinced that traffic in women was a serious problem in Australia and the 1914 Premiers' Conference refused to hear from a

33. AA Series A1108, item vol. 31. Sheila Jeffreys, *The Idea of Prostitution* (Melbourne, VIC, 1997); ch. 1, contains a brief history of these international conventions.
34. Letter Millicent Garrett Fawcett to Andrew Fisher, 17 November 1913, AA Series A1/1, item 1915/5651.
35. Letter from the prime minister to Miss A.B. Witham, hon. secretary, Women's Non-Party Political Association of South Australia, 13 November 1913, AA Series A1108, item 31.

delegation, led by the Women's Political Association of Victoria, on the issue.[36]

What is especially significant about the lobbying of feminists and the response of politicians is the way the focus on the *white* slave traffic deflected attention from the sexual exploitation of Aboriginal women within Australia exposed at the time by the Roth royal commission in 1905. In 1914, the premier of Western Australia could thus write without fear of contradiction, that "the procuration of white women for immoral purposes is not now practised". For feminists, the focus on the *white* slave traffic encouraged a blindness where the traffic in non-white women was concerned.[37]

THE WHITE AUSTRALIA POLICY AND THE WHITE SLAVE TRAFFIC: WORLD WAR I AND THE LEAGUE OF NATIONS

The outbreak of war in 1914, however, was to mark a new departure in the history of government and feminist reactions to the international sex industry. Australian troops fighting in the Middle East frequented the brothels of Cairo, a fact that was generally known both to the authorities and to feminist organizations in Australia.[38] This intercourse drew attention both to the extent of the traffic in women in Egypt and also heightened concern about the relationship between prostitution and venereal disease, and especially about the importation of new, "foreign" strands of the disease to Australia.[39] After the war, feminist concerns about the traffic in women overlapped with eugenicist fears about the impact of sexually-transmitted diseases on racial vigour. The postwar Australian government shared the fears about racial decline and was also concerned that Australia be seen to acquit itself well as a "civilized" and "advanced" society on the international stage. When the League of Nations took over the administration of the international conventions on the traffic in women, Australia was keen to become a signatory and to carry out its obligations under the convention.[40] By the middle of the 1920s, most Australian governments no longer regarded the presence of foreign prostitutes as beneficial or even benign. The advent of the white Australia policy had meant an end to the importation of

36. AA Series A1, item 1915/5651; also AA Series A1108, item vol. 31.
37. Letter J. Scadden, premier of Western Australia, to prime minister, 6 July 1914, AA Series A1108, item vol. 31. See also Raelene Frances, "Australian Prostitution in International Context", *Australian Historical Studies*, 106 (1996), pp. 129–130.
38. AA series CP78/23/1. item 14/89/252 Pt 1; Bruce Scates and Raelene Frances, *Women and the Great War* (Cambridge, 1997), ch. 6.
39. Judith Smart, "The Great War and the 'Scarlet Scourge': Debates about Venereal Diseases in Melbourne during World War I", in Judith Smart and Tony Wood (eds), *An Anzac Muster: War and Society in Australia and New Zealand 1914–18 and 1939–45* (Clayton, VIC, 1992), pp. 58–85.
40. The first two conventions (1904 and 1910) were administered by the French government.

"coloured" Pacific Island and Chinese labourers and the enforced repatriation of most of Australia's existing "coloured" populations. The racial
rationale for tolerating foreign prostitutes to service a large non-white male
population no longer existed. Japanese prostitutes were themselves victims
of the new immigration laws: the door was firmly closed against new arrivals
while most already in Australia were required to leave. French prostitutes
were now targeted as the main contaminating influence, both morally and
physically. After Australia's experiences during the war, it was not hard for
the government to be convinced that a traffic in women did exist and that
the Middle East had a particular role to play as a staging post en route to
Australia and the Orient. In 1927 the director of the Attorney General's
Department referred to impending Commonwealth action due to "a growth
in the obnoxious traffic in this country, organized in Alexandria and Port
Said".[41]

It was also very convenient for Australians to blame foreigners for the
traffic, as this reinforced national stereotypes which had achieved greater
clarity during the war. Thus in 1931, the director of the Commonwealth
Attorney General's Department informed the secretary of the Prime
Minister's Department that: "This gravamen [i.e. persons living on immoral
earnings of women] is very rarely discernible among Australians of British
descent, as such a practice is repugnant to national ethics. The infrequent
cases discovered have been perpetrated by aliens, [...]."[42] The fact that the
League of Nations had endorsed the issue of the traffic in women gave it
an added validity which it had lacked when the main proponents of the
convention could be dismissed as "hysterical" feminists and religious
enthusiasts. The endorsement of the League also meant that there was one
central bureaucrat in Australia who had the responsibility of monitoring the
traffic and reporting back to the League. All these factors combined to
ensure that the matter was treated with much greater seriousness after the
war than it had been before.

Having decided that some action needed to be taken, it is not hard to
see why the policy of exclusion commended itself to the authorities. As the
director of the Attorney General's Department explained:

> As principal executive officer in Australia under the White Slave Convention of
> the League of Nations, I am of opinion that one of the best practical methods of
> dealing with the question of White Slavery is to make it impossible for the
> unscrupulous foreigners to import women of the unfortunate class to Australia,
> and that the best way to do this is to deport any such women who manage to
> enter and who immediately practise their profession here.[43]

41. Letter, H.E. Jones, director, Attorney-General's Department, to the secretary, Home and
Territories Department, 29 July 1927, AA Series 2998/1, item 51/576.
42. Memo, 10 November 1931, AA Series A981/1, item League Wom/11.
43. Letter, H.E. Jones, director, Attorney-General's Department, to the secretary, Home and
Territories Department, 29 July 1927, AA Series 2998/1, item 51/576.

The fact that immigration policy was centrally determined under the Commonwealth made a uniform Australian response to the issue possible, unlike during the nineteenth century when each colonial government devised its own policy. After federation, immigration policy was the one area of control that the Commonwealth government had over the sex industry. Policing as such remained a state concern. Indeed, as the subsequent history of Australia's involvement with international conventions shows, the unwillingness of certain states to adopt policing policies favoured by the Commonwealth government was to prevent Australia becoming a signatory until the 1970s to the more stringent abolitionist conventions under the United Nations.[44] The major problem was that a *de facto* type of regulation of prostitution had existed in Queensland and Western Australia for several decades. After the war, international pressure to abolish regulation was becoming stronger, and scrutiny of Australia's policing methods more sweeping. The Commonwealth government attempted to deflect such international criticism by semantic twists in their response to inquiries from the League. For instance, when in 1926 the League inquired about the existence of licensed houses of prostitution, the official response had to be carefully worded. As the prime minister's secretary noted on the file, "*The point is that the System is not authorised in any of the States* [...]" [original emphasis].[45] Exclusion of alien prostitutes and procurers had the attraction of being uncontroversial in Australia whilst also enabling Australia to present an enlightened face to the rest of the world on the white slave issue.

The effects of Australia's approach to the "white slave traffic", however, were much more ambiguous from the point of view of the abolitionists. As we have seen, the activities of the International Abolitionist Federation and the various conventions which it spawned had considerable impact on immigration policy and policing within Australia. Activists would no doubt have been most gratified at the exclusion or deportation of men allegedly involved in trafficking in women. However, the wholesale deportation of foreign prostitutes, which was carried out as a government strategy to discourage the international movement of sex workers, was more problematic from a feminist perspective. Indeed, the question of the compulsory repatriation and exclusion of prostituted women was a contentious issue in the League of Nations forums, with feminists and civil libertarians arguing

---

44. See AA Series 1838/1, item 856/14/8, part 4. "Abolitionists" sought the abolition of the system of policing prostitution known as regulation, that is, a system whereby prostitutes were required to register with the local police and subject themselves to regular medical examination. The incorporation of the abolitionist principle was first adopted by the Traffic in Women and Children Committee in 1936, and expressed in the 1937 Draft Convention for Suppressing the Exploitation of the Prostitution of Others. However, the outbreak of World War II delayed developments of this draft. AA Series A18382, item 856/14/8, pt. 1.

45. File note on report on licensed houses for transmission to Secretary-General, League of Nations, 7 October 1926, AA Series A981/1, item League Wom/11.

against discriminatory measures. As debates in the League's International Bureau for the Suppression of the Traffic in Women show, civil libertarians were alive to the potential for official abuse of any such measures. Monsieur Reelfs of Switzerland also pointed out that such repressive measures meant that: "The prostitute was being considered as a special class which could be driven from place to place."[46] The women who were subsequently deported from Australia had left Egypt in the wake of changes brought about by the activities of the International Bureau for the Suppression of the Traffic in Women, working in conjunction with the local police. The *Vigilance Record*, for instance, reported in 1929 that: "Port Said, notorious for its traffickers a few years ago, is now a reformed City. Owing to the vigilance of the Police and the work being done by the local branch of the International Bureau, Port Said is utterly changed."[47] As the official files relating to the 1920s deportations show, many, perhaps even most, of the women who came to Australia from France via Egypt intended to become long-term residents. They brought property and established businesses in the relatively lucrative and safe environment of Roe Street in Perth. These women became the unintended victims of the anti-trafficking campaign, forced to sell their property at a loss and to leave a country where they had hoped to achieve modest comfort and security. Indeed, it could be argued that deportation prolonged the working life of prostitutes by forcing them to recoup their Australian losses.

THE DICTATION TEST: AN INTERNATIONAL VAGRANCY LAW?

Given the obvious attractions of a policy of exclusion, the question remains as to why the government chose to use the dictation test, originally designed to exclude non-Europeans, against people engaged in the sex industry. The question needs to be asked because the original Immigration Restriction Act specifically prohibited the entry of "any prostitute or person living on the prostitution of others". The 1912 Amending Act added the word "procurer" after "prostitute".[48] Initially it seems the government relied on this clause.[49] However, increasingly the authorities came to prefer the dictation test because it gave them much more flexibility: it did not require the same kind of proof necessary to proceed under the more specific clause. As the director of the Attorney General's Department put it, "a distinct charge under this

---

46. International Bureau for the Suppression of the Traffic in Women and Children, *Congress Reports*, London, 1930, cited in Jeffreys, *The Idea of Prostitution*, p. 24.
47. Extract from *Vigilance Record*, March–April 1929, in International Bureau for the Suppression of the Traffic in Women Papers, Josephine Butler Archives, Fawcett Library, London, ms. 4/1BS, box 112.
48. Letter, Atlee Hunt to Hon. P. McGlynn, 30 March 1915, AA Series A1, item 1915/5651.
49. *Ibid.*

category is not laid unless the evidence is convincing". Undeterred, however, immigration authorities "invariably charged" "the culprit" with being a prohibited migrant, using the dictation test. The "culprit" was "always deported". Indeed, the effectiveness of this clause, and the inevitable failure of any appeals, eventually ensured that the mere threat was sufficient to ensure the persons targeted left the country.[50]

The dictation test thus came to assume a similar role in the international arena that the vagrancy law performed for local policing. Sue Davies's observations about vagrancy laws can thus be applied with equal validity to the dictation clause of the Immigration Restriction Act:

> Vagrancy laws, in general, were distinct from other criminal legislation because of their preoccupation with character, and their inherent breadth and flexibility. They allowed a degree of discretion in their application, and could therefore be used as a catch-all. In Victoria, and in Britain, the vagrancy provisions were used to prosecute not only the criminal, but also the suspected and the innocent.[51]

As noted earlier, the vagrancy clauses of the Police Act were used in Western Australia to enforce a type of *de facto* regulation of prostitution. Davies's comments about the arbitrary authority of the vagrancy laws are equally applicable to the dictation test. This is nowhere more clearly illustrated than in the case of Mrs Mabel Freer, who was refused permission to enter Australia in 1936.

Mrs Freer was the Indian-born daughter of an English army pensioner and his British wife. In 1936 she was an attractive twenty-six-year-old mother of two, divorced from her English husband, residing in Bombay. Sometime during 1936, whilst living apart from her husband, Mrs Freer met and fell in love with a young Australian army officer. He, too, was unhappily married and separated from his wife. He decided to return to Australia and organize a divorce and she accompanied him on the same ship, hoping to marry him in due course. Unfortunately, their plans were thwarted by the intervention of the Australian Department of Immigration. The young lieutenant's father-in-law, concerned at the course of events, lobbied acquaintances in the army who used their position to persuade the immigration authorities that Mrs Freer was an undesirable immigrant. When the boat carrying the couple reached Fremantle in October 1936, Mrs Freer was given a dictation test in Italian, which not surprisingly she failed. She was promptly declared a prohibited immigrant under the Immigration Restriction Act. Mrs Freer subsequently was given permission to transship to New Zealand, where she appealed against her fate for eight months before finally being allowed to enter Australia. In the meantime, however, she became

50. See memo 10 November 1931, director, Attorney General's Department to secretary, Prime Minister's Department, AA Series A981/1, item League Wom/11.
51. Suzanne Davies, "Vagrancy and the Victorian Social Construction of the Vagrant in Melbourne, 1880–1907" (Ph.D. thesis, Melbourne University, Melbourne, VIC, 1990), pp. 115–116.

something of *cause celèbre* in the Australian press: because the Immigration Department refused to give any reason for her exclusion, the public had no limit when it came to speculation. Was she a spy or a dangerous subversive? Was she a woman of ill-fame? Even engaged in the white slave traffic? Was she a "dope fiend"? Was she, perhaps, really of mixed English and Indian descent? Even when the federal cabinet learned the real history of the case and eventually decided that she should be admitted to Australia, no official explanation was given nor any apology or compensation. As Mabel Freer put it, her "character was ruined".[52] Her solicitor protested to the Australian Attorney-General, "It seems hard to believe that any Government would, in light of the circumstances [...] go so far as to exclude a British citizen from its territory." In his opinion, the way in which the dictation test was used constituted a breach of the basic principles of British justice: a denial of the "primary right to which every British subject is entitled – open accusation and open opportunity for reply".[53]

The reason for this denial of natural British justice was the fact that the Immigration Restriction Act targeted those who transgressed either (or both) the racial and moral ideals of white Australia. Like the vagrancy laws, the dictation test was used to police women's sexuality. Sex workers were an obvious target, but clearly any woman whose sexuality seemed to contravene the ideal of exclusive marital relationships was also vulnerable. Like the sex workers deported in 1929, Mrs Freer was excluded despite her class background. The Freer case shows not just the arbitrary power available to immigration officials under the Act, but also the increasingly narrow definition of "white Australia" between the two world wars. The dictation test gave immigration officials the flexibility to respond to this narrowing definition without having to resort to legislative changes.

REASSESSING WHITE AUSTRALIA AND THE WHITE SLAVE TRAFFIC BETWEEN THE WARS

It is ironic that just as Australia achieved its peak of "whiteness" in the 1930s, the first signs of a fundamental reassessment of Australia's racial policies and practices were appearing. After the First World War, and the advent of the League of Nations, there was a much greater international awareness that the use of the term "white slave traffic" was misleading. This was reflected in the change of name for the 1921 convention to Convention for the

52. Letter from G.P. Finlay, barrister and solicitor, Wellington, NZ, to the Attorney-General of the Commonwealth of Australia, 11 November 1936, Australian Archives (AA) Series A 432/85, item 36/1360. The Mabel Freer case is documented in the following files, held at the Australian Archives in Canberra: Series CP 290/1/1, item 16; Series A422/85, item 43/1139; Series A432/85, item 36/1360; Series A5954/1, item 973/13.
53. Letter from G.P. Finlay, barrister and solicitor, Wellington, NZ, to the Attorney-General of the Commonwealth of Australia, 11 November 1936, AA Series A432/85, item 36/1360.

Suppression of the Traffic in Women and Children. In Australia, however, the full implications of this change were only slowly recognized. As recent work in this area shows, the Australian feminist movement did not become active on the issue of the sexual exploitation of Aboriginal women until 1927.[54] This sudden interest in the plight of Aboriginal women seems to have been prompted as much by events overseas as by developments in Australia. Australian women participating in international conferences in the mid-1920s, such as those organized by the League of Nations, the Anti-Slavery Society, the International Women's Suffrage Alliance and the British Commonwealth League, returned to Australia with a feminist agenda which emphasized the plight of Aboriginal women in a way that previous agendas had not.[55] Mary Montgomerie Bennett was one of the most prominint of these activists. In 1934 she wrote of her concern about what she termed the "white slave traffic in black women" in Western Australia's Kimberley region, where she reported that pastoralists, pearlers and other men were using Aboriginal women as "merchandise".[56] Yet, as earlier noted, this situation was hardly new: the sexual exploitation of Aboriginal women had been a feature of the colonization process across Australia since 1788.[57] The tardiness of Australian feminist responses to this issue is perhaps a product of the consciousness produced by the earlier concentration on "white slavery", with the typical victim being an innocent white girl at the mercy of foreign men, rather than a black woman being sexually exploited by a white man. The shift in attitudes in the late 1920s was made possible partly by the changing international awareness that the traffic in women and children also involved non-white women and children, and partly by a renewed concern with slavery generally. Indeed, the international anti-slavery movement of the 1920s was the more powerful influence on women such as Mary

54. Alison Holland, "Feminism, Colonialism and Aboriginal Workers: An Anti-Slavery Crusade", in Ann McGrath and Kay Saunders with Jackie Huggins (eds), *Aboriginal Workers*, a special issue of *Labour History*, 69 (1995); Alison Holland, " 'Saving the Aborigines': The White Woman's Crusade. A Study of Gender and Race on the Australian Frontier", (Ph.D. thesis, University of New South Wales, 1999); Fiona Paisley, " 'Don't Tell England!': Women of Empire Campaign to Change Aboriginal Policy in Australia Between the Wars", *Lilith: A Feminist History Journal*, 8 (1993), pp. 139–152; Fiona Paisley, "Feminist Challenges to White Australia 1900–1930s", in Diane Kirkby (ed.), *Sex, Power and Justice: Historical Perspectives on Law in Australia* (Melbourne, VIC, 1995), pp. 252–269; Marilyn Lake, "Feminism and the Gendered Politics of Anti-Racism, Australia 1927–1957: from 'Maternal Protectionism to Leftist Assimilationism' ", *Australian Historical Studies*, 110 (1998), pp. 91–108.
55. The importance of international influences on Australian feminists in this case has interesting resonances to the growth of the interest in issues of sexual domination, prostitution, venereal disease and the "white slave traffic" in the prewar period. See Barbara Caine, "Vida Goldstein and the English Militant Campaign", *Women's History Review*, 2 (1993), pp. 363–376.
56. Bennett to *Australian Board of Missions Review*, Rischbieth Papers, MS 2004/12/35, National Library of Australia, cited in Lake, "Feminism and the Gendered Politics of Antiracism", p. 100.
57. Raelene Frances, "A History of Female Prostitution in Australia", in Roberta Perkins, et.al. (eds), *Sex Work and Sex Workers in Australia* (Kensington, NSW, 1994).

Bennett. Fiona Paisley has suggested that the activism of Australian feminists in the late 1920s and 1930s reflected a less defensive strand in relation to Australian nationalism and a greater willingness to risk embarrassing the Australian government in order to advance the cause of Aborigines.[58] I would also argue that as Australia became more confident as a "white nation" in the interwar period, some of its white citizens became less concerned with policing the borders of white Australia and more prepared to reconsider the fate and rights of its indigenous population. The white slave traffic, and attitudes towards it, were an important part of this shifting definition of citizenship.

CONCLUSION

Ann Curthoys has argued that writing a history which embraces the interrelationships between race, class and gender presents almost insuperable difficulties:

> Trying to keep just two of these concepts in play has proved extremely difficult [...]. But if keeping two such concepts in play is hard enough, look what happens when the third concept, be it ethnicity or class or sex, is brought seriously into play. The system, the analysis, becomes too complex to handle.[59]

By focusing on the issue of prostitution, I hope to have overcome some of the difficulties presented by "the three body problem". I have argued that since the inception of white occupation, the sex industry has played a critical part in the way in which governments attempted to construct a society within a particular configuration of racial/ethnic, sex/gender and class factors. However, the precise relationship of these factors to each other, both in the official vision and in practice, varied considerably over time and place.

Initially, maintaining a particular class hierarchy and heterosexual norm assumed primacy over any considerations of racial hierarchies. Official priorities, however, were quickly modified in the light of popular attitudes and colonial realities. As white society achieved supremacy over the indigenous population, and non-white labourers were imported, particularly in the north, the preservation of white supremacy ensured that racial considerations became a major issue for colonial governments and important presssure groups within white colonial society. However, the very fact that racial *hierarchies* were an issue meant that questions of class and status were inextricably linked. Similarly, the predominance of men over women in most non-white immigrant ethnic groups required careful management of the sex industry to ensure that sexual access of "coloured" men to white

58. Fiona Paisley, "'Don't Tell England!'".
59. Ann Curthoys, "The Three Body Problem: Feminism and Chaos Theory", in Women/Australia/Theory, special issue of *Hecate*, 17 (1991), p. 15.

women did not arise as a disturbing element in the colonial social order. On the other hand, white men's access to Aboriginal women formed part of the process of dispossession and domination of indigenous people.

In the early twentieth century, as Australia redefined itself as a modern, independent, "civilized" white nation, racial issues assumed a different, less visible, but equally important role. White men's access to Aboriginal women was now officially deplored as a threat to white racial purity and vigour, but unofficially and clandestinely practised on a large scale. Strict immigration controls ensured that "coloured" labourers were prohibited from entering Australia. The movement of sex workers between Australia and overseas countries came to be seen as a threat both to the racial vigour of Australia's white population and a threat to Australia's standing in the international community. Race was still the issue, but it was defined differently, with "white" increasingly coming to mean British rather than European. Likewise, race was inextricable linked to the maintenance of a white society with a particular class basis. Whereas in the colonial period "coloured" immigrant workers existed as a cheaper rung of the working class, federated Australia deliberately turned its back on such a racially defined sub-class. While immigrant "coloured" workers and their descendents were deported in large numbers, it was not so easy for governments to dispose of the indigenous "coloured" population who also occupied the role of a subservient, poorly paid workforce.[60] As the century progressed it became clear that Australians of Aboriginal descent were increasing in number rather than decreasing according to Social Darwinist prescription. By the end of the 1930s their plight was becoming visible to increasing numbers of white Australians, who were forced to rethink the nature of the so-called "white Australia". The international movement against the "white slave traffic", with its new sensitivity to the exploitation of non-white women, provided a gendered lens through which the class relationship of Aboriginal peoples to white Australia could be reassessed.

60. There is now an extensive literature on this subject, which is reviewed in Ann Curthoys and Clive Moore, "Working for the White People: an Historiographical Essay on Aboriginal and Torres Strait Islander Labour", in Ann McGrath and Kay Saunders with Jackie Huggins (eds), *Aboriginal Workers*, special issue of *Labour History*, 65 (1994). See also Andrew Markus, "Aborigines in Labour History", in Jim Hagan and Andrew Wells (eds), *Australian Labour and Regional Change: Essays in Honour of R.A. Gollan* (Wollongong, NSW, 1998), pp. 41–56; and Raelene Frances, Bruce Scates and Ann McGrath, "Broken Silences? Labour History and Aboriginal Workers", in Terry Irving (ed.), *Challenges to Labour History*, (Kensington, NSW, 1994), pp. 189–211.

International Review of Social History 44 (1999), Supplement, pp. 123–147
© 1999 Internationaal Instituut voor Sociale Geschiedenis

From Muscles to Nerves: Gender, "Race" and the Body at Work in France 1919–1939*

LAURA LEVINE FRADER

In the years before and immediately after World War I, gendered and racialized bodies at work became the focus of debate and discussion in France amongst an informal alliance of engineers, doctors, scientists, employers, workers, and the state.[1] Seduced by the promise of "modernity", and the seemingly endless possibilities of science and mechanization, the state attempted to modernize public services and employers sought new ways to discipline labor for greater productivity. Both mobilized rationalization – Taylorism and work science – in the service of greater efficiency and in an effort to identify the allegedly "natural" qualities that made gendered and racialized workers suitable for certain kinds of jobs and would exclude them from others.[2] A not insignificant dimension of this project lay in how

---

* The author thanks Nancy Green for suggesting the title of this essay, and Eileen Boris, Antoinette Burton, James Cronin, Rayna Rapp, and Eve Rosenhaft for comments on earlier drafts.
1. Gendered bodies were already the site of considerable debate throughout the nineteenth century in discussions about the right to work, social and family policies, the qualifications of citizenship and the problem of male military preparedness. See, for example, Robert A. Nye, *Crime, Madness, and Politics in Modern France: the Medical Concept of National Decline* (Princeton, NJ, 1984); George Mosse, *Nationalism and Sexuality: Respectability and Abnormal Sexuality in Modern Europe* (New York, 1985); and Anson Rabinbach, *The Human Motor: Energy, Fatigue, and the Origins of Modernity* (New York, 1990), pp. 224–228. Rabinbach's work is the most extensive study of work science in English, although the book is not designed to focus on the gender or race dimensions of work science. See also, Mary Lynn Stewart, *Women, Work, and the French State* (Montreal, 1991); L.R. Villermé, *Tableau de L'Etat physique et moral des ouvriers employés dans les manufactures de coton, de laine, et de soie* (Paris, 1971); Leora Auslander and Michelle Zancarini-Fournel (eds), *Différence des sexes et protection sociale. xix'–xx' siècles* (St Denis, 1995); Susan Pedersen, *Family, Dependence, and the Origins of the Welfare State: Britain and France 1914–1945* (Cambridge, 1993) and Seth Koven and Sonya Michel (eds), *Mothers of A New World* (New York and London, 1995); Rachel Fuchs, Eleanor Accampo et al., *Family, the State, and Welfare in Modern France* (Baltimore, MD, 1996); Kathleen Canning, *Languages of Gender and Labor: Female Factory Work in Germany, 1850–1914* (Ithaca, NY, 1996); Laura Lee Downs, *Manufacturing Inequality* (Ithaca, NY, 1995); and Laura Levine Frader, "Social Citizens Without Citizenship: Working-Class Women and Social Policy in Interwar France", *Social Politics*, 3 (1996), pp. 111–135. On the the way in which this collaboration constructed "a new image of class relationships", see Charles Maier, "Between Taylorism and Technocracy", *Journal of Contemporary History*, 5 (1970), p. 29.
2. For examples of the naturalizing discourses addressed to the "inherent qualities" of women, see, for example, Anne Phillips and Barbara Taylor, "Sex and Skill: Notes Towards a Feminist Economics", *Feminist Review*, 6 (1980), pp. 79–88; Harriet Bradley, *Men's Work, Women's Work* (Minneapolis, MN, 1989); Helen Harden Chenut, "The Gendering of Skill as Historical Process: the Case of French Knitters in Industrial Troyes, 1880–1939", in Laura L. Frader and Sonya O. Rose (eds), *Gender and Class in Modern Europe* (Ithaca, NY, 1996), pp. 77–107; and Downs, *Manufacturing Inequality*.

French work scientists began to envision the potential uses of gendered French and colonial labor. The development of the French North-African and Indochinese colonial empires around the turn of the century heightened attention to racialized difference. World War I had opened the opportunity to use racialized colonial bodies, both on the military front and in the factory.[3] Thinking about race and gender characteristics continued to influence work science and its applications in the 1920s and 1930s. Work scientists' experiments to ascertain the physical endurance of colonial male workers and white workers underscored the durability of gender meanings in dealing with white French workers and the instability of those meanings in assessing the abilities of workers of color.

This paper shows how gendered and racialized working-class bodies became the sites of "modernization" after the war and focuses on the science of work as one aspect of the rationalizing impulse in interwar France.[4] Operating from the assumption that gender, race, and class, are mutually constitutive, rather than separate and parallel categories of difference, the paper investigates how race and gender both complicated the notion of "class" as well as inflecting each others' meanings: gender complicated the meanings of race and vice versa, illustrating the instability of meanings often assumed to be fixed.[5] However, the particular meanings of "race" and common uses of racial vocabulary in France between the wars may not have been exactly the same as the meanings of this term in other national contexts. This particularity introduces another level of complexity into discussions of how race operated as a marker of difference. Even though "whiteness" and "blackness" may have functioned as categories within the context of French anthropology, it is not clear how generalized they had

---

3. See B. Nogaro and Lucien Weil, *La main d'oeuvre etrangère et coloniale pendant la guerre* (New Haven, CT and Paris, 1926); Tyler Stovall, "Color-blind France? Colonial Workers During the First World War", *Race and Class*, 35 (1993), pp. 35–55 and Stovall, "The Color Line Behind the Lines: Racial Violence in France During the Great War", *American Historical Review*, 103 (1998), pp. 737–769, which analyses the different responses of the French to North African immigrant labor versus European immigrant labor. Stovall argues that the war lessened tensions between the French and European immigrants whereas it heightened hostility towards colonial workers of color. On immigrant workers, see Gary S. Cross, *Immigrant Workers in Industrial France. The Making of a New Working Class* (Philadelphia, PA, 1983) and John Horne, "Immigrant Workers in France During World War I", *French Historical Studies*, 24 (1985), pp. 57–88, and Horne, *Labour at War: France and Britain 1914–1918* (Oxford, 1991).
4. See Rabinbach's discussion of cultural and social modernity with reference to the science of work in *The Human Motor*.
5. On the mutually constitutive character of these categories, see introduction in Sandra Harding, *The "Racial" Economy of Science: Towards A Democratic Future* (Bloomington, IN, 1993). As Harding writes, "[...] it is clear that "race" and gender, racism and sexism, construct and maintain each other [...]. Class and gender policies have constructed and maintained racial hierarchies just as race policies have done for class and gender hierarchies"(p. 11). See also Carole Turbin, Laura L. Frader, Sonya O. Rose and Evelyn Nakano Glenn, "A Roundtable on Gender, Race, Class, Culture and Politics: Where Do We Go From Here?", *Social Science History*, 22 (1998), pp. 1–45.

become in the popular vocabulary of racial identification in France. In any case, whiteness was never merely about color, alone. The French notion of race was strongly linked to membership in the national community – to Frenchness or non-Frenchness.[6] As I shall suggest below, "French" was coded as white even before "whiteness" entered the popular lexicon in the way it had in, say, the United States, where the consciousness of race was not only the shadow presence of an overseas colonial empire, but where the language of racial difference and the social exclusions of race had long been part of the vocabulary and social fabric of everyday life.

I argue first, that in spite of their claims to "science" – a term that signified neutrality and objectivity – the social and medical investigators who practiced and promoted the science of work in the period from 1900 to 1939, hardly treated the body as a neutral biological entity. As Sandra Harding has observed, science itself is constituted by historical and cultural meanings and practices that are never absent from its cognitive core. For centuries, science has been complicitous in perpetuating racist and gendered as well as Eurocentric assumptions and beliefs.[7] As the object of work scientists' investigations into fatigue and endurance, the working body could never be separated from its gendered, racialized, or cultural meanings and those meanings permeated the investigations of work science.[8] Moreover, work science and employer practices revealed the instability of the meanings of "race" – through their attention to bodies identified as explicitly racialized and through their silences on race. My task here is to look at how employers and the state deployed those meanings in analyzing and appropriating the bodies of workers. I hypothesize that despite its silence on race, racialized

6. I am grateful to Rayna Rapp and to Ann Laura Stoler for conversations on this subject. See Stoler, "Racial Histories and Regimes of Truth", *Political Power and Social Theory*, 11 (1977), pp. 183–206. See also Stoler and Frederick Cooper, "Between Metropole and Colony", in Cooper and Stoler (eds), *Tensions of Empire: Colonial Cultures in a Bourgeois World* (Berkeley, CA, 1997). As Stoler and Cooper write, citing George Stocking and others, "the concepts of culture and race have long served to buttress one another in crucial ways [...] [racism] has long depended on hierarchies of civility, on cultural distinctions of breeding, character, and psychological disposition, on the relationship between the hidden essence of race and what were claimed to be its visual markers" (p. 34). On the links between notions of racial difference and the nation, see Kenan Malik, *The Meaning of Race. Race, History, and Culture in Western Society* (New York, 1996), pp. 128–148; Herman Lebovics, *True France: The Wars Over Cultural Identity 1900–1945* (Ithaca, NY, 1992). On the cultural distinctions of "civility" and their links to concepts of the nation, and to class, see Norbert Elias, *The Civilizing Process* (Oxford and Cambridge, 1994), especially part 1, ch. 2.

7. See Harding, *"Racial" Economy of Science*. As Harding points out, science itself is laden with conflicting tendencies: regressive collaboration with racist and eurocentric beliefs on the one hand; and on the other hand, the progressive effects of "scientific procedures that have proved effective in identfying racist and imperialist tendencies in the sciences [...]", (p. 14).

8. In the words of Roy Porter, "the body must be regarded as mediated through cultural sign systems". See Porter, "History of the Body" in Peter Burke (ed.), *New Perspectives on Historical Writing* (University Park, PA, 1992), p. 215.

categories may have been marginally more important to the state (than to private sector employers) in establishing the quality and efficiency of public services such as the telephone and telegraph service. Secondly, although French industrialists and the state adopted neither Taylorism or work science wholesale, the rationalizing impulse of Taylor as well as that of work science could be found not only in industrial work, but also in the organization of public sector service work, where ideas about gender and race characteristics influenced employment policy.

RATIONALIZING THE WORKING BODY

In late nineteenth- and early twentieth-century France, Taylorism and work science developed as two competing approaches to rendering workers more productive and efficient.[9] Taylorism, imported into France shortly after Taylor's publication of the *Principles of Scientific Management* and other works in the United States, focused on managers' capacity to organize work effectively and efficiently by measuring the motions of the body through time and regulating the body according to plan.[10] In spite of dramatic protests against the implementation of time and motion studies on the shop floor, notably at the Renault automobile works before the war, some workers (notably in the General Confederation of Labor, CGT) promoted Taylorism under the assumption that better organization of the labor

9. On these two approaches and their policy consequences in France and Britain, see Gary Cross, *A Quest for Time: The Reduction of Work in Britain and France, 1840–1914* (Berkeley, CA, 1989), chapter 5. See Rabinbach, *The Human Motor*, which examines the important German (as well as French) contributions of this movement.

10. Taylor's first work published in France in 1907, *Etude sur l'organisation du Travail dans les Usines* was published by the *Revue de la Métallurgie*; subsequent works were published in French within a year of their appearance in the United States. There is a voluminous literature on Taylorism apart from Taylor's own published work. For a sampling of the literature on the reception of Taylorism in France, see Patrick Fridenson, "Un Tournant Taylorien de la Société française (1904–1918)" in *Annales ESC*, 5 (1987),pp. 1031–1060; Yves Cohen, "Ernest Mattern chez Peugeot (1906–1918) ou comment peut-on être taylorien?", in Maurice de Montmollin and Olivier Pastré (eds), *Le taylorisme* (Paris, 1984); Aimée Moutet, *Les logiques de l'entreprise* (Paris, 1997); O. Christin, "Les Enjeux de la rationalisation industrielle (1901–1929)", Mémoire de Maîtrise, Université de Paris I, 1982. See also Maier, "Between Taylorism and Technocracy", on the cultural and political appeal of Taylorism; and Rabinbach, "The European Science of Work: the Economy of the Body at the End of the Nineteenth Century", in Stephen Laurence Kaplan and Cynthia J. Koepp (eds), *Work in France. Representations, Meaning, Organization, and Practice* (Ithaca, NY, 1986), p. 475, n.1. See also Cross, "Redefining Workers' Control: Rationalization, Labor Time, and Union Politics in France, 1900–1928", in James E. Cronin and Carmen Sirianni (eds), *Work, Community, and Power: The Experience of Labor in Europe and America, 1900–1925* (Philadelphia, PA, 1983), pp. 143–172; Aimée Moutet, "Patrons du Progrès ou Patrons de Combat? La politique de rationalisation de l'industrie française au lendemain de la Première Guerre mondiale", in Lion Murard and Patrick Zylberman (eds), *Le Soldat du Travail. Guerre, fascisme, et taylorisme* (Paris, 1978), pp. 449–489. See also Georges Ribeill "Les Organisations du mouvement ouvrier en France face à la rationalisation (1926–1932)", in de Montmollin and Pastré, *Le taylorisme*.

process would make work easier and ultimately provide workers with more leisure time.[11] Taylor's model of scientific management was not simply about measuring the body's effective and efficient performance of tasks; it also involved a new model of managerial authority aimed at the reorganization of the entire labor process through a more refined and intensified division of labor. In its application, gender often played a fundamental role where the body was the site of new forms of labor regulation. Indeed, it may be nearly impossible to speak about Taylorism without speaking at the same time of gender and racialized divisions of labor.[12] The same was true of work science.

At the very moment that Taylorist rationalization found an audience among French industrialists and engineers, important critiques of Taylors' methods emerged from a small but growing group of psychologists and doctors who focused directly on the human body as the site of investigation and regulation. This was not a new development historically; from the late eighteenth and early nineteenth centuries the economic rationality of capitalist work discipline involved regulating the bodies of workers to conform to the pace of industrial time and the rhythm of the machine.[13] But the particular focus on the body of the worker intensified at the end of the nineteenth century and in the years around World War I. Moreover, as Anson Rabinbach has argued, "the science of labor was certainly not, like Taylorism, simply an ideology of management [...]. It was a struggle over energy and fatigue rather than time and money."[14]

Work scientists like Jean-Marie Lahy recognized the importance of the scientific organization of labor, especially given the loss of labor power due to wartime mortality and the employment of women in jobs formerly coded male.[15] However, Lahy argued that Taylor's focus on productivity had led to ignoring the wellbeing of the worker. Taylor's error was that he had assimilated human beings to machines and omitted the "human factor", especially the problem of fatigue. Lahy attempted to determine the fit between workers and their jobs by analysing their psycho-physiological signs of professional inclination – work that would ultimately lead to professional aptitude testing. Studying endurance and fatigue would allow workers to reduce wasted motions, use their energy more effectively, and become more

11. Cross, "Redefining Workers' Control".

12. Hirata, "Division internationale du travail et taylorisme: Brésil, France, et Japon", in de Montmollin and Pastré, *Le taylorisme*.

13. Edward P. Thompson, "Time, Work Discipline and Industrial Capitalism", *Past and Present*, 38 (1969), pp. 56–97.

14. Rabinbach, "The European Science of Work", p. 506, n. 111. The first stage "represented the creation of a disciplined workforce; the second was characterized by the struggle over the duration and value of labor time", *ibid.*

15. Jean-Marie Lahy, *Le Système Taylor et la Physiologie du Travail Professionnel* (Paris, 1921), Préface, p.v. On Lahy's critique of Taylor, see also Rabinbach, *The Human Motor*, pp. 250–252.

productive.[16] In their laboratory experiments, conducted largely on white
French males, Lahy's fellow work scientists Etienne-Jules Marey and Charles
Frémont, Auguste Chauveau, Jules Amar, and Armand Imbert applied the
principles of general mechanics to the human machine, measuring carbon
dioxide–oxygen exchange, muscular effort, and charting the body's motions
in different occupations ranging from mechanics to public speaking.[17] To
this work on the body, in the first decade of the twentieth century, psycho-
technicans Alfred Binet, Charles Henry, and Edouard Toulouse added the
notion that given the seeming inevitablity of overwork and fatigue in
modern labor, experimental and physiological psychologists could help
industry effectively use its human capital by developing methods of selection. Their measures of professional aptitude and aptitude tests led to the
practices of vocational guidance after World War I.[18] Finally, if these work
scientists and their medical and psychologist allies constituted a minority in
France, by the eve of World War I, work scientists had established a broad
international network of journals and conferences. Although historians have
tended to treat the "science of work" that emerged in this period as gender
and race-neutral, differently sexed and racialized bodies most definitely
entered the calculus of work science.[19]

GENDERED BODIES AT WORK DURING WORLD WAR I

In so far as all bodies are sexed, gendered, and racialized, it was impossible
for either studies of the body or the applications of work science not to

16. See Lahy, *Le Système Taylor*, pp. 156–157. Taylorism and work science both shared productivist
goals; Rabinbach, *The Human Motor*, p. 253.
17. As Rabinbach points out, the science of labor had to take account of changes in the labor
process going on outside the laboratories in which it was first conceived. "Concern with fatigue,
time, and motion, reflected deep social changes in the nature of the factory and the emergence of
a workforce that no longer had to be subjected to the moral economy of industrial discipline
outside the workplace. Instead, workers had to be taught to internalize the regularity imposed by
machine technology and adapt to newly intensified work norms", Rabinbach, "European Science
of Work", p. 507. See also Ribeill, "Les débuts de l'ergonomie en France à la veille de la Première
Guerre mondiale", *Le Mouvement Social*, 113 (1980), pp. 3–36; and Claudine Fontanon and André
Grelon (eds), *Les Professeurs du Conservatoire national des arts et métiers. Dictionnaire biographique,
1794–1955*, 2 vols (Paris, 1994). It is quite possible that in measuring the efforts of the white male
body these scientists were also struggling with their own definitions of masculinity. I am grateful
to Antoinette Burton for this suggestion.
18. Ribeill, "Les débuts de l'ergonomie en France", p. 21.
19. The attention to race in the works of work science experts such as Jules Amar was partly
based on early anthropological attempts to classify and evaluate the capacities of humans according
to anthropometrics. See Jules Amar, *Le Moteur humain et les bases scientifiques du travail professionnel*, 2nd edition (Paris, 1923), p. 151. On race in the science of work, see also Elisa Camiscioli,
"Labor Power and the Racial Economy: the Selection of Foreign Workers in France in the Late
Third Republic", paper presented to the conference, "Blurring the Boundaries: Politics and Culture in the French Third Republic", University of Michigan, Ann Arbor, MI, 1997.

incorporate ideas about perceived or socially-constructed gender or racial-ized difference. War provided one arena for the application of work science with distinctly gendered implications. In the 1880s, in the context of the *revanchiste* response to the French defeat during the Franco-Prussian war, work scientists had examined the marching patterns of military men, and promoted gymnastics training for white French schoolboys in the interest of military preparedness.[20] Scientists then linked improving the health and stamina of the white male body to national strength and proposed the rational application of physiology to physical education and diet.[21] These ideas also inspired Jean-Marie Lahy's subsequent tests of machine gunners' reaction times and fatigue in order to understand the "cold-bloodedness" of soldiers – their ability to withstand the psychological as well as the physical duress of war.[22]

As historians like Laura Downs and Patrick Friedenson have shown, World War I proved to be an important testing ground for experimentation with Taylorism, particularly in integrating women into jobs formerly desig-nated as "men's jobs" in the metalworking and defense industries. It was also an important moment for applying the science of work.[23] As Downs has shown, the process of fragmenting the labor process into semiskilled and unskilled work enabled employers to hire women as a separate category of worker to staff the new positions. Women's bodies became a special focus of interest. Employers singled out women's supposedly inherent dexterity and their alleged ability to withstand monotonous, routinized labor, and spoke of their bodies as almost naturally attuned to the movements of the machine in order to justify employing women on certain processes in metal-working.[24] Work scientists also collaborated with employers and the state during the war in attempting to reconcile the strategic objectives of stimulat-ing war production with the occasionally disturbing incongruity of womens' work in jobs formerly gendered male. Marcel Frois' investigations for the

20. The law of 27 January 1880 required gymnastics training for boys in *lycées*; Rabinbach, *The Human Motor*, p. 224. According to Amar, the physiologist Mosso wrote that "the catastrophe of Sedan will go down in history as the victory of German legs"; Amar, *Le Moteur humain*, p. 673.
21. Rabinbach, "The European Science of Work", p. 492; *The Human Motor*, pp. 130–131, 224–227, 265–270. See also Alain Ehrenberg, *Le corps militaire: politique et pédagogie en démocratie* (Paris, 1983).
22. Rabinbach, *The Human Motor*, p. 265. During the war, work scientists investigated the pos-sibilities of rehabilitating wounded soldiers. Amar in particular worked on the re-education of wounded men and on the development of prostheses that would enable war cripples to return to work. His work concerned exclusively white French soldiers. See Amar, *The Physiology of Industrial Organization and the Re-Employment of the Disabled* (New York, 1919), pp. 227–358. See also Hugues Monod, "Jules Amar", in Fontanon and Grelon, *Les Professeurs du Conservatoire national*, vol. 2, pp. 102–103.
23. See Downs, *Manufacturing Inequality*; Annie Fourcaut, *Femmes à l'usine: ouvrières et surinten-dantes dans les enterprises françaises de l'entre-deux-guerres* (Paris, 1982); Simone Weil, *La condition ouvrière* (Paris, 1951).
24. Downs, *Manufacturing Inequality*, pp. 83–84.

French Ministry of Armaments and War Manufactures of the health and
working conditions of women in the newly Taylorized defense industry in
1916 and 1917 demonstrated how investigators used the scientific study of
motion and fatigue to assess the impact of work on the white female body.
Frois concluded that although the bodies of women disqualified them for
work necessitating muscular force or sustained physical effort, their great
motor sensibility (*grande sensibilité motrice*) meant that industry could effectively utilize their distinctive ability to perform rapid and precise movements. As a result, Frois encouraged employers to modify machinery and
production processes in order to hire women.[25]

In addition to the naturalization of the link between women's bodies and
the machines on which they worked, the process of rationalization during
the war also included the establishment of industrial welfare policies
designed to regulate the body of the white female worker, with special
attention to her health and hygiene, pregnancy and domestic life. In the
silence on race in the discussions of labor practices and policies, one detects
the pervasive assumption that women were French and therefore white.[26]
Employers operated on the premise that healthy women would be the most
productive workers, but they were also specifically interested in protecting
the health and hygiene of the "mothers of the race". Women's wartime
munitions work was not to interfere with the reproductive capacities of
white French women.[27] Partly in response to the devastating mortality of

25. *Ibid.*, p. 84; Marcel Frois, *La Santé et le travail des Femmes Pendant la Guerre* (Paris and New Haven, CT, 1926), p. 62. Frois' concerns about the white female working body were echoed by British investigations into munitions workers for the Health of Munitions Workers' Committee in 1917 and 1918. See Cross, *A Quest for Time*, p. 117. Not all work scientists agreed about the employability of white women in "male" jobs. Jules Amar reviewed differences in the cardiograms of French men and women responding to the sound of the fall of a two kilogram weight. He found that the cardiograms showed strong changes in the women tested, but a negligable changes or none at all in the men – the difference attributable to women's sensation of fear and power-lessness and their greater emotional susceptibility; Mathilde Dubesset, Françoise Thébaud and Catherine Vincent, "Les munitionettes de la Seine", in Patrick Fridenson (ed.), *1914–1918: l'autre front* (Cahiers du Mouvement Social, 2) (Paris, 1977), pp. 189–219, 196, fn. 34. Amar's conclusions were bolstered by anthropometric data from the 1860s and 1870s that demonstrated women's inferiority to men in measures of height, weight, lung displacement (*capacité vitale*), thoracic volume, and muscular strength. Amar argued that in general "the shape of the body [...] provides a guide for the workers' choice of one form of work over another [...] normally, men are organized and constructed to work in a certain way because this is the way their work is most economical"; Amar, *Le Moteur humain*, pp. 148 and 148–178. Amar argued that as a general rule physical proportions determined professional aptitides. See also pp. 323–324 for Amar's attempt to classify men according to morphology or the "architecture of their bodies". Thus, he argued that "in the vast majority of work requiring great effort and sustained attention [*une attention puissante*], there is no place for women workers. They are more appropriate for office occupations". *Ibid.*, p. 606.
26. Immigrant colonial workers and workers of color during the war were overwhelmingly men. See below.
27. As Downs notes, the original intentions of the founders of the system, organized around republican feminist Cécile Brunschvicg, were to promote wage parity for women with men, over-

World War I, and French policy geared to improving population growth as a form of social and economic recovery, the women factory superintendents charged with overseeing the implementation of industrial welfare expanded their activities in the 1920s and 1930s and spent more time helping women reconcile their factory labor with maternity. In some of the automobile factories, they also supervised the establishment of home economics schools, sewing schools, and sports teams, all designed to help women maintain healthy bodies.[28] Thus the application of scientific management had a gender-specific dimension. The use of explicitly racialized colonial male labor during the war, however, complicated the attribution of gender characteristics to workers.

GENDER AND COLONIAL LABOR

Racialized male colonial labor was also employed in munitions work, occasionally side by side with white French women, and as Tyler Stovall has shown, French authorities regarded the intermingling of genders and races on the job with real concern. Such intermixing threatened to weaken the color boundaries that normally separated differently gendered and raced workers.[29] Despite the fact that the category "race" only entered work scientists' lexicon when they investigated male colonial workers, their observations of colonial workers threw into relief the ways that the white working-class European body was also a racialized body and simultaneously illustrated the instability of the category gender when inflected by race.[30] It also illustrated how class and race intersected in the minds of work scientists.[31]

During the war, the French government coordinated the hiring of some 222,000 colonial and foreign men from Tunisia, Morocco, Algeria, Indochina, Madagascar, and China on limited-term contracts of up to a year (with the provision that they return to their countries of origin at the expiration of the contract); colonial women did not migrate to France as a form of reserve army of labor. The vast majority of men were employed in munitions work. Work scientists paid close attention to these men's resistance to fatigue, and the experience revealed assumptions about how

see their working conditions, and ultimately to protect "women's maternal capacity through careful administration of the factory's welfare and maternal services"; Downs, *Manufacturing Inequality*, p. 177. Downs makes the important point that this system, managed by a corps of women factory superintendents, functioned as one additional component of the rationalizing impulse of the war and interwar years.
28. *Ibid.*, on the wartime activities of the superintendents, pp. 166–185, and pp. 233–275 on the interwar years; see also Fourcaut, *Femmes à l'usine*, pp. 200–207.
29. Stovall, "The Color Line".
30. I am indebted to Antoinette Burton for calling attention to these points.
31. Of course, these intersections occurred also in practice as Tyler Stovall demonstrates in "The Color Line".

differently racialized bodies governed perceptions of productive work.[32]
According to a report on the use of colonial and foreign workers during the
war, written by B. Nogaro and Lucien Weil (1926), productivity differed
according to the "unequal value and different aptitudes of the diverse races
[...]".[33] The report found Moroccans, Kabyles and Berbers to be "sturdy"
and "energetic", and suitable for industrial work (munitions), whereas Arabs
were more appropriate for agricultural work. The Indochinese (who
included Cambodians, Cochin-Chinese, Annamites, and Tonkinois) on the
other hand, tended to be "soft and submissive" and made good unskilled
workers for powder factories or agriculture. In thus feminizing the body of
the colonial male subject, Nogaro and Weil illustrated how racialized difference altered the gendered characteristics of bodies. In addition to endowing
Indochinese workers with the classically "feminine" characteristics of softness and submissiveness, the report considered that the Indochinese were
especially suitable for work "requiring dexterity as opposed to physical force" – the very characteristics most often claimed for work gendered female,
and associated with beliefs about women's superior fine motor coordination
and their "nimble fingers". "The Indochinese", it concluded, "[have] no
more strength than women".[34] Nogaro and Weil also observed physical differences among white Europeans: Greeks tended to be hardy and strong,
but resisted working out of doors; Portuguese peasants, on the other hand,
had considerable strength and made good agricultural workers. In contrast
to the instability of gender markings of colonial workers, with respect to
European workers, observers assumed both race and gender as stable, if not
normative categories.[35]

STUDYING GENDERED AND RACIALIZED BODIES BETWEEN THE WARS

Quite apart from the specific experience of the war, the cultural meanings
of gender and racialized difference entered the study of the body at work

---

32. See Stovall, "The Color Line", p. 747.
33. Nogaro and Weil, La main d'oeuvre étrangère, p. 26. There were approximately 30,000 North
African workers already in France prior to the war, most of whom worked as unskilled laborers
in mining and industry (p. 5). In 1915, the Undersecretary of State for Artillery and Munitions in
the Ministry of War hired several hundred Kabyle workers for artillery manufacture and the
Minister of Agriculture hired several hundred for agricultural work in the region south of Paris.
A more systematic mobilization of colonial labor began in 1916. On the differences in treatment
of European and colonial labor, see Stovall, "Color-blind France?".
34. Stovall, "Color Blind France?", p. 48. Stovall observes that during the war, such supposed
physical characteristics came to be viewed as a moral deficiency: laziness. Dexterity was the skill
most often associated with women, usually because of cultural beliefs about women's superior
fine-motor coordination and their "nimble fingers". See, for example, Downs, Manufacturing
Inequality, pp. 83–84.
35. Nogaro and Weil, La main d'oeuvre étrangère, pp. 49–50, 54.

independently of issues directly related to the war. Jean-Marie Lahy's critique of Taylor incorporated a gendered model of the industrial worker:

> One cannot abstract the worker from the man who takes part in social activities in which he occupies a more elevated position than in the factory. Head of the family, he assumes all the moral responsibilities that the direction of a household and the education of children imply; as a citizen, he participates in political life among the most active individuals.[36]

Lahy deserves credit for recognizing that work science could not treat the body of the worker as abstracted from the worker's gender or social and political identities, but his assumptions about the social and political significance of gender could not be mistaken. Nonetheless, Lahy's research showed the capacity of work science to move beyond stereotypical views of the productivity of gendered bodies, with potentially positive effects for workers. During the course of a labor conflict where women protested against piece rates that were twenty-five to thirty-five per cent lower than men's hourly wages, the conservative leader of the male-dominated Typographers' Federation, Auguste Keufer, defended the ideal of the *femme au foyer* and rejected women's appeals for the same hourly wage as men. When Lahy was asked to study the productivity of men and women workers to help resolve the dispute, he observed that women linotypists produced results "rarely outdistanced by men" and deserved the same wage as men. As for objections about the insalubrity of the work, Lahy replied that, "where women shouldn't be working, men shouldn't work either", implying that the health of the bodies of both men and women deserved to be taken into account.[37] But this was a relatively rare instance in which work science would abandon historical and cultural ideas about women's weakness or incapacity for work.

The work scientist Jules Amar, in studies published after the war, continued to leave unexamined centuries-old assumptions about the female body, despite the fact that women refused to disappear from industrial work and increased the ranks of public service workers after World War I. The second edition of his *Le Moteur humain*, published in 1923, reaffirmed age-old ideas about male and female difference, confusing physiology and gender. In studying the cranial capacities of French men's and women's brains, for instance Amar insisted that although he could discover no difference between men and women in the "quantity of energy produced" by their brains, he did see a difference in quality. "In the case of the woman, sensibility holds the first place; [...] In man on the contrary, abstract thought and reason come first."[38] Amar's next logical step was to insist that such

36. Lahy, *Le Système Taylor*, p. ix.
37. Ribeill, "Les débuts de l'ergonomie en France", p. 24. See also William H. Schneider, "The Scientific Study of Labor in Interwar France", *French Historical Studies*, 17 (1991), p. 418.
38. Amar, *Le Moteur humain*, 2nd ed. (Paris, 1923), p. 43.

characteristics produced the aptitudes that would allow employers to assess
the fit between workers and jobs and should be used as a basis of professional aptitude testing.[39] Amar's work on physiology consolidated gender
as a category defining the white worker: the maleness or femaleness of white
French workers was unambiguous. The meanings of gender when applied
to racialized workers were much more complex, as his work on colonial
labor demonstrated.

In his studies of the endurance and fatigue of North African men carrying
weights while walking and climbing, Amar attempted to classify racialized
difference, again introducing race as a category only applicable to colonial
subjects.[40] He recruited his subjects from petty criminals housed in the
Algerian prison of Biskra, reminding us of how male colonial subjects could
be mobilized – not only as a reserve army of labor (or as a reserve army *tout
court*), but in the service of European "science" as well. In North Africa he
could find men presenting "the physical and moral temperament of beasts
of burden [*le tempérament physique et moral du boeuf*]".[41] Amar claimed that
examination of the brain did not enable him to arrive at firm conclusions
about racial difference between Europeans and non-Europeans. Although
he claimed to have found that "the brain of the negro [...] is less massive
and less dense [than that of the European]", he argued that there was no
firm relationship between physiological characteristics and the laboring
capacities of colonial male workers.[42] At the same time, he concluded that:

> [...] the Muslims and the Kabyles are superior to all the Arabs in respect of the
> amount of daily labor of which they are capable, and the rapidity of their move-
> ments. More nervously constituted, they instinctively tend to work rapidly, and it
> is difficult to moderate the swiftness of their [motions].
>
> In industry and in the army, speed is a valuable factor, and presupposes a [...]
> neuro-muscular system which reacts without delay. The Berbers appeared to dis-
> play the vivacious reaction of the French workmen, while the other Arabs displayed
> the slowness of our peasants without possessing their tenacity.[43]

Although Amar's North African subjects allegedly showed no difference
from white, French-born subjects when carrying burdens on a flat surface,
Arabs proved to be less powerful than white Europeans or North African
Berbers when it came to climbing. Kabyles were deemed especially well-
suited to industrial work and physical exertion – true beasts of burden.[44]
Although the essential element of difference for Amar lay in the differential

39. *Ibid.*, p. 116.
40. On Amar's study of racialized bodies at work, see also Ribeill, "Les débuts de l'ergonomie
en France", pp. 14–16 and Camiscioli, "Labor Power and the Racial Economy", pp. 4–6.
41. Amar, *Le Moteur humain*, p. x.
42. *Ibid.*, pp. 43–44.
43. *Ibid.*, pp. 219–220. This observation also revealed how white French workers' characteristics
were defined. I am grateful to James Cronin for pointing this out.
44. *Ibid.*, p. 220.

labor power of white European and non-European bodies of color, despite their common racialized "affinity" not even all white Europeans shared the same physical aptitudes for work. Amar distinguished Italian from French workers, arguing that Italians "lacked energy" and did not seem capable of "the continuity of effort which our modern industries require [...]".[45]

This work also incorporated two important issues that preoccupied work science in the 1920s and 1930s in a world where the rationalization and regulation of the working body came to be seen as a solution to both the pervasive sense of cultural crisis and the palpable crisis of productivity in postwar France. One was the idea of selection – the application of work science to measure the worker's aptitudes in order to match the individual to the most appropriate job. Amar believed, along with nineteenth-century "solidarists", that scientific selection would create social harmony between capital and labor and avoid labor conflict. Work could then truly become a form of social integration and an instrument of social progress. These ideas received further attention after the war in the research of Henri Laugier, Henri Piéron, Edouard Toulouse, Julien Fontègne, and Jean-Marie Lahy, who worked in state-sponsored laboratories and institutes such as the *Conservatoire des Arts et Métiers*, the Henri Rousselle Hospital, the National Institute for Vocational Guidance, and research laboratories of the *École des Hautes Études en Sciences Sociales*.[46] A second set of issues concerned social and industrial hygiene and particularly the improvement of occupational health and safety and the prevention of work accidents.[47] It was perhaps not surprising that work science should receive the support of the state in the 1920s and 1930s, particularly since both French entrepreneurs and the

45. Amar, *The Physiology of Industrial Organization*, p. 204. See also Camiscioli, "Labor Power and the Racial Economy", p. 6. The only defect of the French laborer was that "his temperament is impulsive". Amar believed French workers needed better vocational training and better hygiene at work. He also believed that well-trained French workers should travel to the colonies to train native craftsmen. "Moreover, it is the duty of the European worker to direct native labor which is *naturally adapted to fatiguing kinds of work which would not tax the native's endurance as greatly as it would ours* [...]" (p. 210)[emphasis is mine – LLF].
46. See Schneider, "The Scientific Study of Labor". On how the arguments of these men transcended solidaristic arguments for marrying the interests of labor and capital, see Cross, *A Quest for Time*, pp. 120–122. As Cross also points out, in Britain work scientists believed that the increased leisure that would result from a shorter, more efficient working day and higher productivity would allow Britain to "build an improved race [...]" (p. 120). This is a not atypical example of the looseness with which the notion of race was used to reflect both whiteness and nationality. On the vocational guidance applications of work science, see also Mary Louise Roberts, *Civilization Without Sexes: Reconstructing Gender in Postwar France, 1917–1927* (Chicago, IL, 1994), pp. 183–196 and 206–211.
47. Much of the research of these laboratories was specifically directed towards the prevention of industrial accidents and focused on masculine jobs such as those of railway switchmen, tramway and bus drivers, welders, and mine workers. See, for instance, Lahy, *La Sélection psychophysiologique des travailleurs: conducteurs de tramways et d'autobus* (Paris, 1927) and articles in the review *Travail humain* founded by Lahy and Laugier in 1933. See also Schneider, "The Scientific Study of Labor".

state became preoccupied with rationalizing and modernizing industry and state services. Because of the way in which work science and the study of fatigue had defined gender and racialized difference, these issues likewise had gender and racialized dimensions.

RATIONALIZING THE TELEPHONE EXCHANGE

In the interwar years, the French combined elements of both Taylorism and work science in applying rationalization to selection and the division of labor. Although most studies of rationalization have focused on industry, the application of the scientific organization of work to the gendered bodies of workers occurred in service sector work with equal intensity. Office, clerical and secretarial work saw the distillation and implementation of scientific management and work science in the 1920s.[48] Operating under the assumption that "the organization of the office should be inspired by methods of industrial organization", a small number of French managers applied time and motion studies to evaluate the efficiency of office work, reorganize tasks, and replace skilled white male workers with young men and girls. In the accounting division of some offices, where men, long hired as accountants because of their alleged skill with numbers and fine penmanship, gave way to women typists, prized because of their "nimble fingers".

The modernization of the telephone service in this period also involved the application of work science and the scientific organization of labor to the rationalized workplace and illustrates the convergence of discourses about gendered and racialized bodies and workplace practices.[49] The aggressive feminization of the telephone service in the 1880s coincided with both a major economic depression and the dramatic expansion of the number of telephone customers.[50] The new *"dames employées"* constituted a distinct

48. See Delphine Gardey, "Un Monde en Mutation. Les Employés de Bureau en France, 1890–1930. Féminisation, Mécanisation, Rationalisation"; Thèse de Doctorat nouvelle régime. Université de Paris VII, 1995, pp. 824–833. See also Harry Braverman, *Labor and Monopoly Capital: The Degradation of Work in the Twentieth Century* (New York, 1974), pp. 306–326.

49. See "L'organisation méthodique du Travail et son Application aux Postes et Télégraphes", *Annales des PTT*, 8 (1923), pp. 835–976; "Le Téléphone en France et à l'Etranger. Progrès technique, organisation rationnelle", *Annales des PTT*, 8 (1923), pp. 565–598; "Administration industrielle", *Annales des PTT*, 2 (1917), pp. 356–386.

50. This story of the feminization of the French postal and telephone service is well told by Susan Bachrach in *Dames employées: The Feminization of Postal Work in Nineteenth Century France* (New York, 1984), pp. 30–50. See also Jeanne Bouvier, *Histoire des dames employées dans les Postes, Télégraphes, et Téléphones* (Paris, 1930); Dominique Bertinotti, "Carrières féminines et carrières masculines dans l'administration des postes et télégraphes à la fin du XIXe siècle", *Annales. ESC*, 3 (1985), pp. 625–640. The grade, *"dame employée"*, actually included all women working in the postal, telegraph and telephone (PTT) service; Bachrach, *Dames employées*, p. 42. On differential wages, see Bachrach, *Dames employées*; Pierrette Pezerat and Danielle Poublan, "Femmes sans maris. Les employées des postes", in Arlette Farge et Christiane Klapisch-Zuber (eds), *Madame ou Mademoiselle? Itinéraires de la solitude féminine, 18e–20e siècle* (Paris, 1984), p. 123.

division or grade of public-sector worker that was paid less than male operators and would not compete with men. The employment of white women operators as a distinct category moreover, illustrates how the postal and telephone service, *Postes, Téléphones et Télégraphes* (PTT), was already rationalized along gender and racialized lines from the very beginning. Rationalization and fragmentation of the "labor process" operated differently for men. Whereas women were hired as specialized workers from the very beginning, the postal administration was reluctant to force male labor to specialize in order to allow men to move from one job to another as need arose. As the civil service hierarchy grew more refined after World War I, men, too, became increasingly specialized.

Between the end of the nineteenth century and the turn of the twentieth century, the number of women operators soared, from 812 in 1891 to over 3,300 just after the turn of the century. After the war (1921), about 46,000 women worked in all services of the PTT, the vast majority as telephone operators; by 1936 the service employed over 56,000 women.[51] The administration believed that women's distinctive physical attributes made them good operators, although as well shall see below, the same characteristics could subvert the efficient operation of the system. The rationalizating impulses of Taylorism and work science came together in the 1920s and 1930s in the management of telephone operators in three ways: attention to the gendered and raced body in the selection of candidates; scientific studies of the working body; the regulation of physical space and surveillance; and concern about the health of the worker in the modern telephone exchange.

SELECTING THE OPERATOR

Selection of the telephone operator involved the construction of a new kind of public service worker whose class position was ambiguous. It was well known that state public sector work could be a means of upward social mobility. Although the young operator could be working-class, more often she came from the lower middle class, and she had to be armed with at least an elementary school certificate. Indeed, education ranked among the important criteria for selection and both before and after World War I, the administration (of the PTT) favored women candidates possessing teaching certificates.[52] All candidates took a battery of tests that included writing,

---

51. Madeleine Vignes, *Les téléphonistes des PTT* (préface de Madeleine Rebérioux) (Paris, 1984), p. 12; Bachrach, *Dames employées*, p. 69. Figures on the interwar period are not disaggregated by service, see République française. Ministère du Travail, de l'Hygiène, de l'Assistance et de la Prévoyance sociale, *Statistique générale de France. Résultats statistiques du Recensement générale de la Population* (1921, 1926, 1936) (Paris, 1922, 1928, 1937). Women counted for 22.5 per cent of PTT workers in 1906, 30.3 per cent in 1926 and 32.8 per cent in 1936.
52. Bachrach, *Dames employées*, p. 51; Bertinotti, "Carrières féminines", p. 637.

spelling, arithmetic, physical and political geography of France and the colonies, physics, and chemistry. They could also take an optional examination in English, German, Spanish or Italian. In addition, following a training period in telephone communication, successful candidates had to pass a practical test that included techniques of transmission and reception. The administration gave priority to women who were already employed in the postal service or who were the wives, widows, daughters, or sisters of former male employees who were either retired or deceased.[53] Although there was no marriage bar, about half of the women entering postal work were single and tended to remain so over the course of their employment.[54] Just after World War I, candidates had to be between seventeen and twenty-five years of age (except for widows or orphans of men who had been killed in the war or who had died as a result of war-related injuries, who could be as old as thirty); by 1930, the lower age limit had been raised to twenty-one years, presumably following the shift in the legal age of majority.[55] But beyond these formal requirements, selection criteria focused on physical attributes that theoretically could be verified during the course of an obligatory medical examination, but most of which had been already presumed as cultural and racial characteristics of the female body.

Beyond the formal requirements for admission to the examinations that permitted entry into public service work, selection included the more fundamental, gender and race criteria that fixed on the voice and body of the worker as the sites of skill and qualification. The future telephone operator had to be "*française*" and therefore white, living as she did, in the "shadow of colonialism".[56] "White" or "whiteness" did not appear as a formal category, even among those attentive to race, and it is unlikely that the administration of the PTT would have even thought of employing such a category between the world wars. Yet, her whiteness was already inscribed in her Frenchness, a term that by definition did not apply to colonial workers who would have been specifically identified as such. As a representative of the French state in her capacity as a public sector worker, she could by definition not be a colonial immigrant nor of uncertain accent, reminding us of how public sector work could serve as a privileged if not racialized

53. République française. Ministère des PTT, *Bulletin mensuel des PTT Janvier 1890* (Paris, 1890), pp. 315–316; *Bulletin mensuel des PTT*, 18 (1922), pp. 411–415.
54. See Pezerat et Poublan, "Femmes sans maris", pp. 129–130, who report that in 1921, fifty per cent of all female postal workers were widowed, divorced, or unmarried. Although this figure incorporated the effects of male mortality during the war, it was consistent with low marriage rates among women postal workers before the war. The vast majority of male workers, on the other hand, tended to be married.
55. *Bulletin mensuel des PTT*, 18 (1922), p. 411; République française. Ministère des PTT, *Bulletin officiel du Ministère des PTT*, 17 (1930), p. 694.
56. The phrase is Rayna Rapp's, (personal communication to the author). On the requirements for admission to the competency examinations where these criteria were spelled out, see, for example, *Bulletin mensuel des PTT*, 18 (1922), pp. 411–415.

enclave, and reminding us as well that race is also about cultural competence.[57] Colonial women – especially North African Muslim women – would not have passed the tests of cultural competence as the French administration had defined them, even if cultural constraints on work did not exist for them. The post-World-War-I reconfiguration of sexual politics in the African colonies that gave white French women a specific role as the bearers of white Frenchness contained within it an unmistakable subtext against which Frenchness had to be defined. Observers of colonial life called attention to the Muslim women's dissimulation in wearing the veil, suggesting that they were untrustworthy; others criticized Arab cultural practices as "debauchery" and remarked on the hygiene of colonial subjects, which failed to meet French standards.[58] Even the male colonial workers who had been gendered female by work scientists were not admitted to the competitive entrance examination. The future operator was required to submit a certificate attesting to her good moral character [*certificat constatant qu'elle est de bonne vie et moeurs*] signed by the mayor or the police commissioner of her town of residence. Significantly enough, the administration did not require character references for male candidates.[59] After World War I, residents of the provinces of Alsace and Lorraine could take the examination in either French or German, but if they were unable to take it in French, they could only hope to work in the departments of the Haut-Rhin, the Bas-Rhin and the Moselle.[60] Thus, constructing the public service worker also incorporated the reaffirmation of a certain representation of Frenchness and a nationally, if not racially, marked femininity.

57. Cultural competence also incorporated "civility", and itself contributed to the construction of Frenchness within the public service. See Elias, *The Civilizing Process.*
58. See Alice Conklin, "Redefining 'Frenchness': France and West Africa", in Julia Clancy-Smith and Frances Gouda (eds), *Domesticating the Empire: Race, Gender, and Family Life in French and Dutch Colonialism* (Charlottesville, VA and London, 1998), pp. 76–83. Janet Horne places somewhat more emphasis on white French women's "civilizing" work among Muslim women in North Africa whose wearing of the veil was considered a form of dissimulation and whose hygiene was by implication not up to French standards; Horne, "In Pursuit of Greater France: Visions of Empire Among *Musée* Social Reformers, 1894–1931", *ibid.*, pp. 37–41. A somewhat different picture was painted by Hubertine Auclert in her *Femmes arabes en Algérie* (1900). See Julia Clancy-Smith, "Islam, Gender, and Identities in the Making of French Algeria, 1830–1962", in Clancy-Smith and Gouda, *Domesticating the Empire*, pp. 168–172.
59. This difference suggests that nineteenth-century suspicions of the woman worker and especially the single woman worker remained alive in the period after the Great War. On those nineteenth-century suspicions, see Scott, "'L'Ouvrière, mot impie, sordide', [...]" and "A Statistical Representation of Work", in *Gender and the Politics of History* (New York, 1988).
60. Thus, "race" was also complicated by regionality – an employee who spoke with a thick regional accent was not acceptable unless her pronunciation could be "corrected". Moreover, "Frenchness" was still a category that distinguished among and between French women of different social, regional, and educational – as well as racial – backgrounds. I am grateful to James Cronin for raising this point. See République française. Ministère des PTT, *Bulletin mensuel des PTT*, 18 (1922), p. 412; *Bulletin officiel du Ministère des PTT*, 17 (1930), p. 695.

SCIENCE STUDIES THE OPERATOR: THE BODY AS
MACHINE

As work science developed and influenced the thinking of state managers
in the their goal to modernize and improve telephone communication, the
body became a new focus of attention. Women's pleasant voices, their
alleged inherent patience and politeness, self-control, even-temperedness,
aimiability, and "malleable character"; all figured among the "qualities" that
made women desireable as operators, much as these same characteristics had
been used for decades to justify the employment of women in other contexts.[61] But work scientists and vocational guidance experts Julien Fontègne
and his collaborator, Emilio Solari also gave serious attention to women's
physical aptitudes for the work. In their work, the cultural meanings of
gendered bodies underpinned science and what passed for modernity, and
those cultural meanings were also racialized.[62]

Unlike work scientist Jules Amar, who rarely left his laboratory, Fontègne
and Solari studied their subjects in the workplace. They attempted to
develop the specific criteria that would determine whether a young women
had the requisite physical aptitudes to be an operator. They studied the
operator's routinized, repetitive movements performed rapidly and precisely
in response to lights flashing on a switchboard. As soon as a caller picked
up the telephone at home, a light appeared. The operator put a pin [*fiche*]
attached to a cord into the jack, flicked a switch or pressed a button into
the speaking position and immediately said "*j'écoute*" [I hear you]. She then
attempted to secure the number by touching the end of another pin to the
jack of the corresponding number and putting the switch into the listening
position to ascertain if the number was free. If it was, she introduced the
pin into the jack and flicked another switch to signal the caller that the
number was free. Once the person being called picked up the phone, and
the connection was made, the lights went out. At the end of the conversation, the lights corresponding to caller and receipient went on and the
operator registered the call with another switch and removed the pins. The
operator repeated these mechanical movements hundreds of times in the
course of an hour – the operators who Fontègne and Solari studied placed

61. See also Michele Martin, "*Hello Central*': *Gender Technology and Culture in the Formation of
Telephone Systems*. (Montréal, 1991), pp. 58–60; Bachrach, *Dames employées*. See also Julien Fontègne and Emilio Solari, "Le Travail de la Téléphoniste. Essai de psychologie professionnelle",
Archives de psychologie, 17 (1918), p. 92.
62. See Fontègne and Solari, "Le Travail de la Téléphoniste". Roberts argues that in debates about
vocational guidance, the French attempted to "reconcile the ongoing modernization of economic
and social life with time-honored cultural traditions"; Roberts, *Civilization Without Sexes*, p. 187.
I am not so sure there was that much reconciliation to be done in matters of gender. The
points of departure for both modernization and "cultural tradition" were the same: both already
incorporated cultural notions of gendered bodies.

between 160 and 180 calls an hour; during busy periods they had to handle up to 350 calls an hour.[63]

From their examination of the work, Fontègne and Solari developed a list of physical and psychological aptitides of the ideal operator. She should be tall, with long arms and a supple and elastic upper body. She needed good eyesight and hearing, a strong back, clear respiratory passages, and a normal digestive apparatus. In addition, she needed a good auditory memory for numbers; she had to be capable of sustained attention and be ready to respond at any moment. As Fontègne and Solari noted, this activity was very different from that of the office worker "who could put off work from one day to the next". The telephone operator needed to be able to react instantly to a variety of simultaneous stimuli including differently colored flashing lights and the sounds of callers. A good operator had to be able to demonstrate great rapidity and precision of movement. In short, she needed good nerves – a quality that men did not possess and which made them less desireable as operators.[64] So, whereas in many contexts women had been excluded from jobs because of their "nervous qualities", scientists now rejected "muscles" in favor of "nerves", and argued that women's physical difference from men – their allegedly greater nervousness, their ability to move rapidly and react quickly to external stimuli, their capacity to give sustained attention to work, qualified them for the job. The gendered body itself and the nerves in particular constituted the locus of aptitude.[65] The characteristics that Fontègne et Solari described were ideally suited to the Taylorized environment of the telephone exchange.

REGULATION AND CONTROL

Work scientists' criteria for the ideal operator were incorporated into the medical testing of candidates and into the handbook issued to young

---

63. Fontègne et Solari, "Le Travail de la Téléphoniste", pp. 85–86 and 95.
64. *Ibid.*, pp. 93–95. Work science was applied to telephone operators even more aggressively in the Netherlands. See Robert Korving and Gerard Hogesteeger, "Psychotechnik bei der PTT Niederlande", in Helmut Gold and Annette Koch (eds), *Fräulein vom Amt* (Munich, 1993), pp. 120–134. On male operators, see Bouvier, *Histoire des dames employées*, p. 179.
65. Good nerves, of course, were not enough; Amar judged the Muslim and Kabyle men he tested to have good neuromuscular systems and display a capacity for quick reactions to stimuli, but they were never considered for this kind of work in France. Nor is it clear that they performed public sector work in the colonies. The qualities that work scientists and the state believed made women especially fit to be telephone operators illustrated the instability of gendered categories of skill. The shift from muscles to nerves as the desirable female quality that made women good operators involved a reversal of the frequent criticism of women's presumed "nervous" qualities. Thus women's supposedly inherent "nervousness" that made male workers criticize women's inappropriateness for certain tasks in the defense industries during World War I, for example, enabled them to be effective operators in the eyes of the PTT.

operators, the *vade-Mecum de la téléphoniste*.[66] This guide, which instructed new operators in the basic techniques of the work, claimed that unless workers understood the reasons for each task, "unconscious Taylorism" would transform them into robots, deprived of thought and initiative.[67] But the handbook was really designed to regulate and discipline workers. It appropriately reminded operators to instill confidence in and maintain the confidentiality of the customer and guided them in dealing with irate or impatient callers. In addition, it instructed them in the correct placement of the heavy apparatus of headsets and adjustments of the microphone, which had to be kept at a few centimeters from the mouth so as to alleviate unnecessary stretching and straining of the neck.[68] The operator's dress was also important. Metallic necklaces, bracelets, or wristwatches were forbidden because of the possibility of accidents from electric shocks or their ability to inhibit movement.

The rationalized work of the operator involved the meshing of body and machine. She was literally linked to the switchboard by the headset. The left hand operated the keys or switches; the right hand the pins. Even the voice was regulated, especially its timbre: one shouldn't speak loudly; it was sufficient that the voice was clear and articulate. "The syllables must be rhythmically separated so that they can be easily heard. One must not force the voice, but seek to fill the microphone with its volume; [...] one must shape one's words into the microphone [...] Pronounce not a single extraneous word." The motions of the hands had to be supple and precise. All stray motions had to be avoided.[69]

The desire to build a modern and efficient communications network – for greater productivity, in effect – brought with it more rigid organization of space and the body, accompanied by an even more precise definition of the operator's motions.[70] Indeed, the modern telephone exchange proved to be a model of rational discipline and control. It consisted of an enormous, long room whose walls were covered with switchboards. Women sat in straight-backed chairs close to a horizontal board of buttons and switches (the "table") and had to reach up to fit the pins into the appropriate jacks on the board. But discipline and regulation involved more than the spatial rationalization of the body. It also involved intense competition between operators and supervision to keep track of performance as a way of facilitating promotion.[71] Competition between operators became a vehicle of providing rapid and efficient service for customers. It was as if the white

66. E. Rougier, *Le vade-Mecum de la téléphoniste* (Paris, 1927).
67. *Ibid.*, p. 7.
68. *Ibid.*, pp. 10–11.
69. *Ibid.*, pp. 12–13 and 17.
70. Catherine Bertho, *Histoire des télécommunications en France* (Toulouse, 1984), p. 75.
71. See Vignes, *Les téléphonistes des PTT*, p. 23 and Dominique Bertinotti, *Artisans d'hier et communications d'aujourd'hui, 1850–1950* (Paris, 1981), p. 14.

female body had been transformed into a human motor: a tool of modernization of the public service.

The system of supervision and notation established by the administration
also encouraged competition. Stationed at regular intervals in the hall,
women supervisors (one supervisor for every ten to twelve operators) over-
saw the smooth operation of the system. Some walked up and down behind
the operators armed with clipboard and stopwatch to check periodically on
the number of calls operators put through, and kept records of errors,
"grading" the women on their performance. Another group of supervisors
randomly listened in on the operators, monitoring their calls for quality.
Operators found themselves under constant pressure to speed up the placement of calls. Grades became the basis of promotion. Absences from one's
post, even to go to the restroom, were frowned upon – an operator couldn't
simply get up to leave; she had to raise her hand and wait for the supervisor
to give her permission to vacate her post. Although the administration had
women work in shifts during the course of the day (from 7 a.m. to noon
and from noon to 7 p.m., with another shift from 7 p.m. to 9 p.m.) and
established rooms where women could lie down and relax periodically for
fifteen minutes every two hours, managers attempted to extract as much
effective labor as possible from the body of the operator. Thus, women who
worked a shift from 7 am to noon had to return in the evening to put in
another two hours from 7 p.m. to 9 pm. Women who took sick leave were
obliged to put in extra hours (known as a "return", *retour*), upon returning
to work, or lost the rest period. As Jeanne Bouvier, labor organizer for the
CGT remarked in her study of the *téléphonistes*, "[they lost] one franc a day
during [an] absence and invariably [saw] their grades drop, thereby interfer-
ing with [...] possibilities for promotion".[72]

Regulation also extended from the telephone exchange into the arena of
private life. Marriage, housing, and leisure all fell within the purview of the
postal and telephone service. Despite the absence of the marriage bar,
women who wished to marry had to make a formal request, by furnishing
the administration with information about the person whom they intended
to marry.[73] In order to house the large numbers of young women who came
to Paris from the provinces but who could hardly afford Parisian rents, the

72. Bouvier, *Histoire des dames employées*, p. 182. Women did resist some of these practices,
although the majority of the labor struggles were directed not at the constraints of rationalization
and work discipline, but at pay scales, poor opportunities for advancement and the elimination
of the *dame employée* as a separate category with assimilation of women into the categories reserved
for men.

73. See République française. Ministère de Commerce, de l'Industrie et des Colonies, *Bulletin
mensuel de Ministère de Commerce, de l'Industrie et des Colonies*, 1 (1890), p. 315. This requirement
remained in effect through the 1930s. It was based on the principle of incompatibity of certain
public services (operators could not obtain authorization to marry policemen or mayors or assistant
mayors, for example) and operated as another element of regulation. See Bouvier, *Histoire des
dames employées*, pp. 204–205.

administration built dormitories complete with "company" restaurants, such as the *Maison des dames* on the rue de Lille, just behind the former Orsay railway station (now the *Musée d'Orsay*). These dormitories regulated the operator's off-work hours; they could also, by means of the restaurant, provide some control over the health of the worker. In addition, the administration provided artistic, musical and sports clubs designed "to combine grace with dexterity", in an attempt to fill the leisure time of the young worker with rational, self-improving activities.[74]

"LA NEVROSE DE LA TÉLÉPHONISTE"

Although the operator's work seemed to be a model of regulation and control of the human motor, the same physical aptitudes that scientists and employers believed made women especially well-suited for the job also proved to be a liability. The rationalization of the telephone exchange produced a new focus on the body of the worker – occupational illness. Doctors reported on the *"nevrose de la téléphoniste"*, a catch-all term for the nervous exaustion and multiple auditory and psychological problems operators experienced. Operators sought medical help for electric shocks, acute ringing in the ears or facial neuralgia brought on by defective headsets; some presented symptoms of depression, irritability and personality disturbances verging on hysteria. One doctor reported that in the latter, "one finds that the suggestion that the patient return to work is met with cries, sobs, and convulsions". He observed that "women are naturally more exposed to this malady [*la névrose des téléphonistes*] than men".[75] But he also argued that what disturbed the "fragile brains of the *Parisienne*" was defective headsets and overwork. All the frustration of customers fell upon the operator. His solution was to perfect the headsets and recruit only young women with perfect hearing and healthy nervous systems.[76] Other doctors also noted nervousness and headaches, stomachaches, insomnia, and back pain, all of which contributed to this professional illness, "nervous fatigue". Thus, the very qualities of the body that made women desirable workers – their "nerves" – in the rationalized telephone exchange threatened the very rationalization of the system.[77]

74. Rougier, *Le vade-Mecum de la téléphoniste*, p. 24. The focus of these activities as well as of the housing arrangements for operators was the single women who made up the majority of telephone operators. Telephone operators, along with other postal workers, were awarded paid maternity leave in 1911. See (anonymous) "La Poste au Féminin", *Référence*, 7 (1984), p. 17.
75. Dr Clapart (fils), *Maladies et Accidents professionnels des téléphonistes à Paris* (Paris, 1911), p. 12–17. This was very likely because of the fact that the vast majority of operators were women who worked on the busy daytime shifts.
76. *Ibid.*, p. 19.
77. This is probably why Alexander Millerand, Minister of Public Works and the PTT in 1910, had proposed creating a revolving recruitment of young operators who would be encouraged by a system of bonuses to leave the administration at age twenty-five and who, in any case could work no longer than age thirty-five. See "Le Nouveau recrutement des téléphonistes", *L'Action*, 23

ORGANIZED LABOR REACTS

Labor's consent to the claims of work science shows how workers, if not always sympathetic to scientific management, saw promise in work science. Telephone operators' delegates to the 1922 Congress of the National Postal Workers' Union (the *Syndicat national des Agents des PTT* [CGT]) favored work scientists' and doctors' recommendations for aptitude testing. They called attention to the physical effort, the weight of the headset, mental exhaustion, and the large number of sick leaves taken by operators and proposed more careful screening of the body – a more serious medical examination that "would focus on the overall physical constitution [of the candidate] and included a scrupulous auscultation and examination of the respiratory passages [...] [to determine] the physical aptitudes for the work".[78] Delegates' insistence that good selection would permit employers to find the right person for the right job and thus benefit workers was echoed by the claim of other delegates that "[organizing] our working conditions in the most scientific and rational way" would allow workers to obtain "superior productivity with less effort".[79] In 1925, the *Syndicat national* took up the issue of professional training for both men and women, this time both in response to the demands of telephone operators and in reaction to more general complaints about the poor quality of the telephone service. This time workers blamed the engineers of the PTT for the problems with the service and proposed using the research of Lahy, Fontègne, and Solari for guidance to end operators' overwork. This would allow the administration to introduce "more humanity in the length of rotations, breaks, and regulation". Lashing out at the "Taylor system", as "devoid of any humanitarian concern", workers condemned Taylorism as "coming from the cold brain of an engineer who is only concerned with the output of human material", and asked for the development of a psychotechical laboratory in the PTT Administration on the model of laboratories that had been developed in Germany, to investigate scientifically the problem of operators' fatigue.[80] Thus, postal workers argued that work science could be an antidote to the worst abuses of Taylorism.

February 1910. The rationale was to replace an ageing corps of operators with fresh blood. Since they were considered "floating personnel" they could be easily let go, permitting the administration to save money or adopt new technologies without worrying about the seniority of public service workers. The project was never adopted. On the concern with "nervous fatigue", see Cross, *A Quest for Time*, p. 113.

78. Syndicat national des Agents des PTT (CGT), *IVe Congrès des Agents des PTT tenu à Paris les 19–22 avril 1922* (Limoges, 1922). See especially the intervention of Mme Stanko, delegate for the operators, pp. 130–132. On labor's reaction to Taylorism, see Cross, "Redefining Workers' Control", and *A Quest for Time*; Ribeill, "Les Organisations du Mouvement", pp. 127–140; Fridenson, "Un tournant taylorien".

79. *IVe Congrès des Agents des PTT*, pp. 107, 140. See also discussions in this congress on specialization and the scientific organization of labor.

80. Syndicat national des Agents des Postes, Télégraphes et Téléphones (confédéré), *VIIième Congrès national tenu à Toulouse les 10–13 juin 1925* (Epernay, 1925), pp. 268–283. One delegate's

However, employers (and in this case, the state) tended to be more interested in organizing and disciplining the female body at work than addressing the problem of fatigue in more than a perfunctory manner. In a detailed report published in 1958 on work and fatigue, that focused on the operators' "neurosis", the writer expressed astonishment at how little had changed since the findings of Fontègne and Solari early in the century on operators' nervous fatigue.[81] Yet, the comparatively little attention given to the problem was entirely consistent with the productivist, modernizing thrust of economic policies of the interwar period. As Georges Ribeill and others have noted, work science was expensive and time-consuming; the rational organization of labor according to Taylor's principles appeared to give better returns for a smaller investment. And these workers were, after all, only women.

CONCLUSIONS

Historians of the French working class have already begun to show how gender and gendered meanings of work and the worker constituted "class" in the nineteenth and twentieth centuries.[82] But until very recently "race" has been an absent or problematic category in much working-class history of France, where the myth of republican inclusion may have obscured the workings of racial difference in shaping the meanings and cultural practices of class.[83] Re-examining scientists', employers', and the state's attention to working bodies however, suggests that these groups used both gender and racialized difference in defining class. Beginning in the late nineteenth century Europeans could invoke science to measure and regulate the body of the worker in order to serve the logic of capitalist command. The purpose of work science was to provide scientific foundations for the division of labor, not to question the cultural foundations of divisions according to

suggestion that a solution to the problem of operators' fatigue would be to introduce men into the telephone exchanges was laughed off. On the German use of psychotechnics, see Horst Gundlach, "Psychotechnische Untersuchungen bei der Deutschen Reichspost", in Gold and Koch, *Fräulein vom Amt*.
81. Dr D.P. Begoin, *Le Travail et la Fatigue. Le Névrose des Téléphonistes et des mécanographes*, special number of *La Raison*, 20/21 (1958).
82. See, for example, the essays in Frader and Rose, *Gender and Class in Modern Europe*; and Downs, *Manufacturing Inequality*.
83. Tyler Stovall's excellent work, cited above, is an important exception. There has been much work, of course, on the subject of racism in post-World-War-II France. An abundant literature has examined immigration and the salience of cultural and ethnic difference in shaping working class identities in the interwar and post-World-War-II periods (see, for instance, Nancy Green, *Ready-to-Wear, Ready-to-Work: A Century of Industry and Immigrants in Paris and New York* (Durham, NC and London, 1997) especially pp. 188–218 and 251–279). However, most historical work on immigration does not address the category of race nor does it attempt to theorize the meanings of racial difference in France, particularly in relation to France's colonial empire. This work remains to be done.

gender or racialized difference. Rather, with few exceptions, work science, in conjunction with scientific management, reproduced those divisions faithfully and reinscribed differences on the bodies of workers.[84] In doing so they reinforced the meanings of race and gender with respect to white French workers, while their work threw into relief the instability of the meanings of gender in the case of workers of color. In either case, those cultural meanings of gender and race attached to the body helped shape the meanings of class, influenced the shopfloor practices of both managers and the state, and served the French state's flirtation with modernity on the floor of the telephone exchange.[85]

84. Of course, those differences dictated the terms of "scientific" investigation itself.
85. See Roberts, *Civilization Without Sexes*, p. 210, who cites Marjorie Beale, that the French adopted "techniques of social management [...] in order to preserve what they saw as traditional social relations and cultural traditions".

International Review of Social History 44 (1999), Supplement, pp. 149–169
© 1999 Internationaal Instituut voor Sociale Geschiedenis

"Blood Is a Very Special Juice"*: Racialized Bodies and Citizenship in Twentieth-Century Germany

FATIMA EL-TAYEB

The 1999 plan of the Social Democratic government to adjust Germany's 1913 nationality law has generated an intensely emotional debate. In an unprecedented action, the opposition Christian Democrats managed to gather hundreds of thousands of signatures against the adjustment that would have granted citizenship to second generation "immigrants" born in Germany.[1] At the end of the twentieth century, Germans still strongly cling to the principle of *jus sanguinis*. The idea that nationality is not connected to place of birth or culture but rather to a "national essence" that is somehow incorporated in the subject's blood has been strong in Germany since the early nineteenth century and has been especially decisive for the country's twentieth-century history.

The myth of blood has intertwined with that of "race"; both imply the heredity of mental traits that connect people otherwise not related. Images of race belong to the West's "deep structure", voiced in different manners and to different degrees in different political systems and times, but always there.[2] The conjuncture of "race" and "blood" therefore, has proven resistant to political changes. Germany, with its national identity that through almost the whole of the twentieth century and four political systems has been explicitly based on "blood", is a case in point.[3]

This article explores the roots of the German self-definition in larger Western concepts of identity that are deeply racialized and often manifested through gendered constructions relating to sexuality. Legal exclusion generated by those concepts centered on "race" rather than other possible forms of distinction. German blood implicitly meant "white blood", be it in the

---

* Johann Wolfgang von Goethe, *Faust* I (1808), verse 1740.
1. The 1913 law grants the right of naturalization to "ethnic Germans", who have lived outside of Germany for generations, while "ethnic foreigners", who have lived within Germany for generations, are denied the same right. Thereby, an evergrowing number of "cultural Germans" is created, who are treated as foreigners solely because they miss the qualification of "German blood". See Rogers Brubaker, *Citizenship and Nationhood in France and Germany* (Cambridge, MA, 1992).
    The Christian Democrats' action had no direct political consequences since German law does not allow plebiscites on national issues. Nevertheless it has proven decisive, because the government was forced to compromise after losing the majority in the *Bundesrat* (representing the German states) in elections that centered on the issue of nationality.
2. See e.g. David T. Goldberg, *Racist Culture. Philosophy and the Politics of Meaning* (Cambridge, MA, 1993).
3. For the post-World-War-II-period, this article concentrates on the federal republic, the political system transferred to the reunified Germany.

imperial Germany of the 1910s or the federal republic of the 1960s. Accordingly, in this century public and scientific discourses around national identity often centered on relationships between white Germans and blacks as representatives of the most "foreign blood" and on the danger of the latter entering and tainting the "German blood". This thinking caused racist exclusions in systems that did not consider themselves based on racial thinking.[4]

Changes in the political climate had little influence on the attitudes towards interracial relationships, but it did make a difference whether they involved black men and white women or white men and black women. Race and gender appear as interdependent factors, with class being a less significant independent variable in the construction of national identity.

RACE, SEX, AND SCIENCE

With the rise of the Enlightenment in seventeenth-century Europe came a shift from "faith" to "knowledge". Christianity lost its position as sole and unchallenged ideology and the world was no longer divided between the faithful and the unbelieving, but rather between man as rational, responsible being and man as savage. The construction of the white man as the embodiment of all the qualities of civilization and rationality necessarily needed a counterpart that lacked all these qualities and continually confirmed the white race's superiority. The "black race" was systematically built up as this counterpart. This is not to deny that in Europe, men defined women as other before the idea of races even existed. But the hierarchy of races was central to the construction of a modern Western identity that needed to distance itself both from the rest of the world and its own medieval self. Modern Western gender identity therefore was not about being male or female, but about being *white* and male or female.

The alleged connection of physical and mental "racial qualities" immediately gave the concept of races an ideological function; it never was a neutral description of biological facts. Instead it worked to stabilize the new bourgeois order by replacing the aristocracy of "blue blood" with that of "white blood", creating new bonds and loyalties. Meanwhile it justified slavery and colonialism, since the creation of a natural order that granted full humanity only to whites meant that mechanisms of exploitation and oppression unacceptable among them could be labeled "civilizing mission" when directed against other "races": "The races are not meant to play the same role in history, and the lower races have to serve the uses of the higher ones. The uses of the higher ones are the 'aims of humanity', because only they

---

4. The period of National Socialism with its explicit connection of nationality and race will therefore not be considered here.

represent the highest form of intellectual human power."⁵ Divided into numerous small states, Germany played little part in the slave trade and early colonialism, but its intellectuals were crucial to establishing the new world order that constructed the "savage native" as fundamentally and inherently different.⁶ This might be connected to the country's particular geographical position. Placed in the center of Europe, it had always known a mixture of cultures, flows of immigration and emigration. Lacking a national structure, there was little apart from language that connected the regions that were later to form Germany. The invention of a national myth accordingly did not concentrate on an actually shared cultural and political history, but on an idealized German "spirit", passed on not by nationality or culture but by blood.⁷ Since the myth of the "white race" was created on quite similar terms, the concepts intertwined, defining Germans through their position as "crown of the white race".

Following Darwin's theory of evolution, in the late nineteenth century the "science of races" aimed at developing a method that paralleled the growing disciplines of natural, "exact" sciences. Its proponents tried to discover the "natural laws" that governed humans and human society, creating a model of the world that had race – and nothing else – at its core. All over Europe and the United States, men trained in such disciplines as biology, zoology, history, and above all medicine, turned their attention to race as the last answer to all human questions.⁸ Race had always determined the course of history and continued to do so in the present. The antagonisms of gender and class were secondary compared to this, in fact, they had to be overcome in order to strengthen Europe for the great eternal war between the races.⁹ The problem faced by black men and women – that whatever they did they could never be anything but "other", simply because they were not white – took different forms for oppressed groups within white society. But their otherness was not absolute: they were "normal" instead of

5. Ludwig Woltmann, "Die Klassen- und Rassentheorie in der Soziologie", in *Politisch-Anthropologische Revue*, (1905/6), p. 424. All translations by the author.
6. See e.g. Immanuel Kant, *Von den verschiedenen Rassen der Menschen* (1775) and Johann Friedrich Blumenbach, *De generis humanis varietate nativa* (1795).
7. For details on the construction of the German national myth see Helga Schultz, "Mythos und Aufklärung: Frühformen des Nationalismus in Deutschland", *Historische Zeitschrift*, 236 (1996), pp. 31–61.
8. For the influence racist Social Darwinism gained in the West, see e.g. Michael Banton and Jonathan Harwood, *The Race Concept* (London 1975), p. 42; George L. Mosse, *Towards the Final Solution. A History of European Racism* (New York 1978) and David T. Goldberg, *Racist Culture*.
9. While being extremely hostile towards all ideologies that denied the central position of race, some Social Darwinists nevertheless attempted to develop a "Germanic" socialism. They could identify with socialist concepts as long as they were applied only within the "white race" and believed that the white working class incorporated more of the race's "true qualities" than the decadent and weakly middle and upper classes. See e.g. Ludwig Woltmann, *Die Darwinsche Theorie und der Sozialismus* (Düsseldorf, 1899).

"other" in interracial relations, where "white" remained monolithic in spite of actual divisions. White women were considered inferior by white men, as were workers by the bourgeoisie, but non-white people were required to see all whites as superior to them. There was no such requirement for white women where black men were concerned or for white workers regarding a non-white middle class. To save civilization and humanity, after all, the superior, but comparatively few, "pure whites" had to stick together and keep the inferior masses subjected.

Historians often assume that Germans did not participate in the movement of scientific racism, at least where it was concerned with the "black race", that anti-Semitism was somehow Germany's "substitute" to the racism prevailing in other countries.[10] Actually, the German school of "social anthropology" was among the leading in the world and its major journal basically focused on three subjects: northern Europeans and particularly Germans as the "true whites" and therefore perfect humans; the black race as the eternally most primitive variety of humanity; and racial mixing as the source of all social problems and "re-aryanisation", i.e. restrictive population politics, as their solution.[11] Before World War I, much less attention was paid to Germany's Jewish minority; afterwards though, the racism of the social anthropological press became distinctively and aggressively anti-Semitic.

Historians, national economists and anthropologists considered the race scientists' ideas on the white and yellow race oversimplified and extreme.[12] Academia did not doubt, however, that "race" was a useful category in analyzing historical and social processes and concerning their attitude towards the black race, the Social Darwinists were rather mainstream. That Africans constituted the most primitive kind of humanity, separated from the civilized Europeans by a wide biological gap, was a notion that had been well established by the early twentieth century.[13] Even critics of the

---

10. See e.g. Banton/Harwood, *The Race Concept*, p. 42; Reiner Pommerin, "*Sterilisierung der Rheinlandbastarde*': *Das Schicksal einer farbigen deutschen Minderheit 1918-1937* (Düsseldorf 1979), p. 11, and H. Friedlander, *The Origins of Nazi Genocide: from Euthanasia to the Final Solution* (Chapel Hill, NC, 1995).

11. See *Politisch-Anthropologische Revue* (*PAR*), founded in 1901 by Ludwig Woltmann, published until 1914 and then continued under the name of *Politisch-Antropologische Monatszeitschrift*.

12. Criticism was provoked by the race scientists' division of the "white race" into northern, southern and eastern Europeans, leaving the "Nordics" as the only "true whites", while east Europeans were supposedly "tainted" by Asian and south Europeans by black and Semitic blood, and by the assumption that Asia never produced an autochtonous civilization (i.e. one that was not created by "Aryan invaders"). See a.o. Erwin Baur *et al.*, *Grundriss der menschlichen Erblichkeitslehre und Rassenhygiene* (Munich, 1923), pp. 413–415.

13. Nothing was more damaging here, probably, than Georg Wilhelm Friedrich Hegel's judgment of Africa as "the continent without history". In effect it placed Africans outside the realm of humanity but nevertheless for almost two centuries was not really taken into question; *Vorlesungen über die Philosophie der Geschichte* (Stuttgart, 1945), p. 144.

racist ideology merely insisted that blacks could reach the intellectual level of the other races if removed to the right surroundings.[14]

Since the academic world was exceptionally united in its judgment of the black race, society was likely to accept it. Accordingly, the race scientists' obsession with the dangers of racial mixing became common wisdom: miscegenation could only lead to degeneration of the superior white race. This extremely negative attitude logically sprang from the assumption of a strict racial hierarchy. Nothing threatened the "natural order" more than a blurring of the supposedly clear boundaries between the races: the existence of people with a mixed heritage undermined the dogma of the different races being clearly separable and actually mutually exclusive. Accordingly, "mixing" between the black and white race was condemned as "unnatural" and disastrous not only for the offspring itself but for all mankind. Both Social Darwinists and the general public believed that "bastards" were stale, inherited only the negative qualities of their "parent-races" and had such an uneven psychic constitution that they were naturally driven to crime and mental distortions: "The often physically and mentally extremely disgusting products of such relationships tend to combine the drawbacks, weaknesses and mistakes of both races, of the strength of the white father and the beauty of the colored mothers those split-births usually inherit nothing."[15] "Mixed blood" as the ultimate threat to the West meant miscegenation as the ultimate sin. More than any other form of interaction, society outlawed sexual contact between the races. At the same time, all other racial stereotypes were dwarfed by the West's obsession with black sexuality. In fact, this obsession became constitutive for the discourse on sexuality itself.

Retrospectively, the race scientists seem like reactionary fanatics, but they saw themselves – and were seen – as taking part in the pioneering process of substituting fiction with fact, establishing truly objective methods and founding modern Western science. They shared this belief with disciplines such as eugenics and sexual sciences. All these "modern sciences" were based on the idea that the human body, if only scrutinized and categorized neatly enough, was the key to all secrets of human nature. Replacing charity and social politics with the "natural laws" of the body, these Social Darwinists argued, would automatically create the perfect society. A "natural" elimination of the "inferior" and ruling of the "fittest" would reverse the current "degeneration", i.e. the "deviant" dominating the "normal". Race as well as sexuality were key words in this process.

Sexuality was at the very center of the modern civil society; it was, after all, the antidote to civilization. It was nature in its purest form, "the wild animal" in all of us, the one thing that could break down the control of the

14. See e.g. Friedrich Hertz, *Rasse und Kultur* (Leipzig, 1915), p. 150.
15. Friedrich Richter, *Zeitschrift fuer Kolonialpolitik, Kolonialrecht und Kolonialwirtschaft*, 7 (1905), p. 664.

mind over the body and thus of civilization over nature. In this, it recalled another discourse, as Ann Laura Stoler analyzed for the nineteenth century:

> The nineteenth-century discourse on bourgeois sexuality may better be understood as a recuperation of a protracted discourse on race, for the discourse on sexuality contains many of the latter's most salient elements. That discourse on sexuality was binary and contrastive, in its nineteenth-century variant always pitting that middle-class respectable sexuality as a defense against an internal and external other that was at once essentially different but uncomfortably the same. The contaminating and contagious tropes of nineteenth-century sexual discourse were not new: they recalled and recuperated a discourse that riveted on defensive techniques for constant purification'.[16]

Only whites were believed to be able to domesticate their sexual instincts and thereby to create order from chaos. But whereas all other races were viewed as lacking in this respect, blacks were associated with sexual aggression. Similarly "black blood" was seen as especially aggressive in polluting the white race: one drop was enough. As with all the other determinants of modernity, the normalization of sexuality began with a dualistic division. Whites were rational, moral and controlled, whereas blacks were emotional, amoral and driven by their instincts. Only after this division was established and white superiority again confirmed, was the white population itself categorized according to this standard, finally leaving as completely normal only the white, heterosexual, middle-class male. All those who were not, e.g. prostitutes and homosexuals, and often the working class as whole, were deviant exactly for the same reason that blacks in general were. Those groups were not only believed to have the mental, but also the physical characteristics of the "primitive races". At the same time, such "deviations" as prostitution and homosexuality were considered dominant practices within African societies, and blacks were believed to be "natural" members of the working class.[17]

Through this binary division, blacks gained a high symbolic value for a European bourgeoisie that was in the process of defining itself: anti-civilizatory forces were symbolized by unrestrained sexuality and unrestrained sexuality was symbolized by blacks. As this derived from a projection of both Western fears and desires, it resulted in a complex, at times contradictory construction. Dominant however, was the image of Africans in their "natural state", designing to males and females alike an overpowering sexual drive and identifying the threatening, uncivilized, "dark" field of sexuality with the threatening, uncivilized, "dark continent" of Africa. Of course, the reduction of blacks to their alleged sexual nature

16. Ann Laura Stoler, *Race and the Education of Desire: Foucaut's History of Sexuality and the Colonial Order of Things* (Durham, NC, 1995), p. 193.
17. See e.g. Max Dessoir, "Zur Psychologie der Vita Sexualis", *Allgemeine Zeitschrift für Psychiatrie und psychologisch-gerichtliche Medizin*, (1893), p. 142.

had consequences for their perception in terms of gender. Black men were not "real men", since they missed the intellectual and moral qualities that justified male dominance, but at the same time, they symbolized the essence of maleness, an excess of "normal" male sexual aggression. This aggression was assumed to be directed against whites. There was an almost automatic reference to black men's "natural" drive to rape white women, whenever white oppression needed to be portrayed as mere self-defense.

Control over the white female body was a privilege of rational man – and a necessity. Only he could protect her from the black beast. White man's control of the black female body on the other hand, was central to both slavery and colonialism. Literal control in form of rape left no "safe space" and penetrated every aspect of the subjected's life, asserting power over black women and men. Metaphorical control completely objectified the black woman, turning her into the absolute other and the victim into the perpetrator:

> Images of Black [...] women in "heat" versus "frigid" White women mythically elide the history of subordination of Third World women by First World men. The hot/frigid dichotomy implies three interdependent axioms within the sexual politics of colonialist discourse: first, the sexual interaction of Black [...] men and White women can *only* involve rape (since white women cannot possibly desire Black [...] men); second, the sexual interaction of White men and Black [...] women *cannot* involve rape (since Black [...] women are in perpetual heat and desire the White master); and third, the interaction of Black [...] men and Black [...] women *also* cannot involve rape, since both are in perpetual heat.[18]

Scientific analyses of black sexuality focused overwhelmingly on women.[19] In the course of the nineteenth century, black female sexuality came to be viewed as inherently pathological in opposition to the virtuous and passive nature of white women. This not only justified white men's sexual violence against black women, but also their oppression of white women. To keep society in balance and check the potentially subversive force of sexuality, male aggression had to be counterbalanced by female passivity – and not only where sex was concerned. In the white mind, black women not only violated the gender code, but their behavior, deemed pathological, deprived them of male protection. What this meant for her position in a racist society was made quite clear within colonial Germany.

IMPERIAL GERMANY AND THE "OTHER"

Since German colonial activities lasted only from 1884 to 1914, they are often neglected as irrelevant to both the German society and colonial history

18. Ella Shohat/Robert Stam (eds), *Unthinking Eurocentrism: Multiculturalism and the Media* (London, 1994), p. 157.

19. See Arthur Brittan and Mary Maynard, *Sexism, Racism, and Oppression* (Oxford, 1984); Paula Giddings, "The Last Taboo", in Toni Morrison (ed.), *Race-ing Justice, En-Gendering Power* (New

in general.[20] This perception requires correction. German colonialism put the race theories already dominating the public mind into practice on a broad scale. This did not only change the colonized countries but also the colonizer. A movement of "colonial enthusiasm", massive government propaganda supported by the country's strong nationalist groups, buttressed the acquirement of overseas territories. Aiming at presenting colonialism as necessary for Germany's survival as one of the world's "leading nations", it readily deployed Social Darwinist theories.[21] Exhibitions of "natives" in zoos, "scientific studies" distributed freely to schools, and the widely popular colonial novels popularized the racial theories that had already conquered academia.[22] The idea of a necessary domination of Germans over peoples too primitive to govern themselves quickly became commonly accepted. The Social Democrats (SPD), while criticizing colonial "excesses", agreed in principle, even though "colonial enthusiasm" aimed at alienating workers from the increasingly influential SPD by presenting it as "unpatriotic" and "anti-colonialist".[23] Unemployed, i.e. potentially dangerous, members of the working class were supposed to find a new home in the safely removed colonies. According to the Social Darwinist framework, race solidarity would replace class antagonism as whites of all classes were presented with a people that could be formed into a dependent and racially-separated working class. A popular colonial writer stated:

> In the context of world history, only the necessity to give up their free national barbarism and to become a class of servants to the whites gives the natives the right to exist. As for individuals, so it is for peoples that the useless have no right to live and that an existence is the more useful the more important it is for the general development.[24]

York, 1992), pp. 441–470, and Sander L. Gilman, *Sexuality: An Illustrated History* (New York, 1989).

20. The German colonies were Togo, Cameroon, "German Southwest Africa", "German East Africa" and parts of New Guinea, Samoa and the Solomon Islands.

21. There were numerous personal and ideological correspondences between the race scientists and the nationalist organizations, mainly the German Colonial Society (*Deutsche Kolonialgesellschaft*) and the Pangerman League (*Alldeutscher Verband*). The colonial department of the Ministry of Foreign Affairs, in its turn, relied heavily on the expertise of both the colonial society and individual race scientists. See: *Bundesarchiv Berlin* (BAB), R 1001 *Reichskolonialamt*, Bd. 5418, "Rechtsfragen bei Mischehen und Mischlingen".

22. See Sybille Benninghoff-Lühl, *Deutsche Kolonialromane 1884–1914 in ihrem Entstehungs- und Wirkungszusammenhang* (Bremen, 1983). The country's most popular teenage novel, selling half a million copies up to 1918, was Gustav Frensen's *Peter Moors Fahrt nach Südwest* (1906), describing the colonial war in Southwest Africa.

23. See: Gustav Noske, *Kolonialpolitik und Sozialdemokratie* (Stuttgart, 1914), p. 56. The international socialist congresses of Amsterdam, 1904, and Stuttgart, 1907, also principally supported colonialism (*ibid.*, p. 223).

24. Paul Rohrbach, *Deutsche Kolonialwirtschaft* (Berlin, 1909), p. 17. Rohrbach, a colonial inspector who published several "scientific" books on life in Southwest Africa, became the "voice" of German settlers.

The truth of these Social Darwinist beliefs remained unquestioned. Accordingly, the German self-image underwent a crisis when the Herero and Nama in the biggest colony, "German Southwest Africa" (now Namibia), began a revolt in 1904 that, despite using an unheard number of soldiers and amount of money, could not be suppressed until 1907. The German response led to a genocide leaving only one-quarter of the Herero alive. The commander of the German troops justified this extermination by claiming the revolt as "the beginning of a race war".[25] After they regained power, the Germans established a system of control and oppression that was unique in the world and later became model for the South African apartheid system.[26] It included the destruction of the traditional community and family structures, complete expropriation, mass deportations, and passes and workbooks for all "natives" from the age of eight onwards. This system of forced work actually amounted to slavery (including physical punishment, rape and killings of "rebellious workers"). Africans appeared exclusively in terms of the Social Darwinist ideology and neither government nor white population doubted that the "fittest" held the right to oppress the "weak".[27]

The war in Southwest Africa generated much publicity in Germany. In 1906 the Social Democrats voted against further war credits (costs had amounted to almost 600 million Reichsmark) and Parliament was dissolved. The ensuing elections became known as *Hottentotten-Wahlen* ("hottentotts" being the derogatory name for the Nama). They ended in substantial losses for the SPD, since the country's conservative forces managed to present the colonial war as a cause that united all patriotic Germans and isolated those groups that questioned the colonialist practice. The publicity that went with the election campaign not only further established the racist ideology in German society, but also brought violations of the code of strict racial separation into focus.

The vast majority of the 12,000 German settlers in Southwest Africa was male. That relationships between them and African women were common consternated nationalists and race scientists. As early as 1896, the German Colonial Society began to finance the emigration of white women to the colony in order to stop the "bad habit of marriages between German men and hottentotts".[28] African women were triply conspicuous, after all. They were members of the "opposite race", separated from the whites by such a wide gap that the only communication could be that between master and

---

25. Helmut Bley, *Kolonialherrschaft und Sozialstruktur in Deutsch-Südwestafrika 1894–1914* (Hamburg, 1968), p. 205.

26. South Africa took over Southwest Africa as a mandate in 1920.

27. The attitude towards the inhabitants of the Pacific Island colonies was mellower; they were considered "distant cousins" (with the exception of the "Negroid" Papua New Guineans) and an eventual independence due to the cultural "uplifting" by the Germans was seen as a possibility. See Paul Rohrbach, *Die Kolonie* (Frankfurt a. M., 1907), pp. 100–102.

28. *Deutsche Kolonialzeitung*, 1896, p. 197.

servant. They were members of the opposite sex, incorporating all the
aspects of female sexuality that white women were supposed to lack (or
suppress), i. e. basically a wild, primitive, organic nature. And they belonged
to a class that was associated with the animalistic.

The body was the site for these characteristics: early twentieth-century
discourse reduced the black woman to her sexual organs.[29] Their "monstrous
size" proved her monstrous character.[30] White women who violated the
dogma of female sexual passivity, prostitutes and lesbians, were assumed to
have those same physical abnormalities, but black women were abnormal
per definition. Accordingly, the white attitude towards black women was
extremely aggressive: they were portrayed as revolting, but at the same time
assumed to be always sexually available. Their individuality did not have to
be recognized; they were part of an interchangeable, anonymous black mass.
Sexual contacts that reaffirmed this hierarchy were granted, marriages and
long-term relationships were not. After all, the Social Darwinist equation
of body and society meant that individuals had relevance not as such but
only as members of the race.[31] White settlers in mixed relationships therefore
were "race traitors"; in fact they ceased to be proper members of the white
race and degenerated to the level of their black partner. According to
Southwest Africa's governor:

> Not wife and offspring are raised to the level of the white husband and father, but
> the man is sinking to that of the woman. His house will not be the home of
> German ways and German family life, but he will squander and degenerate in his
> hut that will be dominated by the nature of the woman and that will, after initial
> resistance, lower the man to the sphere in which the woman is born and feels
> comfortable in.[32]

The biggest crime, though, was the production of mixed-race offspring that
had access to the German nationality and could therefore irreversibly "pol-
lute the nation's white blood". During the colonial war the authorities had
already taken measures against miscegenation. From 1905 onwards all

29. Sometimes as literal as in the case of Sarah Bartmann from South Africa. After being publicly
displayed in several European cities as an example of black females' pathological sexuality
(symbolized by her enlarged buttocks), she died in 1815. Her genitals were first scrutinized by
several scientists and then donated to the *Musée de l'homme* in Paris, where they are still exhibited.
See Paula Giddings, "The Last Taboo", p. 445.
30. A character, which had been established earlier. Hegel's description of man-eating African
Amazons, a classical castration fantasy, is the only example he gives of African political systems,
(Georg Friedrich Wilhelm Hegel, *Vorlesungen*, p. 142). White racism obviously also includes an
obsession with the size of black male genitals, though they never became the topic of a similarly
elaborate scientific discourse.
31. Or, as contemporary sociobiology puts it, as "carriers of genes".
32. Theodor Leutwein, *Elf Jahre Gouverneur in Deutsch-Südwestafrika* (Berlin, 1908), p. 232. See
also Albert Raibmayr, *Inzucht und Vermischung beim Menschen* (Leipzig, 1897), p. 51.

marriages between whites and "natives"[33] were declared illegal (including those already existing), mixed-raced children were denied access to schools[34] and German men married to or living with African women were excluded from all German institutions in the colony, and could not vote, buy land or get financial support from the government.[35] Social pressure in the colonial society thus resulted not in a loss of class status but in expulsion from a white community that included all classes.

All these measures aimed to prevent people of mixed ancestry legally becoming Germans, which would have both given them the right to acquire property in the colonies and to settle in Germany. Even more important were political rights like voting, which would have turned them from passive objects of German politics into active participants in the decision-making process.[36] Actually, the vast majority of the children of white settlers and black women was illegitimate, and including them with the powerless "natives" posed no legal problem. Only the churches favored bringing up mixed-raced children in special institutions. Removed from their mothers' negative influence, missionaries believed, they could develop the qualities of their fathers' race that made them superior to "pure blacks", so that they later could be used as mediators between white rulers and black subjects.[37]

Despite confirming to the dominant ideas, the government's practice of generally treating non-white and German as exclusive categories violated German laws that did not forbid marriages on grounds of race and granted citizenship to wives and children of German men. In the wake of the war in Southwest Africa, race scientists and nationalist groups started a debate to end this unclear legal situation. They desired either changed laws or reasons to limit citizenship to "pure whites" within the existing system. For the most part, this debate took place in the conservative mainstream press, liberal or progressive papers hardly caring about the subject at all. The only dissenting voice thus came from the churches, but an outline of the debate shows that this dissent was quite ambiguous.

The principled social anthropologists held the first position. They did not mind how large – or small – the mixed-race population in the colonies

---

33. Colonial law for Southwest Africa defined each person as a "native" that had an African ancestor, however far removed. See: BAB, R 1001, Bd. 5418, pp. 364–379.

34. Accordingly, many settlers married to African women sent their children to Germany.

35. See: *Evangelisches Zentralarchiv Berlin* (EZB), 5/3016: *Die deutsche evangelische Gemeinde in Windhuk*, p. 117; "Stärkung des weissen Rassenbewußtseins", *PAR* 1906/7, p. 423. Between 1906 and 1908 similar laws were introduced in the other German colonies.

36. The image of the wicked, but smart mulatto who incites the passive "natives" to rebellion was very vivid in the German imagination. See *PAR* 1905/6, p. 112 and 469; 1906/7, p. 256.

37. At least three such institutions, limiting education to gardening and cooking, existed in Southwest Africa. See EZB, 5/3016, p. 99 and pp. 198–199.

or Germany itself was, one drop of black blood was enough to poison the whole German nation. Miscegenation was a crime against nature and all sexual contacts between the races had to be outlawed.[38] Accordingly, they favored a radical change of laws.[39] The proponents of this most extreme position could use the authority of Germany's leading expert on "racial mixing", the anthropologist Eugen Fischer, who had stated:

> If there is the *probability*, or even the mere *possibility* that bastard blood damages our race without the realistic chance that it will improve us, *any absorption must be prevented*. I take this to be so absolutely obvious, that I can consider any other point of view only as that of complete biological ignorance [...] this is about the *survival* – I choose my words consciously – of our race, this has to be the main criterion, ethical and legal norms just have to be secondary to that.[40]

Those unconcerned with racial mixing as a matter of principle took a second, more pragmatic stand. Their interest lay in preventing any person of mixed ancestry from becoming a German national. Accordingly, they focused on the legitimate children of white settlers and black women, favoring an addition to German laws that would explicitly exclude those children. In 1908, the Colonial Society topped its list of recommendations to the government with the demands that "no colored can acquire the German nationality" and that "marriages between coloreds and whites in the colonies cannot be registered. Children of those marriages are considered coloreds."[41] At the same time, proponents of this position looked for ways of interpreting existing marriage laws in a manner that would achieve their aims, e.g. by claiming that no African could fulfill the legal marriage qualification of "mental sanity".[42]

Both the Catholic and the Protestant churches held a third position.

---

38. Indeed, the numbers were not quite in relation to the reactions. In 1909, there were fifty "mixed marriages" and 4,284 "mulattos" registered in Southwest Africa. See Theodor Gentrup, *Die Rassenmischehen in den deutschen Kolonien* (Paderborn, 1914), p. 32.

39. Twenty-five years later, fascist laws introduced this change by severely punishing all sexual relations between "Aryans" and members of "foreign races".

40. Eugen Fischer, *Die Rehobother Bastards und das Bastardisierungsproblem beim Menschen* (Jena, 1913), p. 303, (italics in original). Fischer, who in the Weimar Republic became head of the *Kaiser Wilhelm Institut*, center for all eugenic and anthropological research, and who successfully continued his career under the National Socialists and in the federal republic, had built his reputation on publishing "the first scientific study" of racial mixing (conducted 1908 in Southwest Africa). Using new methods, namely Mendel's laws, he came to the same old conclusions: "bastards" were inherently inferior, dangerous and unnatural. Interestingly enough, up to this day his work on racial mixing is considered groundbreaking.

41. "Bericht über die Jahreshauptversammlung in Bremen, 12 Juni", *Deutsche Kolonialzeitung (DKZ)*, (1908), p. 441.

42. V. Fuchs, "Zur Frage der Mischehen zwischen Reichsangehörigen und Eingeborenen in Deutsch-Südwestafrika", *DKZ*, (1909), p. 38. See also: H. von Hoffmann, "Die Mischehenfrage", *DKZ*, (1909), p. 793 and J. Friedrich, "Die rechtliche Beurteilung der Mischehen nach deutschem Kolonialrecht", *Koloniale Zeitschrift*, (1909), p. 361.

They vehemently opposed any restriction of marriage rights. Nevertheless, they too condemned interracial marriage and racial mixing. Their opposition mainly sprang from the fact that governors in the colonies had not only outlawed civil but also religious marriage ceremonies between whites and blacks. That was trespassing into a territory that the churches considered exclusively their own. Consequently, they were ready to compromise as long as they remained in control of religious ceremonies. In fact, they were quite eager to show that they principally agreed with the Social Darwinists:

> Christian morality demands – our opponents might say – that the colored wives and mulatto children acquire the German nationality with all legal consequences, Christian morality wants to force the bastardization of the German nation! No, that is not the conclusion. Christianity simply demands that a possible relation between the white [man] and the colored woman should be legitimate, it does not judge on its legal position. Should the German government think it wise to refuse the colored elements entry into the community of citizens, Christianity will not protest.[43]

In 1912, when the Secretary of Colonial Affairs sought legalization of segregationist policies in the colonies, the debate reached Parliament. Social Democrats and the catholic center party managed to pass a parliamentary measure that forbade marriage bans on grounds of race. While this appears quite progressive on the first look, it had no positive effect on colonial practice. Also, supporters of the measure unanimously condemned racial mixing and agreed to a limited citizenship for black Germans. One argued: "As long as the cultural development has not progressed in such a way that the natives are culturally equal to the Europeans, it is acceptable that they [children of mixed marriages] e.g. will have limited voting rights."[44] All parties agreed that "German" and "white" belonged together. The law that the colonial secretary had introduced suggested that a small group of mixed-raced persons should be considered German, whereas the rest forever lost the right to apply for membership in this category. First however, this privileged group had to be legally redefined as "white". Similarly, the opponents of marriage restrictions advocated full civil rights only for those "mulattos" who by looks and character somehow qualified as "white". Of course, this attitude required rather twisted thinking, but left the unity of nationality and race intact.

In practice, both the Secretary of Colonial Affairs, who had ended his speech against the measure with the exclamation: "We are Germans, we are whites and want to stay whites",[45] and the governors of the colonies refused

43. Theodor Gentrup, *Rassenmischehen*, p. 90–91. See also *Denkschrift des Ausschusses der deutschen evangelischen Missionen*, 3 September 1912, p. 61.
44. MP Gröber of the Center-Party in Theodor Gentrup, *Die Rassenmischehen*, p. 42.
45. *Ibid.*, p. 41–42.

to act on the parliamentary decision, so that marriage bans kept on existing
until Germany lost its colonies in the First World War.

This debate over "Germanness" likely influenced parliamentary discussions around the nationality law of 1913. Both cases show the triumph
of biologist definitions of "German". The nationality law took pains to
differentiate between citizens, i.e. persons of German nationality but not
necessarily German ethnicity (as constructed by science), e.g. Poles in Prus-
sia, and Germans, i.e. persons of "German blood" but not necessarily
German nationality, e.g. Baltics. The latter category was seen as the more
relevant, since identity was not built around a community of citizens, but
around the community of "Germans".[46] That this necessarily meant
exclusion and division of the population according to scientifically-sanctified
but highly questionable racial categories became increasingly obvious.

THE CIVIL SOCIETY

The end of the First World War brought about democracy in Germany
and the Social Democrats gained control of the government for the first
time. But this shift failed to transform society's attitude on race. In the first
place, this attitude did not appear to be political; it rather stemmed from
"scientific discoveries". In the new republic, with its numerous social reform
movements and trust in (scientific) progress, Social Darwinism continued
to gain influence.[47] Accordingly, dominant ideas about races still relegated
blacks to the bottom of German society.

The nationality law of 1913 did not deprive mixed raced children fathered
by German men of German citizenship (even though that clearly meant
something different than being German), but Africans from the former
colonies living in Germany could not gain this status, instead they were
handed "foreigners' passports", leaving them – and their families – in effect
without nationality.[48] Naturalization was theoretically possible, but German
authorities assumed that Africans in general could not reach the required
moral, educational and economic level.[49] Of course, this was a self-fulfilling
prophecy. Science had concluded that blacks, when living in a society with

46. See EZB, 5/340: *Reichs- und Staatsangehörigkeitsgesetz*, pp. 3, 7, 8 and 28.
47. An example of continuity in spite of political changes is the "Society for Racial Hygiene".
Founded in 1905 as a politically and religiously neutral organization (only open to whites, though),
by 1916 it included virtually all important biologists and anthropologists in its ranks. By 1920
lectures on racial hygiene were part of the curricula of all German universities and in 1926 the
state-financed *Kaiser Wilhelm Institut* for anthropology began to co-ordinate all research in anthropology, biology and eugenics. See Peter Weingart *et al.*, *Rasse, Blut und Gene. Geschichte der
Eugenik und Rassenhygiene in Deutschland* (Frankfurt a. M., 1988).
48. A parliamentary motion to grant citizenship to children of German women married to stateless
men (aimed at Danes in Northern Germany) failed out of concern that it would cover those
mixed marriages. See BAB, R 1001, 61 Kol DKG 1077/1, p. 230.
49. BAB, RKA–4457/7, p. 64.

whites, due to their genetic inferiority automatically formed the underclass.[50] Therefore, their choice of work was restricted to what was considered appropriate for their race. An unusually high number of Africans in Germany had come to study, but the majority ended up as musicians, circus artists and manual workers.[51] A fairly typical black German family history recalls:

> My father, Kala King, was born in 1895 in Duala, Cameroon, which was a German colony then. He came to Germany before World War I [...]. He studied to become a teacher. His idea and that of the Germans was that he'd return to Cameroon after finishing his studies. But things turned out different: he met his wife and decided to stay in Germany. As an African, he couldn't work in his profession of course, no one would have given him a job as a teacher. So they decided to become Vaudeville-dancers.[52]

Moving to the men's home countries was not an option for interracial couples, either. German planters and companies, still largely in control of the excolonies' economies, strictly refused to employ Africans married to white women.[53]

In the colonial period already, it had become obvious that relationships between black men and white women were even more threatening to the white world order than the reverse case, which had dominated discussions in the 1910s. Central argument to the rejection of interracial contacts had been "the honor of the white woman". It was in danger when white men preferred black women, but more so, of course, when she was directly involved and in the worst case, actively. Imperial Germany was shaken by several scandals around relationships between white women and African men. The press reacted with great shock, especially because the women involved were from respectable middle class backgrounds.[54]

The Social Darwinist literature, of course, completely ignored the possibility of consensual relationships. It could not fathom this worst threat to the natural order – the white woman, mother of the race, betraying it, mating with black men and producing "bastards". Instead, the supposedly enormous sexual drive of black males, "naturally" directed towards unwilling white women, became the most popular argument for the necessity of the racial hierarchy. Half-hearted attempts at explaining this drive were secondary to describing its effects. Blacks had so long been characterized as

50. See e.g. Baur *et al.*, *Erblichkeitslehre und Rassenhygiene*, p. 412.
51. See: Katharina Oguntoye, *Eine afro-deutsche Geschichte. Zur Lebenssituation von Afrikanern und Afro-Deutschen in Deutschland von 1884 bis 1950* (Berlin, 1997), pp. 56–60.
52. Astrid Berger, "Sind Sie nicht froh, daß Sie immer hierbleiben dürfen?" in Katharina Oguntoye *et al.*, *Farbe bekennen. Afro-deutsche Frauen auf den Spuren ihrer Geschichte* (Berlin, 1986), p. 115.
53. See BAB, R 1001, 61 Kol DKG 1077/1, p. 86.
54. See BAB, R 1001–1077/1, p. 219 and DKZ 1909, p. 593/4. As a consequence of the scandals the Ministry of Foreign Affairs prohibited the immensely popular public exhibitions of "natives". See Sander L. Gilman, "Black Sexuality and Modern Consciousness", in Rheinhold Grimm and Jost Hermand (eds), *Blacks and German Culture* (Madison, WI, 1986), p. 36.

irrational, impulsive and overtly sensual, that it seemed only logical that they could not exercise the sexual restraint that was so central to contemporary Europeans. Therefore, permanent white male control was necessary to produce the ideal black male: childlike, subservient, asexual and non-threatening. Any divergence from this principle immediately evoked elaborate visions of the black beast, bent on raping white women and destroying the white race. The French occupation of the Rhineland in 1919 exposed the extent of this paranoia.

That part of Germany was controlled by the French "archenemy" was a visible and exploitable symbol of Germany's defeat. Of a much higher symbolic value, however, was the presence of several thousand Asian and African soldiers among the French troops. As soon as the peace talks began, the Social Democratic German government based its protests against the occupation, meant to last for fifteen years, on the presence of these troops. Subsequently, they became targets of a campaign against the "Black Horror on the Rhine" that was orchestrated by the government, financed by the industry and supported by all influential groups of society: political parties (only excepting the communists), churches, nationalist groups, women's organizations, professionals and scientists. The hysterical campaign, that had hundreds of thousands followers all over Europe and North and South America focused on the image of the "primitive African beast" that roamed around the streets of a civilized nation raping and killing: "Victims of the endless bestiality of the black monsters are found dead in fields and trenches, their clothes torn to pieces, some with bites that clearly show how the animal fell upon its pitiful victim."[55] The numerous propaganda material indulged in detailed descriptions of alleged acts of sexual violence, giving the campaign a pornographic tinge. This focus on the most powerful racist image succeeded in creating a racial solidarity that overcame deep national and political antagonisms.[56] From an aggressor responsible for the first "world war", Germany was turned into a helpless victim of black aggression.[57]

There were marked differences to the discussions of the 1910s, most notably rape in the earlier case had not been a topic, since the men involved were white and the victims black, but there were also crucial similarities. Again, despite the small number of mixed-race children, warnings against the "bastardization" of Germany abounded. And not only in propaganda-pamphlets, a medical journal asked: "Shall we silently endure that in future

55. Joseph Lang, *Die Schwarze Schmach. Frankreichs Schande* (Berlin, 1921), p. 8.

56. For an overview of the campaign and the decisive role e.g. the British socialists played in it see Robert C. Reinders, "Racialism on the Left: E.D. Morel and the 'Black Horror on the Rhine'", *International Review of Social History*, 13 (1968), pp. 1–28.

57. An inquiry conducted by the British Foreign Office in 1920, that showed the unfoundedness of the accusations against the black soldiers, did not have any influence on the continuous propaganda. See *ibid.*, p. 10.

days not the light songs of white, beautiful, well-built, intelligent, agile, healthy Germans will ring on the shores of the Rhine, but the croaking sounds of greyish, low-browed, broad-muzzled, plump, bestial, syphilitic mulattos?"[58] The massive reactions to several hundred black Germans among millions of white compatriots reveals the impact of the racist Social Darwinism: every single black German had a high symbolic value. To admit that one at the same time could be German and black had become impossible, since both terms were treated as contradictory racial categories. The systems' logic demanded that exceptions were impossible. Only within this line of thought does the genuine belief make sense that "in the long run this is about the survival or decline of the white race".[59] Accordingly, black Germans and the relationships that produced them had to be defined as deviant, as consequences of an abnormal situation: "Those mulatto children are either products of violence or the white mother was a whore. In both cases there is not the least moral obligation to this racially foreign offspring [...]."[60] They violated an idea of racial normality that was so crucial to the country's identity that it made more sense to adjust reality to ideology than the other way round:

> May France and other countries handle their race matters as they please, for us there is only one thing: elimination of anything foreign, especially in those damages caused by brute violence and immorality [...]. Sterilization of all mulattos that the Black Horror on the Rhine left us![61]

Since the children, usually referred to as "Rhinelandbastards", for the most part were born to unmarried German women within Germany, a Germany that was still under observation of the Allies, there could be no denial of citizenship. Also, contrary to the nationalist groups within Germany and supporters in other countries, the German government did its best to suppress the subject of mixed-race children, since research among the white mothers had shown that only one of them claimed to have been raped – a fact that was considered quite embarassing.[62] Nevertheless, the government initiated lists of mixed-race children (not only those fathered by soldiers) and considered several solutions to the "problem". That the existence of black Germans did constitute a problem was beyond doubt for the authorities. The original idea of transferring all of them to Africa had to be given up, since Germany had lost its colonies and could not expect co-operation

---

58. Friedrich Rosenberger, *Ärztliche Rundschau*, Nr. 47/1920, in Heinrich Distler, *Das Deutsche Leid am Rhein. Ein Buch der Anklage gegen die Schandherrschaft des französischen Militarismus* (Minden, 1921), p. 56.
59. Joseph Lang, *Die Schwarze Schmach*, p. 16.
60. Hans Macco, *Rassenprobleme im Dritten Reich* (Berlin, 1933), p. 13–14.
61. *Ibid.*, p. 16.
62. Reiner Pommerin, *Sterilisierung der 'Rheinlandbastarde': Das Schicksal einer farbigen Deutschen Minderheit 1918–1937* (Düsseldorf, 1979), p. 23.

from other colonial powers. The second plan of sterilizing them could not
be put into practice since the necessary consent of the mothers could not
be gained and it was feared that the Allies would not react favorably to such
a measure.[63]

The National Socialists, gaining power in 1933, were not disturbed by
such considerations. Using the existing lists and the enthusiastic support of
the race scientists, forced sterilizations of several hundred black Germans
began in 1937. According to fascist laws, they also lost their citizenship, the
right to work, go to school or study and to own property, and an unknown
number of them was sent to concentration camps.[64]

"DON'T LOOK SO SAD, JUST BECAUSE YOU'RE A LITTLE NEGRO": BLACK GERMANS IN THE FEDERAL REPUBLIC[65]

The second German democracy attempted to break with certain traditional
structures that had proven fatal, but national identity was not among them.
The citizenship law of the young republic was the same one that defined "Germanness" since 1913 in a restricted, biologist sense that showed no trace of *jus
soli* aspects. Accordingly, the confusion of race/ethnicity and nationality that
went with it remained; it was assumed that in the case of Germany the different categories were indeed one. This meant that the situation of those who
violated the image of German ethnic uniformity did not change. Black Germans, who had lost their citizenship under National Socialism, had massive difficulties regaining it in the Federal Republic. One woman recalls:

> I reapplied for German citizenship. And 1963 I got it, finally. They even asked me
> whether I had a voucher for losing it. What madness! I had to write a German
> essay to prove I could write without mistakes. My certificate of baptism and all
> other documents didn't count, I was treated like a foreigner.[66]

Since the existence of a population that was not white and still German was
as unthinkable after 1945 as it was before, history was both ignored and
repeated. The persecution of black Germans under fascism, the hysteria
around the "Rhinelandbastards" and the anti-miscegenation laws miracu-
lously vanished from public consciousness. At the same time, the old

63. Pommerin, *Sterilisierung der "Rheinlandbastarde"*, pp. 94–95.
64. See Robert W. Kesting, "Forgotten Victims: Blacks in the Holocaust", *The Journal of Negro History*, 77 (1992), pp. 30–36.
65. In 1952, "Mach nicht so traurige Augen, weil du ein Negerlein bist" by Leila Negra, a black German teenager, was a Top-Ten hit song in Germany. See Gisela Fremgen, *und wenn du dazu noch scharz bist. Berichte schwarzer Frauen in der Bundesrepublik* (Bremen, 1984), p. 110.
66. Anna G. und Frieda P., "Unser Vater war Kameruner, unsere Mutter Ostpreussin, wir sind Mulattinnen", in Oguntoye et al., *Farbe bekennen*, p. 81.

positions continued to guide discussions about non-white Germans, this time under the heading "occupation children" (*Besatzungskinder*).

In 1952, not only did "Don't Look So Sad" make the top of the German charts, but scientific "race studies" revived within the academy. Responsible was the former *Kaiser Wilhelm Institut* for anthropology, founded 1926 in the Weimar Republic, headed for sixteen years by an anthropologist who had built his reputation on "bastard studies" in the *Kaiserreich*, and reaching a peak of activity with fascism.[67] It was one of the few German scientific centers that was not closed down by the Allies (it was renamed, though). Seven years after the end of the war, the institute published a study on mixed-raced children based on material gathered during the preparation of the forced sterilizations. It ended with the conclusion that "[e]specially the children's strong animalism will surely cause certain problems".[68]

Just as the unchanged nationality law revealed a consistent political attitude towards race matters, the work of the institute showed the consistency of the scientific positions. It is not much of a surprise, therefore, that public reactions to "racial mixing" did not change either. In the 1950s black Germans once again were defined as unnatural, a product of extraordinary circumstances; the label "occupation children" targeted this.[69] Again, the public viewed black soldiers foremost as potential rapists, white women in relationships with them as whores and their children as mistakes of nature.[70] Again, removal of the children to a more appropriate surrounding, i.e. Africa or the US, was seen as the preferable solution. After all, as a 1952 parliamentary debate on the issue concluded, "the climate in this country does not suit them".[71] Continuing its colonial tradition, the Protestant church established at least one "mulatto village" to house black children in preparation

67. Apart from continued "bastard studies" and expertise on race, the Institute initiated Mengele's "experiments" in concentration camps. See Weingart *et al.*, *Rasse, Blut und Gene*, pp. 399–423.
68. Walter Kirchner, "Untersuchung somatischer und psychischer Entwicklung bei Europäer-Neger-Mischlingen im Kleinkindalter unter Berücksichtigung der sozialen Verhältnisse", quoted in Benno Müller-Hill, *Tödliche Wissenschaft*, p. 115.
69. Of the 66,730 "occupation children" officially registered by the German authorities in 1955, i.e. children fathered by allied soldiers, 62,000 were white; public, scientific and political interest was focused exclusively on the black children, however. See Klaus Eyferth *et al.*, *Farbige Kinder in Deutschland und die Aufgaben ihrer Eingliederung* (Munich, 1960), pp. 11–12.
70. Several studies conducted in the 1950s show the population's negative attitude towards "'the niggerlovers' and their bastards", Luise Frankenstein, *Uneheliche Kinder von ausländischen Soldaten mit besonderer Berücksichtigung der Mischlinge* (Genf, 1953), p. 29; see also Eyferth *et al.*, *Farbige Kinder in Deutschland*, pp. 74–78. Magazine articles and stories of the 1950s had a less aggressive attitude towards the children, rather portraying them as "tragic mulattos", but presented their fathers in "black horror" tradition as drunken, animal-like rapists. See Rosemarie K. Lester, "Blacks in Germany and German Blacks", in Grimm and Hermand, *Blacks and German Culture*, pp. 122–128.
71. See Fremgen, *und wenn du dazu noch schwarz bist*, p. 98.

for their later emigration. But in spite of support by Albert Schweitzer and the NAACP, this did not prove a workable solution.[72]

While IQ tests showed no difference between black and white children, the vast majority of two hundred teachers of black students who had been surveyed agreed that "mulattos" were generally less intelligent.[73] This belief was manifested in the extraordinary small number of black children recommended for higher education.[74] Job recommendations for girls were restricted to washerwoman, chambermaid, factory worker or typist, for boys it was circus artist, musician, mechanic or elevator boy.[75]

When black children reached puberty, public interest focused again on the girls' sexuality. Numerous magazine articles dealt with topics such as "How colored girls seduce white men" or "Drama of a mulatto girl in Germany: she had to love them all".[76] Far from being seen as part of the population, black German women embodied "exotic fun". But where serious relationships were concerned, the fun ended. Female and male black Germans were believed to have minimal chances of finding a (white) marriage partner; their existence was perceived as a mistake that should not be repeated. A contemporary study on mixed-race children concluded:

> Racial mixing is almost exclusively seen as something negative, even threatening. Superstitious ideas, memorized as biological laws, are connected with it, e.g. that always the negative characteristics are transmitted, so that children of mixed relationships are mentally and physically inferior. Or it is said that it is never certain whether a parent looking relatively little Negroid might have a totally black child with kinky hair and thick lips [...]. Even though this fear of racial mixing is not justified, it has to be taken into consideration in the future.[77]

CONCLUSION

Attitudes towards interracial relationships in twentieth-century Germany were surprisingly consistent. Six decades and four different political systems did not change the fact that Germans perceived blacks – be they African, Afro-American or German – almost exclusively in terms of their alleged sexuality. Differentiation among class lines did not occur, since blacks automatically appeared as working-class. This brings into focus the similar stereotypes that were used in the discourses around the "lower races" and the "lower classes". Political groups as well as scientists, on the other hand, offered "race solidarity" as a means to overcome class conflict within the

72. Lester, "Blacks in Germany", p. 121.
73. Eyferth *et al.*, *Farbige Kinder in Deutschland*, p. 8.
74. *Ibid.*, p. 54.
75. *Ibid*, p. 77.
76. Fremgen, *und wenn du dazu nich schwarz bist*, p. 65. See also Lester, "Blacks in Germany", pp. 128–130.
77. Eyferth *et al.*, *Farbige Kinder in Deutschland*, p. 105.

white society, deeming (biologically defined) class differences unimportant where the "war of races" was concerned. German publics judged sexual relationships between blacks and whites as immoral and unnatural, but the interaction of gender and race images led to a harsher reaction to relations between black men and white women. The fear and rejection of "racial mixing" and people of mixed ancestry, though, seemed less dependent on gender, the important factor here was to keep the German nation "white".

Racial construction assigned opposite mentalities to the races. Only whites were granted differentiated personalities and societies. This differentiation could include class and gender conflicts as internal problems, while the West saw conflicts around race as external, imposed by black outsiders who embodied everything whites were not (or should not be). Loss of "racial purity" was therefore equated with loss of identity. This idea required that the separation of races was presented as necessary and natural. The acceptance of a mixed raced population within the white West would have shown that cultural identity is not connected to "race". That this acceptance never took place shows that the West still depends on race to define itself. The massively negative reactions that relatively small numbers of interracial relationships and non-white Germans repeatedly invoked are an example of how central and deep-seated this racial definition is. Science's clinging to the validity of the race concept also reflects this.[78] And references to "science" continue to justify racist exclusion, while "racist excesses" are condemned, but never analyzed within the context of this illusory concept of the pure white West. Without recognition of the historical construction of ideas about race, exclusionary policy continues to find ample justification, as the recent debates on German national identity have re-emphasized.

78. Be it in the form of sociobiology that holds positions similar to those of the social anthropologists and nevertheless receives favorable treatment in the mainstream press, as e.g. the reception of Murray's and Herrnstein's *The Bell Curve* shows; see Stephen Frazer, *The Bell Curve Wars* (New York, 1995). Or in the modified variation of "invincible cultural differences" between the "races", see Berrin Ozlem Otyakmaz, *Auf allen Stühlen: Das Selbstverständnis junger türkischer Migrantinnen in Deutschland* (Cologne, 1995).